COACHING
An Effective Behavioral Approach

COACHING

An
Effective
Behavioral Approach

GARRY L. MARTIN, Ph.D.

Professor
University of Manitoba
Winnipeg, Manitoba, Canada

JOAN A. LUMSDEN

Winnipeg, Manitoba, Canada

with 120 illustrations

TIMES MIRROR/MOSBY
COLLEGE PUBLISHING
St. Louis   Toronto   Santa Clara   1987

Editor: Nancy K. Roberson
Editorial Assistant: Jeanne Hantak
Editing and Production: Top Graphics
Designer: Susan E. Lane

Cover Photo: 1986 Cary Wolinsky: CLICK/Chicago
Credits for all materials used by permission appear before the index.

Copyright © 1987 by Times Mirror/Mosby College Publishing

A division of The C.V. Mosby Company
11830 Westline Industrial Drive, St. Louis, Missouri 63146

Printed in the United States of America

Library of Congress Cataloging in Publication Data

Martin, Garry L., 1941-
  Coaching: an effective behavioral approach.

  Bibliography: p.
  Includes index.
    1. Coaching (Athletics)—Psychological aspects—
Study and teaching. I. Lumsden, Joan A. 1949-
II. Title.
GV711.M36 1987   796'.07'7   86-5868
ISBN 0-8016-3152-1

AC/VH/VH 9 8 7 6 5 4 3 2 1   12/A/227

To
Jack Whelpton, a natural coach
and
Carl Roberts, a dedicated teacher

G.L.M.

Preface

General Purpose of the Text

Coaching: An Effective Behavioral Approach has a twofold purpose: *first*, it is intended as a how-to-do-it manual to guide the student through the critical components of an effective behavioral approach to coaching; and *second*, it is designed as an easy-to-use handbook to assist coaches to effectively apply behavioral methods and techniques to everyday coaching concerns. Among other things, effective behavioral coaching encourages coaches to identify desirable athletic behaviors in observable terms, frequently monitor and chart athletic behaviors, and adopt a consistent positive approach to changing behaviors of athletes. Moreover, it encourages coaches to frequently assess their own behaviors as an important step to self-improvement. Although this approach is applicable to all levels of coaching, areas of emphasis vary depending on the age and level of the athletes being coached. Some of the examples and applications in this book are based on college athletics. The major emphasis, however, is on preparing students to coach participants in youth, junior high, and high school sport programs.

For Whom Is It Written?

The book is addressed to two main audiences: physical education students taking courses in the principles and procedures of coaching; and students and coaches in grade schools, junior high and high schools, community clubs, and service organizations. Effective behavioral coaching is based on behavior modification. Behavior modification represents the most powerful nonmedical technology for influencing behavior that is available today. That technology is now being made available to the world of sports. This book is one means of access to that technology. It assumes no specific prior knowledge about psychology or behavior modification on the part of the reader. It was written for use. It is easy to read, easy to understand, and based on proved techniques. We hope that it's also enjoyable.

Specific Goals and Organization of the Text

On the assumption that a how-to-do-it book does not have to be the stuff of which boredom is made, the goals, and the means by which we have tried to achieve them, can be summarized as follows:

1. To teach the basic characteristics of effective behavioral coaching in a style that is both informative and enjoyable. The first two chapters portray the flavor of situations and problems to which effective behavioral coaching can be applied, and provide an overview of the general characteristics of effective behavioral coaching. Throughout the remainder of the text, these characteristics are illustrated by example.

2. To teach practical "how-to" skills, such as identifying goals for athletes in terms of behaviors and results that can be measured; using behavior modification procedures to teach new skills and to maintain previously taught skills at a high level; motivating beginning athletes for optimal performance at practice and during competition; and organizing and administering an athletic program. To accomplish these ends, the book contains numerous pedagogical aids.

3. To provide practical guidelines for coaches to monitor, evaluate, and improve their own coaching behaviors. Coaches are encouraged to regularly self-evaluate, experiment, and reevaluate the specific coaching behaviors that help to guarantee success. We also provide a chapter on time management that describes strategies to help a coach juggle his or her time and energy between coaching responsibilities, a full-time job, and a personal life—strategies to help a coach make the most of available time.

4. To present this material in a way that will provide students with an easy-to-read, easy-to-use handbook to deal effectively with the challenges faced by coaches in a wide variety of sports. The style and organization have been carefully crafted with the *student* in mind.

Pedagogical Features

Coaching: An Effective Behavioral Approach contains the following pedagogical features:

1. *Introductions.* An introductory paragraph is included to introduce the contents of each chapter so that students can more readily grasp what they can expect to learn.

2. *Checklists.* Sport-specific checklists are found throughout the text for use by athletes or coaches and are drawn from a wide variety of sports, to help athletes improve and maintain specific sport behaviors.
3. *Questionnaires.* Questionnaires of a general nature are included and can be used for precompetition assessments by athletes in all sports.
4. *Illustrations.* Cartoons, photographs, and tables are used to reinforce the concepts and promote reader interest.
5. *Summaries.* Each chapter contains a summary to assist students in understanding and retaining the salient points of the chapter.
6. *Coach's checklists.* Checklists at the end of Chapters 3 through 16 are provided as practical guidelines for readers to monitor, evaluate, and improve their own coaching behaviors.
7. *Review questions.* Review questions are listed at the end of each chapter to promote mastery by students and to be used by professors to help evaluate student performance.
8. *Mini-lab exercises.* These exercises at the end of Chapters 2 through 16 encourage students and coaches to analyze, interpret, and develop behavioral programs for athletes in a variety of settings.
9. *References.* A reference list and up-to-date bibliography at the end of each chapter are included to facilitate access to important material in the field.

Instructor's Manual and Test Bank

Considering the extensive study aids already incorporated in the text, we believe that the most helpful additional material we can give an instructor is a detailed answer key to the review questions in the text. Such an answer key can be a tremendous time saver for instructors and can greatly facilitate accurate and consistent grading by teaching assistants. The instructor's manual therefore contains answers to all the review questions in the text. The form of the suggested answers varies somewhat according to the question asked. For questions in which variations in answers are acceptable, we provide at least one typical answer. For instructors who prefer multiple-choice or true-false questions, we have provided a pool of such questions on a chapter-by-chapter basis. The multiple-choice and true-false questions were chosen so as to be closely related to the material contained in the answers to the review questions. This was deliberate, so that students who master the text material by learning answers to review questions will perform well on the multiple-choice and the true-false questions.

Acknowledgments

The writing of this book was made possible by many individuals. We wish to express our appreciation to Claudia Milton for efficiently and cheerfully typing several drafts of the manuscript. Grateful acknowledgment is due many students for their constructive feedback on earlier drafts; the many athletes who helped us to field test aspects of the technology and who volunteered to serve as subjects for the photographs; Peter Marinelli for the photograpy, and Ian Pauley for some of the illustrations; and Brunata Smyk and Nicole Duy for their help in the preparation of the instructor's manual. Special appreciation is expressed for the many excellent suggestions and helpful criticism of the following reviewers:

Boyd Baker
University of Arizona

Don Bethe
California State University. Northridge

Ralph Bibler
University of Colorado

Barbara Drum
University of Maryland

Evelyn Hall
Louisiana State University

Jack Johnson
University of South Carolina

Thomas Meinhardt
Towson State University

Mimi Murray
Springfield State College. Massachusetts

Bob Olsen
Northern State College. Aberdeen. South Dakota

Lelani Overstreet
California State University. Fresno

Ferne Price
Indiana State University

Marc Rabinoff
Metropolitan State University. Denver

Keith Tennant
University of Florida

Maureen Weiss
University of Oregon

Contents

COACHING
An Effective Behavioral Approach

STEPS TO EFFECTIVE BEHAVIORAL COACHING

Introduction

"Let's see a little concentration out there. You should hardly ever miss lay-ups in drills!", shouted Jim Dawson at basketball practice. Jim was coach of the Clinton Junior High basketball team in Columbus, Ohio. He was concerned about the players' execution during a series of drills that he used to open each practice. There was also an attitude problem. "Some of them just aren't team players," he thought to himself. "Some of them really have a bad attitude."

ILLUSTRATION OF EFFECTIVE BEHAVIORAL COACHING

Jim Dawson is one of the many coaches you'll read about in this book. The challenges he faced are, sooner or later, faced by all coaches—challenges such as teaching new skills, improving skill execution, increasing work output at practices, encouraging attention and interest, encouraging hustle and a "positive attitude," and maintaining some semblance of order in group activities.

How did Coach Dawson deal with his concerns with the basketball team? With the help of Dr. Daryl Siedentop of Ohio State University, he worked out a motivational system in which players could earn points for performance in lay-up drills, jump shooting drills, and free throw drills at daily practice. In addition, they could earn points by being a "team player" and encouraging their teammates. Points were deducted if Coach Dawson saw an incidence of lack of "hustle," or of "bad attitude." The points were recorded by volunteer students who served as team managers. All of this was explained to the players in detail. In addition to reviewing their record of points earned at each practice, players who earned a sufficient number of points were rewarded with an "Eagle Effort" award at a post-season banquet, and their names were posted on the Eagle Effort board in a conspicuous place in the hall leading to the gymnasium. Overall, the system was highly effective. Performance in lay-up drills improved from an average of 68% before the system to an average of 80%. Jump shooting performance improved from 37% to 51%. Free throw shooting at practices improved from 59% to 67%. However, the most dramatic improvement was in the "team player" category. By the end of the season, said Jim, "We were more together than I ever could have imagined." Teachers would stop Jim and ask, "What in the world is going on in your practices?" He would reply in all honesty, "We've started to really help each other" (Siedentop, 1980, p. 53).

The strategy developed by Dawson and Siedentop illustrates what is referred to as effective behavioral coaching. Among other things, this approach encourages coaches to identify desirable athletic behaviors in observable terms, frequently monitor and chart athletic behaviors, and adopt a consistent, positive approach to changing behaviors of athletes. Moreover, it encourages coaches to frequently assess their own coaching behaviors as a surefire way to self-improvement. Although this approach is applicable to all levels of coaching, areas of emphasis vary depending on the age and level of the athletes being coached. Although some of the examples and applications in this book are based on college-level athletics, the major emphasis is on coaching participants in youth, junior high, and high school sport programs. This approach will help you to deal effectively with many of the challenges faced by coaches.

SOME CHALLENGES FACED BY COACHES
Coach Jones' Problems with the Football Team

Charlie Jones had a problem. For the past 3 years he'd been coaching a Pop Warner football team of 9- and 10-year-olds. His team was doing pretty well this year. They'd won a fair share of their games. The problem was that some of the parents thought there was too much emphasis on winning, too much competition between team members. Mrs. Davis said the kids ought to be having more fun—not feeling depressed about getting yelled at when they lost a football game. On the other hand, some of the parents were critical of Mrs. Davis and the "goody-goody, namby-pamby" types. The world is competitive, they argued. Learning how to win in sports teaches a kid how to win in life. Michael Appelbaum's mother kept quoting Joe Namath: "When you win, *nothing* hurts!," she said. If that attitude was good enough for Joe Willie. . . .

Coach Jones was caught in the middle. Somehow, it should be possible to find a happy medium: balance—between competition and skill development, between wanting to win and enjoying the game. Individual players *should* receive praise and recognition for playing well, regardless of the score at the end of the game. And there *should* be more emphasis on positive feedback rather than lots of hollering and reprimands for mistakes. He believed all of that. But believing it and doing something about it are two different things.

And if the parent thing wasn't bad enough, there was his backfield to worry about. At the start of the season he gave each player a playbook and told them to memorize the plays. All they had to do was look at the diagrams and follow the instructions. Even so, he took time to explain the individual plays to the backfield. They spent at least half of every practice rehearsing those plays. And he pointed out their mistakes—often.

That was 17 practices and five games ago. Many mistakes were still there. And Michael Appelbaum's father, who was keeping statistics on the team's performance, kept pointing it out.

"Charlie," he said, "I gotta tell ya, the backfield's averaging only 60% correct execution. And they're not getting any better, Charlie. No way."

Charlie was painfully aware that Appelbaum was right. Trouble was, he didn't know where to go from here.

Challenges illustrated by this example include:

- How can a coach walk the fine line between emphasizing winning, encouraging young people to develop, and ensuring that the young athletes have fun?
- What's an effective strategy for improving team play, such as execution by the backfield on a youth football team?
- How should a coach respond when caught in the middle between parents with conflicting views on the purpose and value of participation in youth sport?

A Lesson in Golf? Or a Guide to Frustration?

Tom Simek was watching a golf instructor give a lesson. The guy who was getting the lesson looked frustrated, and more than a little confused. Tom hid a sympathetic grin. "Poor guy," he thought, "there's got to be a better way to teach golf." It was an interesting problem. *Was* there a better way to teach the finer points of golf? Tom Simek was working toward a master's degree in psychology. He knew that behavioral psychologists had developed specific techniques for teaching complex behavior. He also knew that these techniques were

being applied in subareas of sports and physical education. Why not apply them to golf? Inasmuch as he was a two-handicap golfer himself, he figured he knew the game pretty well. All he needed was a workable technique for teaching it. Tom and Dr. Richard O'Brien, from the Department of Psychology at Hofstra University, began investigating the possibilities of designing a step-by-step program to teach golf. Convinced, finally, that it could be done, they began a research project to prove that it worked (Simek and O'Brien, 1981).

Challenges illustrated by this example include:

- What is the optimal amount of instructional information to present to a beginner learning a new skill?
- What signs should a coach watch for that might indicate that a beginner is experiencing "stimulus overload"?
- What is the best way to teach a complex skill, such as executing a "good" golf swing?
- How can a coach experimentally evaluate the effectiveness of her or his coaching techniques?

Julie Carver! Mary Lou Retton! And Back-Walkovers

The gymnasium at Hailover High School bustled with activity as the girls' gymnastics team lined up to begin their practice session. Julie Carver jostled for position in line, anxiously awaiting her turn. "Mary Lou Retton, I'm not," she thought, "but I'm going to perfect this back-walkover if it kills me." Silently, she ran through the steps again in her mind. "As I walk over, my lead foot should touch down about $1\frac{1}{2}$ to 2 feet behind my hands. My lead leg shouldn't bend too much at the knees. Have to keep my other leg straight—toes pointing. Arms straight, head between my arms, facing backward."

When her turn came, she moved into position and started the movement. As her lead foot touched down right behind her head, her arms crumpled and she fell, smacking her face on the floor. Barbie Dickson sauntered by as she was getting to her feet.

"You okay?," Barbie asked casually.

"Ouch!," she answered, rubbing the bruise on her nose. "I'm going to master this thing if it kills me!" As a grin began to spread across Barbie's face, Julie nodded glumly, "Yeah, I know. It probably will!"

Challenges illustrated by this example include:

- How should complex skills be practiced by young athletes?
- What's the best way to encourage young athletes to practice skills independently, especially if independent practice is likely to be accompanied by frequent failure?
- Can young athletes improve their independent practice if they learn self-management techniques such as self-instruction, self-monitoring, self-evaluation, and self-reinforcement?
- Can young athletes be efficiently taught to practice in pairs, giving each other corrective feedback and encouragement?

Coach Hill and the Juniper High School Tennis Class

Twang . . . thump! Mary Henderson hit her third serve in a row into the net. "Mary!," her tennis coach hollered, "Don't try to be Chris Evert Lloyd! Just do what I told you!"

Mary took another ball and got ready to try again. She placed her left foot behind the baseline at a 45-degree angle and her right foot parallel to the baseline. With both hands and the racket in front of her, she repeated her serve. Twang . . . thump!

"No, Henderson! How many times do I have to tell you! Your racket is supposed to drop behind your neck, not out to the side!"

Mary Henderson was one of 12 students in the Juniper High School tennis class. This was the third class in a row that Linda Hill had devoted to instruction on how to serve. At the start of each class,

Coach Hill discussed and demonstrated the proper components for serving correctly. After her instruction session, each of the players was given a chance to practice while Hill observed and pointed out errors. Coach Hill had a real knack for finding mistakes.

Twang . . . thump! Another one into the net. By the end of the session, Mary was feeling pretty discouraged. Coach Hill walked off the court, shaking her head and muttering to herself. Mary walked away feeling that she would never learn to play tennis.

Challenges illustrated by this example include:
- How can a coach strike a balance between a well-meaning desire to help an athlete learn and the negative effects of overemphasizing mistakes?
- When teaching skills to young athletes, what are alternatives to the strategy of giving feedback following errors?
- Is there an optimal ratio of instances of praise to instances of error correction?

Will Fred Thister Achieve His Goal with the Swimming Team?

Fred Thister worked in a hardware store . . . and dreamed of being a full-time coach. Not an average, run-of-the-mill coach, but the kind who wins a state championship. At the moment, Fred was an assistant coach for the Shaftsbury Sharks, a small age-group competitive swimming club. A few years ago, Fred had won three "firsts" as a competitive swimmer in the state finals. He had also, briefly, held the state record in the 100-yard freestyle. He'd read books written by guys like James Councilman and Don Schollander. He knew swimming.

Fred knew what the team was supposed to be doing. He could see where each swimmer was making mistakes. Problem was, he had difficulty communicating. Somehow, the swimmers just didn't listen. When the head coach was at practice, the swimmers were terrific. They listened to instructions and swam hard during drills. When the head coach was away, however, and it was up to Fred to run the show, the practices turned into chaos. The swimming mistakes were bad enough!—things like unnecessarily changing strokes, failing to swim up to and touch the pool lane wall, not pushing off against the wall to start a new lap. What really upset him, though, was the "brat syndrome," the loud smacks echoing throughout the pool area as paddleboards were slapped against the water. Mike and Davey flipping their goggles at each other like elastic bands. Packy McFarlane filling his bathing cap with water and pitching it around like a balloon. Packy always looked like he was having such a good time that, before he was finished, every kid on the team was doing the same thing. Fred couldn't take much more. "If I really want to be a coach," he fretted, "I have to do something! It's not enough just to know the fundamentals of the sport."

Challenges illustrated by this example include:

- What are effective strategies for communicating with young athletes?
- What is a reasonable list of "dos and don'ts" for young athletes at practices?
- What's the best way to develop fair rules for participation and reasonable consequences for rule violations?
- Are there positive approaches that can be used to decrease problem behaviors of young athletes at practices?
- When a positive approach doesn't work, then what?

Meet Disorganized Dick, Head Coach of the Senior High Baseball Team

Sixteen very bored 17- and 18-year-olds were sitting in the dugout at the baseball diamond, looking at their watches and grumbling:

"Practice was supposed to start half an hour ago!"

"Where's the coach?"

"If we had some equipment, we could get started ourselves!"

"The equipment is in the coach's car."

"If he remembers to bring it, that is!"

"Hey! Here he comes!," yelled Jimmy Danners, as a station wagon pulled into the parking lot.

Coach Dick Mitchell hopped out and started digging through the debris in the back of his wagon. After he'd pushed aside his briefcase, some books that were overdue at the library, and a couple of empty Big Mac cartons, he finally uncovered the equipment and started to get ready for the fourth practice of the season.

"When's our first game, coach?," asked Jimmy.

"That reminds me, I've got some new schedules for you guys. Jimmy, go look in my black briefcase, and bring those schedules over."

Just then, another car pulled into the lot. A woman got out and yelled, "Dick! Mr. Kragan just called! You were supposed to be at a meeting with him half an hour ago."

"Oh no! I forgot all about that!," muttered Dick.

"Hey, coach!," hollered Jimmy from the back of the station wagon, "I can't find your black briefcase in all this stuff. Are you sure it's here?"

Challenges illustrated by this example include:
- How can a coach balance coaching commitments, family commitments, and a number of other commitments?
- Has an effective approach to time management and personal organization been developed for use by coaches?

PURPOSE OF "COACHING: AN EFFECTIVE BEHAVIORAL APPROACH"

Do these situations sound familiar? They probably do, especially if you coach at the grade school, junior high, high school, or even college level, or if you coach for a community club, service league, or volunteer organization. If you're a physical education student looking forward to a career in coaching, then you will undoubtedly encounter these and many other challenges. Coaching is *not* easy! As Yogi Berra said, "Ninety percent of this game is mental, the other 50% is physical."

See what we mean? The stress can make you talk funny. The problem, of course, is that *good* coaching *is* difficult. Every time you step on the field or court or pool or rink, you face many questions. And it's difficult finding answers, at least the kind that will help you to be a better coach. You have probably already read considerably on the subject of coaching. Numerous articles in publications such as the *Athletic Journal* and *Coaching Review* discuss plays and practice drills for various sports. You can also find books on every sport known to our culture. Books that describe, in detail, the skills that are needed to play well. Hockey, football, basketball. You name it, somebody wrote a book about it. And every book written will tell you what to teach. Some will even tell you what kind of person you have to be in order to succeed as a coach. What to teach and who to be: what else is there to know?

Perhaps the most important thing: *how* to teach. And how to *become* that person they call a "Good Coach." That's what this book is about. There's a big difference between knowing what to teach and actually teaching it effectively. The key word is *effective*. There's a difference between knowing what should be practiced and running a practice session that keeps everyone active and productive (especially when you are coaching beginners). There's a difference, too, between knowing what your athletes should do during a competition and communicating that knowledge to your players so that they compete to the best of their ability.

Is it possible for coaches to be more effective at teaching individual skills? Yes! Is it possible for coaches to hold attention, gain respect, teach athletes to perform to their full potential, and *at the same time* make the learning fun? Yes! Are there practical methods to help a Linda Hill or a Charlie Jones solve their coaching problems? Yes!

We are certain that the answer to such questions is "Yes!" The proof comes out of 30 years of research in behavioral science. During those 30 years, behavioral scientists have investigated and developed practical techniques for changing behavior. The approach is called behavior modification or applied behavior analysis.* In helping professions such as education, social work, psychology, and rehabilitation medicine, the results are clear in experiment after experiment. In situations where someone wanted to improve, behave differently, learn a new skill, develop persistence, or eliminate a bad habit, behavior modification procedures have been used, and most often used effectively. Most of the time, they work. And during the past few years the research has shown that the techniques can be helpful to coaches in a wide variety of sports (*see* Martin and Hrycaiko, 1983). In a general sense, effective behavioral coaching is the consistent application of behavior modification techniques to deal effectively with challenges faced by coaches. Many difficult coaching situations, such as those described earlier in this chapter, have been successfully dealt with through the use of behavior modification. The purpose of this book is to describe these techniques in an easy-to-understand fashion so that you, as a coach or physical education instructor, can adapt them to any sport. You will find a description of practical, proved methods for teaching basic skills, correcting errors, motivating players for practices and endurance training, developing team spirit and cooperation, maximizing performance in competition, and effectively integrating coaching duties with your other responsibilities and commitments.

Review Questions

1. Briefly list some of the characteristics of effective behavioral coaching (*see* p. 4).
2. Coaches face many challenges—challenges that can be successfully met through effective behavioral coaching. List several challenges faced by coaches.
3. In a general sense, what is effective behavioral coaching (*see* p. 11)?

---

*The terms behavior modification and applied behavior analysis are used interchangeably in this text. For a comparison of these and related terms, *see* Martin and Pear (1983).

References

Martin, G.L., and Hrycaiko, D., eds. (1983). Behavior modification and coaching: Principles, procedures, and research. Springfield, Ill.: Charles C Thomas.

Martin, G.L., and Pear, J.J. (1983). Behavior modification: What it is and how to do it. 2nd ed. Englewood Cliffs, N.J.: Prentice-Hall.

Siedentop, D. (1980). The management of practice behavior. In W.F. Straub, ed., Sport psychology: An analysis of athletic behavior. Ithaca, N.Y.: Mouvement Publications.

Simek, T.C., and O'Brien, R.M. (1981). Total golf: A behavioral approach to lowering your score and getting more out of your game. Huntington, N.Y.: B-Mod Associates.

Selected Readings

Donahue, J.A., Gillis, J.H., and King, K. (1980). Behavior modification in sport and physical education: A review. Journal of Sport Psychology 2:311-328.

Martens, R., Christina, R.W., Harvey, J.S., Jr., and Sharkey, B.J. (1981). Coaching young athletes. Champaign, Ill.: Human Kinetics Publishers.

Murphy, P. (1985). Youth sports coaches: Using hunches to fill a blank page. Physician and Sports Medicine 13(4):136-142.

Rushall, B.S., and Siedentop, D. (1972). The development and control of behavior in sport and physical education. Philadelphia: Lea & Febiger.

Siedentop, D., and Taggert, A. (1984). Behavior analysis in physical education and sport. In W.L. Heward, T.E. Heron, D.S. Hill, and J. Trapp-Porter, eds., Focus on behavior analysis in education. Columbus, Ohio: Charles E. Merrill.

Effective Behavioral Coaching: What's It All About?

In general, effective behavioral coaching refers to the consistent application of the principles of behavioral psychology to the improvement and maintenance of athletic behavior. In one sense, behavioral coaching is everything in this book. There are, however, certain characteristics of the approach that make it distinctive. Effective behavioral coaching:

1. Identifies goals for athletes in terms of specific behaviors and results that can be accurately measured, and uses those measures to evaluate the effectiveness of specific coaching techniques.
2. Encourages coaches to use specific behavior modification procedures for which effectiveness has been experimentally demonstrated in numerous studies.
3. Recognizes the distinction between developing new behavior and maintaining (or motivating) existing behavior at acceptable rates, and offers positive procedures for accomplishing both.
4. Encourages athletes to record and chart their performance and to compete and improve against their own previous performance as much as against others.
5. Encourages coaches to frequently record, self-evaluate, and continually improve their coaching behaviors.

6. Emphasizes the need for continually including the views of the athlete in evaluating goals, the acceptability of coaching procedures used to achieve those goals, and the desirability of the results obtained.

In this chapter we discuss, in a general way, these characteristics of effective behavioral coaching, to set the stage for the specifics of the how-to-do-it chapters that follow. We also review some cautions and disclaimers about effective behavioral coaching.

GENERAL CHARACTERISTICS OF EFFECTIVE BEHAVIORAL COACHING
Specific and Frequent Measurement of Athletic Performance

An important characteristic of behavioral coaching is that it emphasizes specific, detailed, and frequent measurement of athletic behaviors and the use of these measures as the primary means for evaluating the effectiveness of specific coaching techniques. The first step in a behavioral approach in any area of application is to prepare a preliminary list of target behaviors that need to be changed or maintained. For example, for a coach of a group of beginners in an age-group competitive sport, such a list might include the following:

1. Desirable behaviors by athletes at practices:
    a. Attendance at practice
    b. Good listening to instruction (in groups or individually)
    c. Practice of proper skill technique after instruction
    d. Practice of proper components of good technique during endurance training
    e. Continuous repetition of skill without frequent stopping
    f. Practice of skills with intensity and speed at least equal to that required in the final desired performance
    g. Practice of relaxation techniques and imagery (so that they might be used just before competition)
2. Desirable behaviors by athletes at competitions:
    a. Stretching, warm-up, and imagery to prepare to compete
    b. Good skill performance leading to measurable performance improvement (e.g., time, distance)
    c. Good team spirit and mutual support of group members
    d. Desirable sportsmanlike behaviors and minimal behavior problems (e.g., shaking hands with opponents, calm acceptance of calls by officials)

Preliminary lists of behavioral categories similar to this could be prepared to cover all major categories of behaviors that coaches consider important. Obviously, such categories are quite broad and vague and require further specification before precise measurement. The second step in a behavior modification approach is to prepare detailed assessment systems for monitoring specific component behaviors that make up the general categories. The data collected from such assessments serve as the foundation for effective behavioral coaching. Some assessments would be concerned with monitoring improvement of beginners in basic skills. For example, the checklist in Fig. 2-1 might be used by a swimming coach to regularly monitor improvement of beginning swimmers performing the backstroke.

Other data might emphasize results rather than form, for example, goals scored in hockey, baskets made in basketball, or number of tackles made in football. In some situations these statistics may be the primary concern for a coach, even though they tell the coach nothing about the form displayed to achieve those results. For example, it is difficult to imagine a coach being terribly concerned with the form with which the star center has just scored 46 points in a basketball game in which the team won the state championship. However, some young athletes compile impressive statistics at local levels of competition even though they have major flaws in technique or form. If that athlete happens to be coached by someone who is not concerned with form but is overly impressed with results, that athlete is likely to encounter difficulties when he or she goes on to higher levels of competition. The optimal strategy for a coach is one that emphasizes monitoring form as well as results. The data can then be used to evaluate the effectiveness of variations in coaching techniques. It is this data-based approach that places behavioral coaching on a firm, scientific foundation and that ultimately will lead to maximum effectiveness in coaching strategies.

Often we hear coaches talking about such things as "getting psyched up" or "developing the will to win" or "showing determination and dedication" or having "mental toughness." Some people might call these kinds of statements "goals." Some may even believe that these are the goals toward which a winning coach should strive. Well, maybe they should. Unfortunately, such things are usually not well defined. Often these statements are made when a coach cannot explain why players performed well or badly in a given situation. For example, if the bottom team in a league manages to beat the top team in the league, the coach of the top team might explain the loss by saying, "That team was really playing over their heads!," or "My players just weren't psyched up today." The coach might just as well say, "Something really

Assessing Backstroke

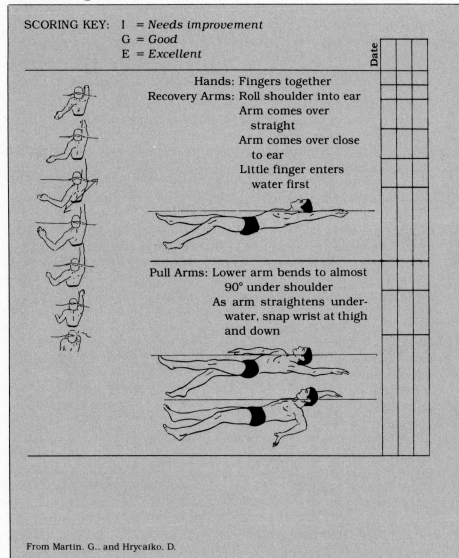

SCORING KEY: I = *Needs improvement*
G = *Good*
E = *Excellent*

Date

Hands: Fingers together
Recovery Arms: Roll shoulder into ear
Arm comes over
straight
Arm comes over close
to ear
Little finger enters
water first

Pull Arms: Lower arm bends to almost
90° under shoulder
As arm straightens under-
water, snap wrist at thigh
and down

From Martin. G.. and Hrycaiko. D.

FIGURE 2-1

	Date		
Legs: Leg action begins at hips			
Knees move up and down very little			
Knees do not break surface			
Toes point down at bottom of kick			
Toes just break surface at top of kick			
Body: Hips kept high in water			
Hips kept as flat as possible			
Head: Tilted up slightly, ears in water			
Head kept stationary; do not rock			

went wrong out there today, but I haven't got a clue what happened!" In behavioral coaching, we try to avoid vague statements such as "playing over your head." A behavioral coach strives to deal in specifics, the specifics being *behavior* that the coach can observe, assess, measure, and most important, teach!

Frequent Use of Proved Behavior Modification Procedures

A second characteristic of effective behavioral coaching is that this approach relies heavily on the *proved* principles of behavior modification to help athletes learn and improve. These principles have been studied both in the laboratory and in the "real world" in applied settings. Thirty years of study and application have produced a complex and rapidly expanding body of knowledge about behavioral psychology (*see* Martin and Pear, 1983). It is a simple fact that the most successful approach in psychology for changing behavior is the application of behavior modification principles. It makes sense, then, to apply the principles of behavioral science to the main problem faced by coaches: influencing behavior change in athletes. If you master the principles and procedures that we describe in the chapters that follow, you can be more effective at teaching new skills, maintaining those skills in game or contest situations, and organizing and administering an athletic program.

Distinction Between Developing and Maintaining Behavior

A third important characteristic of behavioral coaching is that this approach makes a distinction between *teaching* new skills and *maintaining* existing skills at a high level. And it offers practical behavior modification procedures to help coaches with both areas. The teaching procedures include techniques such as instruction, demonstration, role-playing, physical guidance, shaping, immediate reward for progress, and immediate corrective feedback for errors. These techniques are described in more detail in later chapters. All coaches use at least some of these techniques, but the coach who uses all of them, and uses them systematically, is rare indeed. Recent evidence shows that some coaches rely far too heavily on instructions and negative consequences (Rushall, 1983). Fortunately, there are better ways to coach. In later chapters we will discuss in detail positive ways to get a point across to the athletes that you coach.

With regard to maintaining previously learned skills, some coaches try to use the thrill of victory and the agony of being hollered at as their strategy for maintaining top performance in competition.

However, neither strategy is enough to ensure maintenance of a previously learned skill. An effective behavioral coach, on the other hand, watches for and keeps records of newly acquired skills of individual players *during* competition. He or she then uses both the records and a systematic system of goal setting, and praise or feedback to *maintain* those skills—independent of winning or losing! This approach is not only effective, it is also a lot of fun for the athletes!

Encouragement of Athletes to Compete Against Own Previous Performance

A fourth characteristic of behavioral coaching is that it emphasizes competition with oneself rather than against standards of others. Athletes are encouraged to set performance goals and to self-monitor progress. Self-monitoring involves recording objective indicators of performance and charting the data in a way that clearly displays progress.

Goal setting and self-monitoring are not new ideas. Today many coaches encourage serious athletes to keep personal diaries, set personal goals, and keep track of their own progress. Effective behavioral coaching, however, advocates a high degree of goal setting and self-monitoring for the beginning athlete as well. This approach can help counteract potential problems for the beginning athlete that can stem from overemphasis on winning. Consider, for example, a possible situation in age-group competitive swimming. In a club that has six 10-year-old members who compete against each other, there are bound to be one or two who consistently outperform the others. If the swimming coach places a great deal of emphasis on winning when competing against someone else, this situation becomes a discouraging environment for the young athletes who are always fifth or sixth on the totem pole. They can't win against the "superstars," so they can't win, period. Their athletic experience becomes one long agony of defeat with no hope in sight for the thrill of victory. We doubt that any coach really wants to put a beginner in this type of situation. And a coach doesn't have to. In effective behavioral coaching, each athlete is encouraged to improve against his or her own previous performance. Number Six on the totem pole can compete against herself or himself, not the superstar. The result? Number Six frequently beats his or her own previous score. In a sense, a beginner *can* win! And win often enough to make the whole experience of participation in sports a genuine pleasure.

By permission of Johnny Hart and News America Syndicate.

This whole area of "competition" and "winning" has sparked a fair bit of controversy with regard to amateur sports. In today's sports community, many coaches would probably be reluctant to say outright that winning is everything. It would be difficult, however, to find anyone who does *not* believe that winning makes you feel good. There is no doubt that achievement and success can make an athlete feel terrific. The problem with regard to amateur sport is that winning is often defined as being better than the opponent, regardless of whether the opponent is a teammate or a player in opposition. In effective behavioral coaching, winning is defined as being the best that *you* can be, regardless of what the opponent is doing. That may be a small distinction, but it is important. Sports events are already structured so that the rewards go to Number 1. The "best" player is always acknowledged. And there is nothing wrong with that, as far as it goes. But a good coach wants to add a dimension to sports that will be appreciated by *all* the young athletes in her or his care. That dimension consists of encouraging *each* athlete to compete with himself or herself to accomplish *realistic goals of personal improvement.* Effective behavioral coaching provides methods whereby that dimension can be achieved.

In addition to benefitting beginning athletes, self-monitoring is also a useful tactic for maintaining skills of experienced athletes. Consider, for example, the skilled player who goes into a slump. Sometimes, such a player's poor performance is discussed in vague terms: "He's down." "She's been psyched out." "His concentration is poor." In short, no one really knows why the player is suddenly playing badly. And sadly, the player often cannot explain it either. Logically, however, we can assume that the player's behavior has changed in some way. In some cases this might be caused by boredom, injury, or fatigue. In other cases, however, there might be one small or subtle behavior change that literally turned a formerly good skill into a presently poor skill. An athlete who is self-monitoring is more likely to notice imme-

FIGURE 2-2
Charting results can improve performance.

diately that a change has occurred. He or she is also in a better position to correct a fault before it affects his or her entire performance. Self-monitioring as it is used in effective behavioral coaching can help the athlete stay on top of this type of situation. At the very least, the notion of recording one's own performance and competing against oneself can provide a player with a step-by-step means of pulling out of a slump. At its best, a self-monitoring system might help to prevent the occurrence of a slump in the first place. There is always a reason for athletic performance that has changed. A coach who emphasizes self-monitoring can help athletes locate behavioral change and correct the change if it's negative or maintain the change it it's positive. Examples of self-monitoring are shown in Fig. 2-2.

Behavior Modification of Coach's Behavior

The fifth characteristic of effective behavioral coaching is perhaps the most interesting one from the coach's point of view. So far, we've talked about the athletes—about their performance, their skills, their learning needs, and their behavior. But what about the coach's needs and the coach's behavior? As a coach, you may want very much to learn to use the objective approach we've talked about, but you know that sometimes your *own* behavior gets in your way. You're only human after all. You can be irritable and inconsistent. You can get angry and tired. Sometimes you do things as a coach, but you don't actually know why. You may feel that it's a bad habit, but you find yourself doing it anyway. And sometimes you have a sense that things aren't going well, but you don't know what you're doing wrong. Effective behavioral coaching can help coaches as well as athletes. This approach to coaching emphasizes the need (and provides the methods) for you to learn to objectively keep track of your own skills as a coach. Self-assessment for coaches is one way to help you put into practice the procedures we describe in this book. More than that, it will help you to be fair and consistent in your dealings with the athletes in your care. An effective behavioral coach learns to regularly ask (and answer) questions such as the following:

1. Have I encouraged athletes to set, and write out, individual and team goals at the start of the season?
2. Have I encouraged the athletes to write out their goals for practices?
3. Have I identified specific training strategies to help them accomplish these goals?
4. During practices and games, do I dispense more rewards than reprimands to the athletes?

5. Do I take advantage of opportunities to give immediate corrective feedback for errors?
6. Do I correct errors in a way that is nonthreatening and not embarrassing to the athletes?
7. Am I aware of the personal needs of the athletes (needs that may have an effect on their performance)?
8. Do I take the time to praise small improvements, especially with beginners, even though overall performance may still need lots of improvement?

Many of these questions can be answered by regular self-evaluation. It is also possible to ask someone else (parent, volunteer, assistant coach) to observe, score, and give you feedback on your behavior during games and practices. Effective behavioral coaching requires that coaches constantly study and improve their coaching behavior.

Learning to objectively assess your coaching behavior can be a useful and rewarding experience. If nothing else, objectivity with regard to your own behavior can help you to bypass emotions such as confusion, guilt, anger, or that sense that "Something's wrong, but I don't know what." It is easier to change inappropriate behavior into positive behavior when you can clearly see what you're doing wrong. Remember, too, that objectivity and self-evaluation can also tell you what you're doing *right*. Some people think that being honest with yourself only means finding the flaws in your behavior. A behavioral coach is willing to objectively look at and change flaws, but is also aware of the value of knowing that he or she is doing something well. Knowing when you're good makes it easier to keep on being good. Regular self-evaluation, experimentation, and reevaluation of your coaching behavior helps to guarantee success as a coach.

Social Validation from Athlete's Point of View

The final characteristic of effective behavioral coaching is important. In behavioral psychology this characteristic is called *social validation* (Martin and Pear, 1983), which refers to procedures or standards to ensure that techniques employed by a psychologist are selected and applied in the best interests of the client. As applied to behavioral coaching, social validation requires that a coach constantly seek answers to three questions:

1. What do the athletes (and perhaps their parents or guardians) think about the *goals* of the coaching program?
2. What do they think about the *procedures* used by the coach?
3. What do they think about the *results* obtained by those procedures?

In many situations, coaches have had total control over deciding the answers to at least the first two questions.

By permission of Johnny Hart and News America Syndicate.

Often it is the coach who sets the goals, and the coach alone who decides on the adequacy of his or her coaching procedures. In some cases it is also the coach who decides on the acceptability of the results, a situation that sometimes has meant that acceptable equals winning at all costs. In effective behavioral coaching, beginning athletes are encouraged to set many of their own goals. They are also encouraged to indicate how they feel about the goals that are set by the coach. Goals that are set by mutual agreement between the athlete and the coach are goals that are more likely to be achieved. An effective behavioral coach constantly monitors how the athletes feel about the procedures that are used. As described in Chapter 10, this is accomplished through direct observation of athletes' reactions or with questionnaires. In general, procedures that are aversive to the athlete should be minimized. Instead, procedures should be used that emphasize positive interaction between coaches and athletes. And finally, the athletes have something to say about the results that are obtained. In effective behavioral coaching, greater emphasis is placed on the achievement of realistic personal goals than on the concept of winning at all costs. Athletes have a right to a positive experience in sports. Their opinion matters. It is the coach's responsibility not only to teach the young athlete effectively, but to ensure that he or she is enjoying the learning experience. The concept of social validation (of goals, procedures, and results), when applied correctly to the coaching situation, is certainly one way to assess whether that happens.

POSSIBLE PITFALLS TO EFFECTIVE BEHAVIORAL COACHING: SOME CAUTIONS

In general, there are two major approaches to coaching: coaches can try to influence their athletes in a positive way by liberally rewarding desirable behaviors, or they can attempt to control their athletes with a negative approach that emphasizes the use of punishment and criticism. Most coaches employ a mixture of these two methods. Unfortunately, the mixture often favors the negative (Rushall, 1983). Thus, our first caution is that you should take steps to ensure that you dispense as many or more positive consequences and feedback than reprimands and negative feedback. That, however, is easier said than done. We can certainly sympathize with situations in which coaches find themselves, especially when coaching young athletes. Young athletes make errors. Coaches must constantly deal with "bonehead" plays, lack of attention, daydreaming, screw-ups, and frequent mistakes. It is understandable that a coach might criticize, put down, be sarcastic, and generally disapprove of mistakes. However, research has indicated that punishment has a number of highly undesirable side effects (Martin and Pear, 1983). It causes emotional behavior in the individual that interferes with performance. Punishment *does not teach new behavior;* it simply suppresses old behavior. Punishment can cause a person to behave in a hostile way and to become less receptive to instruction. Perhaps most important, punishment becomes associated with the activity itself. Thus, if an athlete experiences a lot of punishment while participating in a sport, he or she may decide not only to quit that sport but to avoid other, similar sports. Dr. John Dickinson, author of *A Behavioral Analysis of Sport,* wrote:

> After receiving punishment for one sport, therefore, a large number of similar sports may be affected and participation in those sports may not occur simply because of the avoidance reaction through stimuli with which they are associated. I feel fairly certain that this phenomenon accounts for many of the non-participants amongst adults. Performance in sports at school has been punished in some way and the avoidance has generalized to a large number of sports (1977, p. 45).

Does this mean that coaches should not correct errors because it might be unpleasant to the athlete to have an error pointed out? Of course not. However, a coach should pay careful attention to the *ratio* of instances of positive and negative feedback that he or she issues to the athlete. In fact, we highly recommend that all coaches should regularly try the following exercise. Purchase or borrow two wrist counters used for keeping count of golf scores. During practice of the sport that you coach, each time you praise or speak positively to an athlete, count it on one of the wrist counters. Each time you disapprove, yell, criticize, or show sarcasm, count that on the other wrist counter. We would be willing to bet that the majority of coaches will find that they give far more negative feedback than positive feedback. Some research, however, indicates that a desirable ratio of positive to negative feedback with kids in educational settings is 4:1 (four positive, one negative) (Martin and Pear, 1983). Although we know of no research examining the most effective ratio for coaching young athletes, we suggest that the ratio should at least favor the positive over the negative. By negative feedback, by the way, we mean behavior such as yelling, criticism, and sarcasm. We are *not* referring to *corrective feedback*. Corrective feedback refers to coaches' reactions to errors in which the coach provides suggestions or guidance for correct performance (e.g., "Follow through more with your left hand." "Don't bend your wrist so much on your backswing."). Siedentop (1976) recommends that physical education instructors also adopt a goal of providing positive feedback versus corrective feedback at a ratio of 3 or 4:1.

Another caution for effective behavioral coaching is to resist the temptation to continuously tell athletes how they *should* be performing. It is almost always possible to identify something a beginning athlete *could* be doing better. It is difficult for a coach, even though praising the athlete, to resist the temptation to point out all of the things the athlete could be doing better. Resist the temptation! The "Yes, but" approach (e.g., "Your hand entry was really good, but . . .") can get out of hand. If a coach consistently pairs praise for good performance with criticism for bad performance, the praise will eventually lose much of its effectiveness. Be constantly on the lookout for desirable improvements to praise. Also, when you spot an inappropriate behavior, provide some corrective instruction. But be wary of continually praising one thing and criticizing several others in the same interaction.

A third caution: Try to resist being influenced by outmoded, unscientific ways of thinking about behavior. When discussing the positive approach to coaching, some coaches react with the following kind of statement: "I don't believe in using too many rewards. I believe in giving the kids responsibility. They'll grow up to be better people if they learn to show initiative, to do things on their own without being praised all the time, to take some responsibility for their own actions. After all, when they grow up, no one is going to be praising them all the time for what they do." We have several reactions to such statements. First, most experts on learning recommend the positive approach to behavior modification (e.g., Alberto and Troutman, 1982; Kazdin, 1984; Walker and Shea, 1984). Second, if someone suggests that students learn without rewards, that someone simply has not reliably observed the rewards that influence all of us, day in and day out, in all parts of our daily lives (e.g., Martin and Pear, 1983). Third, our observations indicate that coaches who argue against the positive approach are coaches who use a high ratio of negative versus positive feedback with their athletes. The coach who claims to be "giving the kids responsibility" is in fact "controlling" through use of threats, sarcasm, criticism, and other forms of punishment. Fourth, these coaches are ignoring what we identified earlier in this chapter as the sixth characteristic of behavioral coaching. They are ignoring *what the athletes think about the procedures used by the coach.* As indicated by the research of Smith and co-workers (1979) at the University of Washington, when given the choice, young athletes much prefer to work with a coach who emits a high frequency of rewarding behaviors. Fifth, we would like to point out that behavioral coaching might not be acceptable to everyone. Some coaches will feel very uncomfortable with behavioral coaching and will not adopt the approach. Also, some parents may prefer that their children be taught by other coaching methods— methods that incorporate "lots of good old-fashioned discipline" (which usually means a much higher dose of the negative approach and a much lower dose of the positive). That, of course, is their choice. However, we predict that many coaches and parents will prefer the positive approach advocated in effective behavioral coaching.

Finally, we want to express a disclaimer. When reading a book such as this, some coaches might reply, "So what's new about behavioral coaching? I do all of those things." And, of course, they're right. Coaches do use instructions, modeling, guidance, positive reinforcement, and most other behavior modification procedures. We don't mean to imply otherwise. We do suggest, however, that there is room for improvement in (1) the *consistency* with which behavioral procedures are applied to developing desirable behavior of athletes, and organizing and administering athletic programs, and (2) the *extent* to which coaches employ detailed data systems to thoroughly evaluate the effectiveness of their coaching procedures. It takes practice to become skillful at behavioral coaching. Coaches, like the athletes they train, learn, make progress, and change as the season unfolds. You are most likely to master the steps of effective behavioral coaching if you yourself are assessed and receive reports on how well you do. Chapters 3 through 16 conclude with a Coach's Checklist" to use to monitor and evaluate the development of your effective coaching behaviors, a set of review questions for examination purposes, and some mini-lab exercises to help you practice the chapter content.

SUMMARY

This chapter reviewed six distinguishing characteristics of effective behavioral coaching: specific and frequent measurement of athletic behavior; use of positive behavior modification procedures; distinction between developing and maintaining desirable behaviors; encouragement of athletes to compete against themselves as well as against the standards of others; regular self-evaluation, experimentation, and reevaluation by coaches to continually improve their own coaching behaviors; and frequent involvement of athletes in validating coaching procedures and results. Stress was placed on both the need for coaches to use detailed data systems to evaluate coaching effectiveness and the need for improved consistency with which behavioral procedures are applied to various coaching situations. Specific cautions for those who practice effective behavioral coaching include recommendations for coaches to (1) carefully monitor the ratio of instances of positive to negative feedback to ensure that the ratio favors the positive; (2) frequently praise athletes for improved components of skills rather than overemphasizing those aspects of a skill that were performed incorrectly; and (3) resist outmoded, unscientific ways of thinking about behavior.

Review Questions

1. What is the first characteristic of effective behavioral coaching? Describe two examples that fit this characteristic.
2. Some people believe that coaching is a science. Others believe that it is an art. Which do the authors believe, and why?
3. Why is the distinction between developing and maintaining athletic behavior important?
4. Behavioral coaching emphasizes self-monitoring and competition with self. Describe the desirable aspects of this characteristic.
5. What does effective behavioral coaching have to say about the behavior of the coach?
6. The sixth characteristic of effective behavioral coaching involves social validation. What three questions does social validation attempt to answer concerning coaching?
7. In a sentence or two each, what are three cautions for those who try to practice effective behavioral coaching?
8. In brief, what are four undesirable side effects of excessive use of punishment by the coach?
9. What does the research say is the most desirable ratio of positive to negative feedback with young people?

10. Why should coaches avoid the "Yes, but" habit?
11. Some coaches don't believe in using rewards. Why do the authors object to this view?

Mini-Lab Exercises

1. Consider the six characteristics of effective behavioral coaching. Now consider one of your former coaches. List those characteristics of behavioral coaching that your former coach practiced. Also, briefly describe how he or she practiced them.
2. Ask a coach that you know for permission to attend one of her or his practices and to sit on the sidelines and observe specific coaching behaviors. Throughout a practice, tally the frequency with which the coach dispenses praise or positive feedback to the athletes. In another column, tally the instances in which the coach yells, criticizes, shows sarcasm, or disapproves of athletes. Count the frequency of instances rather than the specific words. For example, if a coach says to an athlete, "Good hustle, Charlie. Keep it up," that is one instance. The purpose of this exercise is not to put you in a position of giving feedback to an experienced coach, but to make you aware of the ratio of positive to negative feedback that might be dispensed by a coach at a typical practice.

Acknowledgment

The material in this chapter is paraphrased from Martin, G., and Hrycaiko, D. (1983). Effective behavioral coaching: What's it all about? Journal of Sport Psychology 5:8-20. Champaign, Ill.: Human Kinetics Publishers.

References

Alberto, P.A., and Troutman, A.C. (1982). Applied behavior analysis for teachers. Columbus, Ohio: Charles E. Merrill.

Dickenson, J. (1977). A behavioral analysis of sport. Princeton, N.J.: Princeton Book Co.

Kazdin, A.E. (1984). Behavior modification in applied settings, 3rd ed. Homewood, Ill.: Dorsey Press.

Martin, G.L. (in press). Applied behavior analysis in sport and physical education: Past, present, and future. In L. Hamerlynk, and R.P. West, eds., Designs for excellence in education: Legacy of B.F. Skinner, Lawrence Erlbaum.

Martin, G.L., and Hrycaiko, D. (1983). Effective behavioral coaching: What's it all about? Journal of Sport Psychology 5:8-20.

Martin, G.L., and Pear, J.J. (1983). Behavior modification: What it is and how to do it, 2nd ed. Englewood Cliffs, N.J.: Prentice-Hall.

Rushall, B.S. (1983). Coaching styles: A preliminary investigation. In G.L. Martin and D. Hrycaiko, eds., Behavior modification and coaching: Principles, procedures, and research. Springfield, Ill.: Charles C Thomas.

Siedentop, D. (1976). Developing teaching skills in physical education. Boston: Houghton Mifflin.

Smith. R.W.. Smoll. F.L.. and Curtis. B. (1979). Coach effectiveness training: A cognitive behavioral approach to enhancing relationship skills in youth sport coaches. Journal of Sport Psychology 1:59-75.

Walker. J.E.. and Shea. T.M. (1984). Behavior management: A practical approach for educators. St. Louis: C.V. Mosby.

Selected Readings

Donahue. J.A.. Gillis. J.H.. and King. H. (1980). Behavior modification in sport and physical education: A review. Journal of Sport Psychology 2:311-328.

Martin. G.L.. and Hrycaiko. D. (1983). Principles and procedures of applied behavior analysis with illustrations from sport and physical education. In G.L. Martin and D. Hrycaiko. eds.. Behavior modification and coaching: Principles. procedures. and research. Springfield. Ill.: Charles C Thomas.

Orlick. T.. and Botterill. C. (1975). Every kid can win. Chicago: Nelson Hall.

Rushall. B.S. (1977). Two observation schedules for sporting and physical education environments. Canadian Journal of Applied Sport Sciences 2:15-21.

Siedentop. D.. and Taggart. A. (1984). Behavior analysis in physical education and sport. In W. Heward. T. Heron. D. Hill. and J. Trapp-Porter. eds.. Focus on behavior analysis in education. Columbus. Ohio: Charles E. Merrill.

Smith. R.W.. Smoll. F.L.. and Hunt. E. (1977). A system for the behavioral assessment of athletic coaches. Research Quarterly 48:401-407.

Behavioral Assessment

Batman and Robin! Romeo and Juliet! Rowan and Martin! Abbott and Costello! Mantle and Maris! Trottier and Bossy! Gretzky and Kurri! Linus and his blanket! Tom and Jerry! Simon and Garfunkle! Hawkeye and B.J.! Anthony and Cleopatra! A behavioral coach and his or her data sheet!

A behavioral coach and his or her data sheet? Yes! Like the famous pairs listed above, you can't think of one without remembering the other. As we indicated in Chapter 2, the Number 1 characteristic of behavioral coaching emphasizes specific, detailed, and frequent measurement of athletic performance, and the use of those measures to evaluate the effectiveness of specific coaching techniques. If an athlete or team is not performing satisfactorily, the first step is behavioral assessment: detailed and careful assessment of present level of skill or performance.

Sometimes it is useful to obtain data on two or three specific behaviors. You will recall from Chapter 1 that Coach Dawson recorded whether his basketball players made their lay-ups, free throws, and jump shots during their practice drills. At other times the assessment task may be to evaluate all of the players on all of the fundamentals. Such might be the case when a new coach takes over a team and wants to begin by evaluating the players' strengths and weaknesses on the basic skills. A third assessment situation involves breaking a new skill into its component parts for instructional purposes, and so that improvements can be accurately monitored. A fourth assessment situa-

31

tion involves assessing the components of team play. In this chapter we present specific guidelines for conducting behavioral assessments in each of these areas, and include some precautions to ensure that the assessments are accurate. A number of benefits of behavioral assessments are also discussed. Finally, some ethical considerations are reviewed to ensure that behavioral assessments are conducted with the best interests of the athletes in mind.

STIMULI, BEHAVIOR, REWARDS, AND STIMULUS CONTROL

Before reading about behavioral assessment, it is necessary to know about stimuli, behavior, rewards, and stimulus control, some of the building blocks of behavior modification. A *stimulus* is any physical event or object in the environment. Some examples of stimuli include the sound of a basketball hitting the backboard, the sight of a baseball curving toward the strike zone, the twang of a hockey puck hitting the net, the sight of a swimmer's toes at the surface of the water in backstroke, the sound of signals called by the quarterback, and the words of a referee warning a boxer about a low blow.

A *behavior* is anything that a person says or does. Some commonly used synonyms for behavior are activity, performance, reaction, and response. Bouncing a ball, shooting a basket, hitting a ball, catching a ball, skating, performing a back-walkover in gymnastics, and making a tackle in football are all examples of behavior. Another term sometimes used synonymously with behavior is skill. Skating, for example, might also be referred to as a skill. Performing a back-walkover might be referred to as a skill. While the term skill has additional meanings in some texts (e.g., Magill, 1980), we use the terms behavior and skill interchangeably.

People learn to make certain responses in the presence of some stimuli and not others. As can be seen by comparing the examples of stimuli and behaviors above, a person's behavior can constitute a stimulus to which another person might respond; that is, a word spoken by a coach might be a stimulus for the behavior of an athlete. Nonverbal behavior can also constitute a stimulus for an athlete; for example, the expression on a coach's face often provides a stimulus for athletes to show attentive listening behavior. An athlete's behavior may also serve as a stimulus with respect to further behavior of that athlete. Many golfers can tell whether they've hit a good shot just by the feel of the swing. The tactile or kinesthetic feeling of muscle movement serves as a stimulus for further muscle movement for that athlete.

What is it that causes people to learn to make certain responses in the presence of some stimuli and not others? Consider the following. A golfer is standing on a putting green and is about to hit a 5-foot putt toward the hole. In the presence of the stimuli provided by a flat putting green, the golfer who responds by aiming directly at the hole will be rewarded by making the putt (assuming the ball is hit with appropriate force). However, in the presence of the stimuli provided when there is a slope on the green, the golfer who responds by hitting the putt directly at the hole will not make the putt (it will curve off in the direction of the slope). After several trials, the golfer learns to hit the ball directly at the hole only when the putting green is flat. In more general terms, a behavior is likely to occur in the presence of the stimuli that were present when previous instances of that behavior were rewarded; a behavior is not likely to occur in the presence of the stimuli that were present when previous instances of that behavior were not rewarded or, perhaps, were punished. This sequence of events is diagrammed as follows:

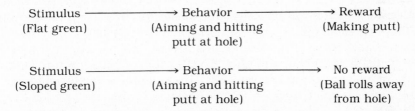

Technically speaking, a *positive reinforcer* refers to a consequence that, when presented after a behavior, tends to increase the frequency of that behavior. The term positive reinforcer is roughly synonymous with reward. Guidelines for effective use of rewards by coaches are described in later chapters.

When specific responses are linked to specific stimuli, we say that *stimulus control* exists. For example, stimulus control is demonstrated several times within the sequence of components that characterize a good golf shot. The sight of the golf club positioned immediately behind the ball and the feel from the stance constitute stimuli for a golfer to start the backswing. The position of the arms and the cocked wrists at the top of the backswing constitute stimuli for the golfer to begin the downswing. And so on. It is crucial for coaches to ensure that certain stimuli exert control over certain behaviors of their athletes in competition. The successful quarterback must be able to pick out the pass receivers quickly, even in the face of charging linemen from the opposing team. An effective counterpuncher must be able to detect and avoid punches from an opponent boxer, and to throw the correct combination of counterpunches. The distance and terrain of a golf course must exert appropriate stimulus control over the correct selection of clubs in order for a golfer to hit the ball the correct distance consistently. Basketball players must know when to shoot versus when to pass. All of these examples involve stimulus control, situations in which specific stimuli control the occurrence of specific behaviors.

ASSESSING FREQUENCY OF A SPECIFIC BEHAVIOR

Sometimes a behavior is simple to define and easy to accurately record. Consider the situation faced by Coach Keedwell of the Manitoba Marlin Swim Club. "We have a big meet coming up in 3 weeks," she said to the swimmers in lane 4 at the start of practice. "To do your best, you have to be in good shape. I want you to swim all the sets without stopping or touching down in the middle. You also have to practice your racing turns." "You know me, Coach," said Tyson, "I never stop in the middle." "I always do my turns," chimed in Tammy. A few minutes later, after watching some of her older swimmers in the fifth lane, Coach Keedwell went back to lane 4. There was Tyson, in the middle of a set, stopping and adjusting his goggles for the fourth time. Tammy and three other swimmers swam to the end of the lane, touched the bulkhead with their hands, and began swimming again without executing the proper turn. "It's time for some formal behavioral assessments," thought Coach Keedwell.

Clayton Cracklen, a psychology student from the University of Manitoba agreed to run a project with the swimmers. For the next four practices, Clayton and some additional students sat on the bulkhead and observed the swimmers in lane 4. They recorded the frequency of improper turns and unscheduled stops during sets. The results showed an average of approximately 20 of these inappropriate behaviors per swimmer per practice. At the start of the fifth practice, Coach Keedwell had a meeting with the swimmers in lane 4, and explained some new rules (Fig. 3-1).

With the new rules in effect, the swimmers each averaged only three stops or missed turns for the entire fifth practice, a total of 21 for the group. Subsequent research demonstrated that the improvement was clearly due to the treatment program of showing the swimmers a graph of their performance and requiring them to earn relays by meeting a certain goal. Not only did they improve dramatically, 11 of the 15 swimmers who participated in the project said that they preferred earning relays. Two said they preferred having relays without having to earn them, and two said that they did not care one way of the other. These results suggest that not only can fun activities be used to motivate

FIGURE 3-1
Coach Keedwell explains new rules to swimmers in lane 4.

improved performance of swimmers at practice, but also that such activities continue to be fun for most swimmers, even when earned (Cracklen and Martin, 1983).

You're probably thinking, "Yes, but improper racing turns and stopping while swimming are simple behaviors that are easy to count and to change. Besides, swimming is a close-ended sport. What about more complex skill development? What about open-ended individual and team sports where there's a lot more action than during swimming?" And of course, you're right. Improper racing turns and stopping during the set are simple behaviors that are easy to count. Every sport, however, has some simple behaviors that are easy to monitor. The point here is that behavioral assessment is an important first step to changing such behaviors. Increased output by swimmers at practices (McKenzie and Rushall, 1974), improved physical fitness activities (Keefe and Blumenthal, 1980), picking up the weights in a college weight room (Darden and Madsen, 1972), returning pool cues to the recreation center (Pierce and Risley, 1974), decreasing late arrivals at practices (McKenzie and Rushall), keeping your head still while putting (Simek and O'Brien, 1978), decreasing off-task behaviors of figure skaters (Hume et al., 1985), and passing accurately to a "setter box" placed along the net in volleyball (McKenzie and Liskevych, 1983) are examples of such behaviors that have been easily improved in formal research projects.

ASSESSING BASIC SKILLS

Casey Stengel once said, "I had many years that I was not so successful as a ball player, as it is a game of skill." May the wisdom that was Stengel's never be forgotten! Successful performance in any sport requires mastery of the basic skills, an appropriate level of physical fitness for performing those skills, and lots of practice. It's part of the coach's job to ensure that players acquire the skills, attain the desired level of physical fitness, and demonstrate effective practice performance. The cornerstone for monitoring improvement in all these areas is behavioral assessment. Obviously, swimmers attempting racing turns or stopping in the middle of a set were easy behaviors for Cracklen to observe and record. Other concerns require more complex assessment systems, for example, an increase in the number of behaviors to be assessed. Imagine being faced with the task of evaluating the strengths and weaknesses of basic skills of 12-year-old players trying out for a hockey team that will represent the city of Minneapolis in an international tournament in Canada. An initial step might be for several experienced coaches to observe skating, passing, shooting, and puck-handling skills of the players trying out for the team. They would probably want a quick summary of the strengths and weaknesses of the players on these basic skills. A common aid to this type of problem is a behavioral checklist of the basic skills to be assessed. An example of such a checklist is shown in Fig. 3-2.

ASSESSING COMPONENTS OF A SINGLE SKILL

A behavioral checklist such as that shown in Fig. 3-2 can provide a useful summary of an athlete's strengths and weaknesses on the basic skills of a sport. Such a checklist can be helpful for planning a training program for preparing a team to represent Minneapolis in a Pee-Wee ice hockey tournament in Winnipeg. But what if you want to help a beginner improve several aspects of a single skill? This leads to another type of complexity in behavioral assessment: analyzing the components of a single skill. This subarea of behavioral assessment is called *task analysis*, or breaking a new skill into its component parts so that they can be taught effectively and improvements can be accurately monitored. The checklist shown in Fig. 3-3 was designed by Dr. Dennis Hrycaiko, coach of the University of Manitoba varsity football team, to assess a football player performing the drive block. Task analyses of basic skills of other sports appear throughout this book.

ASSESSING COMPONENTS OF TEAM PLAY

Complexity in behavioral assessment systems is also present in assessing team play. Remember Charlie Jones, the coach of the Pop Warner football team from Chapter 1? The statistics that had been gathered by Michael Appelbaum's father showed that the backfield was averaging 60% correct execution. Although those stats told Coach Jones that there was no improvement in the play execution of his backfield, they did not tell him *who* was making mistakes or *which* mistakes were being made. Now, you may have guessed that Charlie Jones is a fictitious character. Fred Barnett, however, is not. Fred was the coach of a Pop Warner football team in Atlanta. He joined forces with Dr. Komaki, a behavioral psychologist, and began experimenting with behavioral coaching techniques to try to improve the play execution of his backfield (Komaki and Barnett, 1977). He had been coaching for two seasons. All of his current players had at least 1 year of experience in organized football. Barnett and his fellow coaches had spent a great deal of time working with their team on fundamentals

CHECKLIST

Fundamental Skills for Age-Group Hockey Players

SCORING KEY: N = *Needs improvement*
              G = *Good (average for age)*
              A = *Advanced (for age)*

Date

Skating Forward

1. Starting
2. Striding
3. Speed
4. Turning right
5. Turning left
6. Turning from forward to backward
7. Stopping right
8. Stopping left

Skating Backward

1. Starting
2. Gliding
3. Speed
4. Turning right
5. Turning left
6. Turning from backward to forward
7. Stopping

Puck Handling

1. Carrying puck with two hands
2. Carrying puck with one hand
3. Stick handling forward
4. Faking to backhand and moving to forehand
5. Faking to forehand and moving to backhand

FIGURE 3-2

	Date							

Passing

1. Forehand pass delivery while standing
2. Forehand pass delivery while skating
3. Backhand pass delivery while standing
4. Backhand pass delivery while skating
5. Forehand pass receiving while standing
6. Forehand pass receiving while skating
7. Backhand pass receiving while standing
8. Backhand pass receiving while skating
9. Passing accurately to stationary targets
10. Passing accurately to moving targets

Shooting

1. Forehand stationary wrist shot
2. Forehand wrist shot while skating
3. Backhand stationary wrist shot
4. Backhand wrist shot while skating
5. Snap shot while standing
6. Snap shot while skating
7. Slap shot while standing
8. Slap shot while skating

Steps to Effective Behavioral Coaching

C H E C K L I S T

Assessing Drive Block

SCORING KEY: I = *Needs improvement*
 G = *Good*
 E = *Excellent*

Date

Arms crossed at wrist with palms up
Initial step taken with foot closest to defender
Drive out of stance, short initial step(s) toward target
Arms brought up and forward on rotation, aiming at chest of target

As rotation of arm starts, there is good arch of back, with head up. Forward thrust is from low position
On impact, block is delivered with forearms, not head. Side view will reveal that both elbows are ahead of head
Both fists (closed) against chest (not away from body)
Elbows at blocker's chest level, not above shoulders
If fists open, palms should face opponent, or rotation not complete

Blow is delivered from wide base. Balanced stance avoids easy slip-off, and opponent receives full impact of blow
Follow through with short, choppy steps (footfire), from wide stance. Take defender in direction he wants to go (control of man essential)

From Martin, G., and Hrycaiko, D.

FIGURE 3-3

such as tackling, blocking, passing, and receiving. Each player had been given a playbook that described some 30 different plays. Coach Barnett's concern, at the time he and Dr. Komaki began this study, was the offensive play of his backfield.

After some 13 practices and three games, Coach Barnett thought he saw an improvement in the backfield's execution of plays. But he couldn't be sure. He decided that he needed more accurate records of what was happening when particular plays were run during a scrimmage and during an actual game. He chose three plays for investigation. Each required different activities on the part of the players and was not simply a variation on the same play. Coach Barnett's first step in behavioral assessment was to make a list of fundamental skills involved in executing each play. For example, for the quarterback option play, the basic skills included the quarterback-center exchange, the quarterback—right halfback fake, the fullback sprinting toward and blocking the defensive right end, the quarterback moving down the line and making a decision to pitch or keep the football, and the quarterback—left halfback action in which the quarterback either keeps the ball or pitches to the left halfback, who catches the ball and runs upfield.

Coach Barnett's next step was to make a checklist to monitor progress (Fig. 3-4). During seven practices and three games, Coach Barnett's assistants kept track of the backfield performance with regard to execution of the plays. During that time he followed his usual coaching routine. After analyzing the information collected on his checklists, he discovered that his backfield was not improving. It was averaging approximately 62% correct execution. There was only one instance where an entire play had been perfectly executed (according to the steps he had listed on his checklists). More important, performance during the first few practices and games was about the same as during the last few. In short, his checklists proved that there was no improvement.

Once Coach Barnett knew for sure that the backfield was not improving, he and Dr. Komaki designed the following behavioral coaching procedure:

Step 1. Each player was shown the checklist (Fig. 3-4), and told that play execution was being graphed.

Step 2. The players "walked through" the play several times while the coach demonstrated the correct movements and gave verbal instructions to each player regarding the correct execution of the play.

C H E C K L I S T

Assessing Quarterback Option Play _____

SCORING KEY: √ = Correct X = Incorrect	Individual Assessment Trials							
	1	2	3	4	5	6	7	8
Quarterback-center exchange								
Quarterback–right halfback fake								
Fullback blocks end								
Quarterback decision to pitch or keep								
Quarterback action								
PERCENT SCORES								

From Komaki. J.. and Barnett. F.

FIGURE 3-4

Step 3. In addition to pointing out errors, Coach Barnett strongly emphasized the things that were done right and praised his players enthusiastically for their correct performance.

Step 4. During scrimmages and during games, as soon as possible after the play was executed, the players checked with the coach to see how well they had done.

This four-step procedure was pretty simple overall. The results were positive! Over the remainder of the season, play performance improved to an average of 82%! And there were many instances where play execution was 100% correct. Barnett and Komaki repeated this procedure for two additional plays, and got the same positive results. How did the players feel? Terrific! The checklist apparently made games more fun than ever. The backfield was fascinated by the checklist and often got into long discussions regarding the finer points of various stages of a play.

Thus far in this chapter, our examples of behavioral assessment have included counting the frequency of specific, simple behaviors (improper turns and stopping during sets while swimming), rating the quality of a number of skills on a checklist (skating, puck handling, passing, and shooting in hockey), evaluating the components of a single skill (the drive block in football), and evaluating the execution of team play (a backfield performing the quarterback option play in football). These represent only a small number of the different behavioral assessments that can be used to enhance coaching effectiveness. Many other examples are described throughout this book. To be useful, however, your assessments must be accurate.

ARE YOUR ASSESSMENTS ACCURATE?

A list of the basic skills of your sport, and a checklist for assessing them will help you achieve at least one of the goals of effective behavioral coaching. You'll have a clearer, more objective picture of your players' strengths and weaknesses and a solid basis for judging improvements. Often, however, you will have to go into more detail in describing basic skills than simply listing them in a word or two. This is especially true if several assistant coaches or volunteers are helping you to assess the players. For example, if Coach Barnett scored the quarterback-center exchange as correct when his backfield ran a quarterback option play during a game, and an assistant coach scored it as incorrect while watching the same play, the two coaches would have to get together on just what they considered to be correct execution of the quarterback-center exchange. In fact, anticipating just such a problem, Coach Barnett and his assistant prepared detailed descriptions of each of the components of the play in their checklist. Two of these are described in Fig. 3-5; similar descriptions were prepared for the re-

Components of Quarterback Option Play _____

1. *Quarterback-center exchange.* On correct count, center "snaps the ball," that is, raises ball between the legs and quickly places ball in hands of quarterback (QB). QB should have the ball firmly in his hands.

2. *Quarterback—right halfback fake.* With the ball in his hands, QB moves quickly down line as right halfback (RHB) goes toward middle of line. QB fakes handoff to RHB, that is, places ball in hands of RHB. As RHB bends over and runs low, appearing to have ball. QB pulls ball back and continues going down line.

From Komaki. J., and Barnett. F.

FIGURE 3-5

maining three components of the quarterback option play, and for the components of the other two plays studied. By studying the detailed descriptions of the items in the checklist before using it, Coach Barnett and his assistant avoided potential disagreements while assessing the backfield.

The problem of observers disagreeing on how to score items in a checklist might be encountered in any situation where behavioral assessments are being used. It is important to prevent this problem. A coach has to have confidence that the data collected from assessments are "the real McCoy," that is, they accurately reflect the performance of the athletes. To alleviate such doubts, a coach might consider the following precautions before using behavioral assessments:

1. Ensure that your observers agree on how to score the behaviors being assessed. This might require preparation of more detailed descriptions of the items, such as the descriptions prepared by Coach Barnett and his assistant for scoring the quarterback option play (*see* Fig. 3-5). In some cases, picture prompts might be placed on the data sheets (*see* Figs. 2-1 and 3-2).

2. Two or more observers might practice with the definitions and compare scores obtained for a particular athlete (assessed by the two observers at the same time). Accurate assessment would be reflected by identical or very similar scores. A formal comparison of the scores obtained by two observers who scored the same behavior of the same athlete at the same time is referred to as *interobserver reliability* (IOR). There are formulas for computing an IOR score between two observers. For example, in the Cracklen and Martin (1983) study, in which observers recorded the total number of undesirable behaviors of swimmers (improper turns and unscheduled stops during sets), IOR was calculated by dividing the smaller total number of undesirable behaviors recorded for the swimmers in a lane during a session by the larger number recorded by a second observer during the same session, and multiplying by 100. In the Komaki and Barnett (1977) study, the backfield coach and another coach concurrently recorded the stages of the plays that were performed correctly each time the play was run. They then compared their records to assess the number of times they agreed that a particular stage of a play was run either correctly or incorrectly, and the number of times that they disagreed. The formula for computing IOR that they used was the number of agreements, divided by the sum of the number of agreements plus the number of disagreements, times 100. (For a more detailed discussion of the computation of IORs, see Martin and Pear, 1983). In general, in behavior modification re-

search, IOR scores of at least 80%, using the above formulas, are considered necessary for recorded observations to be considered reliable (Kazdin, 1984).

3. When recording performance measures, the observers should be positioned so as not to influence each other but so that they can clearly observe the athletes who are performing. Inaccurate results might be a reflection of distractions in the observation field.

4. Observers should discuss guidelines for using the scoring code. For example, in Fig. 3-2 the scoring key is N = Needs improvement, G = Good, and A = Advanced. But how good does a skater have to be to score a G or an A? Usually observers can solve these kinds of problems by identifying particular athletes to use as their standard for comparison, or by writing out quantitative or qualitative standards for their judgments.

5. Consideration should be given to whether the conditions at the time of assessment are really those in which you're interested. It is one thing to assess athletes who are tired at the end of a practice, and another to assess them under game conditions when they're fresh. For example, if you ask young swimmers to demonstrate their best freestyle stroke at the start of a practice, they might show you very deliberate strokes that are technically quite correct. If you assess them at the end of practice, or put them in a race, however, their technique will likely break down. As described earlier in this chapter, the stimulus control of the behavior being assessed is very important. A rule of thumb is: take data under game conditions if you are most interested in assessing what performance will look like in a game; assess under typical practice conditions if you are interested in having a record of performance during practice.

6. Finally, it is important to keep in mind that the use of assessments such as described does not exhaust the possibilities for behavioral assessment of athletic skills. More detailed guidelines are provided in later chapters.

BENEFITS OF BEHAVIORAL ASSESSMENTS

At this point you might be thinking, "These assessment techniques sound great if you have unlimited assistants, but I don't have the time nor the manpower to do all of this assessment and monitoring." And you're right. Behavioral coaching is a lot of work. However, don't despair. In later chapters we describe several strategies for using volunteer help to obtain the needed manpower. We also discuss strategies for prioritizing and time-lining some of the assessment and intervention strategies so that you can use those that might be most helpful to you. It is not necessary to use all the checklists to practice effective behavioral coaching. Finally, although these assessment techniques may be time consuming, we want to emphasize the following benefits of conducting behavioral assessments.

1. The information in behavioral assessment is essential for teaching your players, because it helps you, as a coach, to identify those specific parts of a player's performance that need improvement.

2. Repeated use of a checklist to assess the finer components of a skill provides a coach with solid proof that there either is or is not improvement. It is proof on paper; facts recorded at the time the performance was occurring. A checklist can free a coach from the burden of relying on memory to recall the facts after the practice or game is over. After all, "Quite literally, a man's memory is what he forgets with."—*Odell Shephard.*

3. The proof in checklists and graphs that there is real improvement can provide a powerful incentive for athletes to practice more and maintain the progress they've gained. Do you remember how much the backfield studied by Komaki and Barnett enjoyed examining and discussing the results on the checklist of their performance? Other studies on the use of checklists to improve performance have been described for bowling (Kirschenbaum et al., 1982), golf (Johnston-O'Connor and Kirschenbaum, in press; Kirschenbaum and Bale, 1980), swimming (Martin et al., 1983; McKenzie and Rushall, 1974), baseball (Ross et al., 1984), basketball (Bradshaw, 1984), and figure skating (Hume et al., 1985).

4. Checklists can also function as useful "report cards" for young and advanced athletes alike. Sending a copy home with a beginner helps to focus discussion with parents on both strengths and weaknesses, encourage realistic appraisal of skills by both parents and athlete, and help the young athlete to set realistic personal goals for improvement. Formal assessments for more advanced athletes will provide them with satisfaction for progress shown or skills acquired, realistic information for goal setting, and identification of areas requiring extra practice time or off-season training programs.

5. Behavioral assessments can help a coach more accurately account for his or her actions. Often, administrators, parents, and sometimes coaches make statements about athletic performance, or offer explanations for it, with considerable certainty, for example, "Her weight transfer is off," or "He didn't follow through," or "She's executing better now than early in the season." When such statements are made, it is always fair to ask, "Let me see the data supporting that," or "Do you have accurate before and after measures demonstrating a change in performance?" You might even ask, "How do you know that improvements were the result of your coaching? Did you use an acceptable research design?" More about that later. The point here is that the 1980s have been described as the decade of accountability in government, teaching, and numerous other areas. Accurate behavioral assessments help a coach become more accountable for his or her actions. (Accountability is discussed in more detail in Chapter 16.)

SOME ETHICAL CONSIDERATIONS

Most coaches adopt some type of code of ethics. Frequently that code is littered with noble words—words such as integrity, fair play, honesty, the rights of the athlete, and the granddaddy of all ethical words in sports, good sportsmanship. These are fine words. Terrific ideas. But they mean nothing unless they have an impact on the *behavior* of the coach. From a behavioral point of view, the term "ethics" refers to certain standards of behavior (Martin and Pear, 1983). An ethical coach behaves in ways that meet standards set by the coaching profession. An ethical coach behaves in a way that others would describe as honest, or fair, or sportsmanlike. The ethics of behavioral coaching are discussed in more detail in Chapter 15. Right now, let's consider some ethics of behavioral assessment.

It goes without saying that a coach should always conduct behavioral assessments with the best interest of the athlete in mind. To ensure that this is not forgotten, a coach should show the following ethical behaviors:

1. Explain to an athlete what behavior is being assessed and why it is being assessed.
2. Clearly and concisely explain the results of the assessment to the athlete.
3. Clearly explain to the athlete how the results of the assessment will be used to improve athletic performance.

A more detailed discussion of the ethics of psychological assessment of athletes is provided by Nideffer (1981).

SUMMARY

Stimuli, behavior, and stimulus control are some of the building blocks of behavior modification. A stimulus is any physical event or object in the environment. A behavior is anything that a person says or does. The term stimulus control refers to the observation that certain behaviors occur in the presence of some stimuli and not others, that is, that certain stimuli and responses are linked.

Stimuli, behavior, and stimulus control are also important components of behavioral assessments. Four types of behavioral assessments that can be used to enhance coaching effectiveness include counting the frequency of specific simple behaviors; rating the quality of a number of skills on a checklist; evaluating the components of a single skill; and using checklists to evaluate the execution of team play. When coaches use checklists to assess the performance of their athletes, it is important that they take the necessary steps to ensure that their assessments are accurate. It is also important for coaches to ensure that they meet acceptable ethical standards, which include communicating to the athletes being assessed something about the purpose of the assessment, the results, and the potential benefits of the assessment for improving the athletes' performance.

Although behavioral assessments can be time consuming, they do have a number of benefits. They can be used to identify performance areas that need improvement; provide proof of improvement; serve as an incentive for athletes to practice and maintain progress; function as useful "report cards" for young athletes; and help the coach to be accountable to administrators, parents, and others.

Coach's Checklist

The first step in effective behavioral coaching is to clearly identify the basic skills or behaviors that you want to improve in your athletes. The second step is to prepare a checklist for assessing those behaviors. If necessary, you might also have to prepare more detailed descriptions of the basic skills that you are assessing. The third step is to use the checklist to obtain a clear, objective picture of your players' strengths and weaknesses.

Armed with good checklists, you can be sure that your plans for the team won't miscarry through lack of aim. You'll be a coach who knows which harbor you're headed for! To help you to make doubly certain that you don't fall asleep at the helm, we have provided one final checklist for your inspection. This checklist is for you. It lists the steps that you should take for conducting preliminary behavioral assessments. An effective behavioral coach keeps watch over his or her own behaviors as well as those of the athlete. The Coach's Checklist presented in Fig. 3-6 is one simple way to do that.

Review Questions

1. Define stimulus. Describe three examples from sports.
2. Define behavior. Describe three examples from sports.
3. List three synonyms for behavior.
4. Describe an example of how a behavior of a coach can be a stimulus for an athlete.
5. Describe an example of how a behavior of an athlete can also serve as a stimulus with respect to further behavior of that athlete.
6. Define stimulus control. Describe an example of stimulus control.
7. Define positive reinforcer. What was the positive reinforcer applied by Coach Keedwell? What was the positive reinforcer applied by Coach Barnett?
8. Cracklen and Martin argued that, to improve performance of age-group swimmers in practice, fun should be earned. Briefly describe their experiment that supported the argument.
9. Define task analysis. Describe an example.

COACH'S CHECKLIST

Conducting a Behavioral Assessment _____

	Date Completed
1. Make a list of the athletic behaviors to be assessed.	
2. Clarify the defining characteristics of the behaviors to be assessed.	
3. Make a checklist for recording the behaviors to be assessed.	
4. Explain to the athlete(s) what behaviors are being assessed and why.	
5. Discuss your scoring code with your observers.	
6. Practice scoring to make sure that you and your observers agree on how to use the checklist.	
7. Select a time of assessment with due consideration for such factors as the fatigue, motivation, and awareness of the athlete as well as distractions in the situation.	
8. Carry out a sufficient number of assessments to obtain a reliable measure of current level of performance.	
9. Clearly communicate the results of the assessment to the athletes and explain how they will be used to improve their performance.	

FIGURE 3-6

10. What is meant by interobserver reliability?
11. If, during swimming practice, one observer scored 37 unscheduled stops by a swimmer, and another observer scored 40 unscheduled stops by that swimmer, what would be the IOR score for those two observers?
12. Briefly describe five benefits of behavioral assessment.
13. Describe three ethical behaviors that a coach should practice when conducting behavioral assessments.

Mini-Lab Exercises

1. Choose a sport that you have played or would like to coach. Prepare a checklist of the fundamental skills for beginners in that sport, similar to the checklist of fundamental hockey skills shown in Fig. 3-2.
2. Consider the list of fundamental skills that you prepared in answer to the previous question. Pick two of the skills and prepare detailed descriptions of them so that observers could accurately score them. Try to arrange an opportunity so that you and another observer can go to a practice where young athletes are practicing those two skills. Using your definitions, you and the other observer score the skills on several trials; then compare your scores and evaluate your interobserver reliability.

References

Bradshaw. D. (1984). Motivation through basketball statistics. Coaching Review **7** (May/June):52-54.

Cracklen, C., and Martin, G.L. (1983). Earning fun with correct techniques. Swimming Technique **20**:29-32.

Darden, E., and Madsen, C.H. (1972). Behavior modification for weightlifting room problems. College Student Journal **6**:95-99.

Hume, K.M., Martin, G.L., Gonzalez, P., Cracklen, C., and Genthon, S. (1985). A self-monitoring feedback package for improving freestyle figure skating practice behaviors. Journal of Sport Psychology **7**:333-345.

Johnston-O'Connor, E.J., and Kirschenbaum, D.S. (in press). Something succeeds like success: Positive self-monitoring for unskilled golfers. Cognitive Therapy and Research.

Kazdin, A.E. (1984). Behavior modification in applied settings, 3rd ed. Homewood, Ill.: Dorsey Press.

Keefe, F.J., and Blumenthal, A.J. (1980). The life fitness program: A behavioral approach to making exercise a habit. Journal of Behavior Therapy and Experimental Psychiatry **11**:31-34.

Kirschenbaum, D.S., and Bale, R.M. (1980). Cognitive behavior skills in golf: Brain power golf. In R.M. Suinn, ed., Psychology in sports: Methods and applications. Minneapolis: Burgess Publishing Company.

Kirschenbaum, D.S., Ordman, A.M., Tomarken, A.J., and Holtzbauer, R. (1982). Effects of differential self-monitoring and level of mastery on sports performance: Brain power bowling. Cognitive Therapy and Research 6:335-342.

Komaki, J., and Barnett, F.T. (1977). A behavioral approach to coaching football: Improving the play execution of the offensive backfield of a youth football team. Journal of Applied Behavior Analysis 10:657-664.

Magill, R.A. (1980). Motor learning: Concepts and applications. Dubuque, Ia.: Wm. C. Brown Publishing Co.

Martin, G.L., LePage, R., and Koop, S. (1983). Applications of behavior modification for coaching age-group competitive swimmers. In G.L. Martin and D. Hrycaiko, eds., Behavior modification and coaching: Principles, procedures, and research. Springfield, Ill.: Charles C Thomas.

Martin, G.L., and Pear, J.J. (1983). Behavior modification: What it is and how to do it, 2nd ed. Englewood Cliffs, N.J.: Prentice-Hall.

McKenzie, T.L., and Liskevych, T.N. (1983). Using the multi-element baseline design to examine motivation in volleyball training. In G.L. Martin and D. Hrycaiko, eds., Behavior modification and coaching: Principles, procedures, and research. Springfield, Ill.: Charles C Thomas.

McKenzie, T.L., and Rushall, B.S. (1974). Effects of self-recording on attendance and performance in a competitive swimming training environment. Journal of Applied Behavior Analysis 7:199-206.

Nideffer, R.M. (1981). The ethics and practice of applied sport psychology. Ithaca, N.Y.: Mouvement Publications.

Pierce, C.H., and Risley, T.R. (1974). Improving job performance of neighbourhood youth corps aides in an urban recreation centre. Journal of Applied Behavior Analysis 7:207-215.

Ross, S.A., O'Brien, R.M., and Mullins, W.C. (1984). Two types of feedback to improve hitting in collegiate baseball. Paper presented at the 92nd Annual Convention of the American Psychological Association, Toronto, Ontario, Canada, September 1984.

Simek, T.C., and O'Brien, R.M. (1978). Immediate auditory feedback to improve putting quickly. Perceptual Motor Skills 47:1133-1134.

Selected Readings

Anderson, W. (1980). Analysis of teaching physical education. St. Louis: C.V. Mosby.

Cautela, J.R. (1981). Behavior analysis forms for clinical intervention, vol. 2. Champaign, Ill.: Research Press.

Curtis, B., Smith, R.E., and Smoll, F.L. (1979). Scrutinizing the skipper: A study of leadership behaviors in the dug-out. Journal of Applied Psychology 64:391-400.

Hersen, M., and Bellack, A.S. (1981). Behavioral assessment: A practical handbook. Elmsford, N.Y.: Pergamon Press.

Keefe, F.J., Kopel, S.A., and Gordon, S.B. (1978). A practical guide to behavioral assessment. New York: Springer.

McKenzie, T.L., and King, H.A. (1982). Analysis of feedback provided by youth baseball coaches. Education and Treatment of Children 5:179-188.

Metzler, M. (1981). A multi-observational system for supervising student teachers in physical education. Physical Education 38(3):152-159.

Quarterman, J. (1980). An observational system for observing the verbal and nonverbal behaviors emitted by physical educators and coaches. Physical Educator 37(1):15-20.

Rushall. B.S. (1983). Coaching styles: A preliminary investigation. In G.L. Martin and D. Hrycaiko. eds.. Behavior modification and coaching: Principles. procedures and research. Springfield. Ill.: Charles C Thomas.

Rushall. B.S.. and Smith. K.C. (1979). The modification of the quality and quantity of behavior categories in a swimming coach. Journal of Sport Psychology **64**:391-400.

Siedentop. D. (1983). Recent advances in pedagogical research in physical education. The Academy Papers. Washington. D.C.: American Association of Health. Physical Education. Recreation and Dance. pp. 82-94.

GUIDELINES FOR SKILL DEVELOPMENT AND MOTIVATION

4

Teaching New Skills

In Chapter 3 we explained that when we use the word "behavior" or "skill," we are referring to the things an athlete does. Athletic behavior includes actions, reactions, a single movement, overall performance, a simple response, or the execution of a play. Passing, shooting, turning, twisting—all are behaviors. Some are simple behaviors. Some are more complex. All can be taught. All can be changed through correct application of basic behavioral laws. In this chapter we present guidelines that can help a coach strengthen desirable behaviors and teach basic skills. In the next three chapters, we discuss behavioral techniques for decreasing persistent errors, motivating athletes, and managing disruptive or problem behaviors.

How does a coach decide whether a behavior or skill is simple or complex? There is no universally accepted answer to this question, but we can provide some guidelines. Many athletic skills involve the repetition of relatively simple mechanical movements that can be performed quickly. Examples include performing chin-ups, kicking movements in freestyle swimming, or stationary dribbling in basketball. At the other extreme are the athletic skills that involve the linking of a successive series of movements in response to changing or moving features of the sports environment. For example, Larry Bird, after pulling down a rebound and passing to Danny Ainge, streaks down the sidelines, receives a return pass from Ainge, and sinks a spin-around jump shot, all in a few seconds.

Between the extremes of the relatively simple skills and the complex series of movements is a range of athletic skills that vary in complexity. There are also other types of behaviors that are relatively simple and, from the coach's point of view, equally valuable for athletes to acquire, for example, listening attentively to the coach, picking up equipment after a game, practicing an exercise as instructed, stopping an activity and going to a particular place on the playing field when the coach blows a whistle. These are the kinds of behaviors that a coach sees in what are often referred to as "coachable" athletes.

The teaching guidelines that we provide in this chapter are helpful for strengthening many kinds of behavior. They are especially applicable for improving relatively simple behaviors or for refining the performance of more complex behaviors and skills that have been partially mastered. These guidelines are also useful in developing the behaviors that are characteristic of coachable athletes. If you are attempting to teach complex skills from scratch with beginning athletes, however, the guidelines presented in this chapter might have to be supplemented by some of the strategies described in Chapter 5.

PRELIMINARY CONSIDERATIONS

> If learning is to be directed and purposeful, the learners . . . must have a clear idea of what is to be learned and must get regular feedback about their performances.—*Daryl Siedentop*

Daryl Siedentop is one of the leaders in the area of behavioral approaches to physical education. Like him, we believe that guidelines for strengthening simple behaviors should be centered around two main concerns. One set of guidelines helps the coach give the athletes a clear idea of the skills to be mastered. Another set of guidelines tells the coach about the most effective ways of providing feedback to strengthen those skills. Both sets are presented in this chapter. However, before reviewing the two sets of guidelines, there are some preliminary considerations to which a coach should attend.

1. Begin at athlete's level. As emphasized previously, behavioral assessment of an athlete's current level of performance has to be one of the first steps of effective behavioral coaching. There's no sense trying to teach a young hockey player to stick handle and make fancy passing plays if the child can't skate. On the other hand, young athletes will become bored if you spend a lot of time reviewing fundamentals they're already skilled at. To help maximize enjoyment and progress for all, begin at the athlete's skill level. There are, of course, some difficulties that must be overcome when one coach has to deal with a large group of athletes. Your beginners will undoubtedly be at different skill levels. There are several possible solutions to this problem. First, identify some drills and activities that tend to be independent of skill level, for example, activities to improve their level of physical fitness. These can be interspersed throughout practices. Second, spend some pre-season time locating and training volunteer assistants. Third, identify competence levels for various skills. During a part of each practice, organize your athletes into small groups for drills appropriate to their individual levels. Fourth, design activities that the athletes can work on in cooperative pairs (taking turns performing and observing each other). In general, the more pre-season time and energy you can spend in identifying strategies to enable you to begin at each athlete's present skill level, the greater the likelihood that each athlete will experience some success early in the program.

Finally, this is also the time to consider levels of fitness that are appropriate for the skills that you plan to teach (*see* Chapter 8). The fitness and strength development exercises that you implement must also begin at the athlete's personal level. An appropriate mixture of simple skills and physical fitness exercises that require a certain amount of "stretch" or "reach" (just beyond the athlete's current level) will help to guarantee success for all of the athletes.

2. Prepare task analyses of complex skills to be taught. We indicated in Chapter 3 that task analysis refers to breaking a new skill into its component parts so that they can be taught effectively and improvements can be accurately monitored. This usually requires the identification of both the individual behaviors in sequence and the stimuli that should control each of the behaviors. Examples of task analyses thus far include the components of the backstroke and the drive block in football. Task analyses should be prepared for each of the fundamental skills of the sport that you will be teaching. Shooting foul shots in basketball, putting in golf, blocking in football: what are the basic skills for the sport that you teach? For each such skill, you will likely be able to find books and coaching articles that have already task analyzed the skills in considerable detail. After you have collected your task analyses, the next step is to prepare checklists (*see* Figs. 2-1 and 3-3) to monitor the progress of your beginners. Not only are such checklists used widely when instructing beginners, they are becoming increasingly common features of instruction for advanced athletes as well. For example, Karen Linde, coach of the women's softball team at Sierra College in Rockman, California, uses one of her checklists regularly in practice to monitor improvement of her pitchers working off the rubber and practicing the whip-action delivery for the windmill-style right-handed pitch (Fig. 4-1).

C H E C K L I S T

Softball Pitcher: Whip-Action Delivery for Windmill-Style Right-Handed Pitch _____

Name_____ Date_____

PITCHING FROM MOUND

Technique	OK	Needs Improvement	Coach's Comment
Feet about shoulder width apart			
Ball of right foot on right edge of pitcher's mound			
Ball of left foot on left edge of pitcher's mound			
Hips facing target			
Shoulders in line with first and third			
First step with left foot			
Proper left foot placement			
Hips open to third base			
Left shoulder facing target			
Eyes fixed on target			
Arm up, back of hand facing up			
Wrist rotates, faces first base as arm reaches top of arc			
Upper arm brushes against hair			
Right foot pivots on ball of foot, toe points toward third			
Proper shifting of body weight			

From Hoehn, R.G.

FIGURE 4-1

3. **Arrange practice conditions so that athletes experience natural rewards.** As stated in Chapters 2 and 3, an extremely important component of the learning process is positive reinforcement: providing rewards for desirable behaviors. Behaviors that are rewarded tend to be repeated. Those that are not rewarded tend to decrease. Additional guidelines for effectively using rewards are provided later in this chapter. In this section, we want to distinguish between "natural," or intrinsic, rewarding consequences and "extra," or extrinsic, rewarding consequences. There are two types of intrinsic rewards. One is the sensory feedback that is inherent in the performance of a task. This type of reward may involve the visual, tactual, and auditory sensory feedback that comes from performing the task well. The "feel" of the solid contact when you hit a golf ball "in the screws"; the sight of your first hit in baseball arcing to the outfield; personal satisfaction (in terms of both self-talk and the internal feelings it elicits) from swimming the length of the pool for the first time; the sight of the basketball dropping through the hoop, and the swish of the net—all of these are natural rewarding consequences in that they are not deliberately programmed by the coach or teacher. Another type of intrinsic reward is the natural (as opposed to deliberately planned) reaction of others. A cheer from teammates for a good play; the roar of the crowd when a touchdown is scored; another player "giving you five" after a home run—these are examples of natural rewards.

By permission of Johnny Hart and News America Syndicate.

Extrinsic, or "material" rewards are rewards deliberately introduced to influence someone's performance. For example, if a coach introduces a scoring system in which points are awarded to players for showing specific practice behaviors, and if the players who earn the most points at practice earn the starting positions for games, then the points constitute extrinsic rewards.

As much as possible, coaches should try to structure early learning experiences so that beginning athletes experience natural, rewarding consequences. For example, in their behavioral approach to teaching golf, Simek and O'Brien (1981) proved that it is more effective for golf instructors to first teach beginners to make 10-inch putts. Why? Because a powerful natural reward for a golfer is hitting the ball into the

Complete Golf Chain and Mastery Criteria _____

Shot	Mastery Criterion
10-inch putt (between clubs optional)	4 putts consecutively holed
16-inch putt (between clubs optional)	4 putts consecutively holed
2-foot putt, clubs removed	4 putts consecutively holed
3-foot putt	4 putts consecutively holed
4-foot putt, some break	2 holed, 2 of 4 within 6 inches
6-foot putt	4 consecutively within 6 inches
10-foot putt	4 consecutively within 12 inches
15-foot putt	4 consecutively within 15 inches
20-foot putt	4 consecutively within 18 inches
30-foot putt	4 consecutively within 24 inches
35-foot chip 5 feet off green, 7-iron	4 of 6 within 6 feet
35-foot chip 15 feet off green, wedge	4 of 6 within 6 feet
65-foot chip	4 of 6 within 6 feet
25-yard pitch	4 of 6 within 10 feet
35-yard pitch	4 of 6 within 15 feet
50-yard pitch	4 of 6 within 15 feet
75-yard shot	4 of 6 within 30 feet
100-yard shot	4 of 6 within 40 feet
125-yard shot	4 of 6 within 45 feet
150-yard shot	4 of 6 within 54 feet
175-yard shot	4 of 6 within 66 feet
200-yard shot (if within your range)	4 of 5 within 90 feet
Driver	

From Simek. T.C.. and O'Brien. R.M.

FIGURE 4-2

hole. So they started with a task that was immediately followed by a reward: making 10-inch putts. Gradually the shot was advanced to longer putts, then to short chip shots, to longer chip shots, to short pitch shots, to longer pitch shots, to middle-iron shots, and eventually to hitting fairway woods shots, and finally using a driver. The detailed progression used by Simek and O'Brien is shown in Fig. 4-2. Similar progression charts could be used to teach skills in other sports. The more a coach can arrange early instruction so that beginners experience the natural rewards of performing a skill, the greater the chances those beginners will achieve sufficient success to maintain their effort and improvement.

GUIDELINES FOR INSTRUCTING ATHLETES ABOUT SKILLS TO BE MASTERED

As indicated previously, the coach must give the athletes a clear idea of the behaviors to be performed. Effective techniques for doing so are described below.

1. Combine modeling with instructions. When you begin to teach, your best approach is to *show* and *tell* simultaneously, especially with beginners. Show the athletes what you want them to do by demonstrating (modeling) the correct skill. While you (or one of the athletes) model, describe specific body movements and subtleties that the beginner would otherwise miss. For some skills, you may want to use pictures to help display (model) the performance. For example, if you were a swimming coach presenting the correct form for hand entry movements in the freestyle for first-year members of the club, you might:

1. Display pictures showing a sequence of freestyle arm movements.
2. Bend over and demonstrate (out of the water) the same movements as in the pictures while you describe the specific arm and hand positions.
3. After demonstrating correcting performance, model two or three common errors or incorrect movements that beginners often make, exaggerating the differences between the correct and incorrect movements so that the swimmers can clearly see what you mean by "correct" movement.
4. Repeat your demonstration of the correct movements one more time (i.e., model and describe correct arm and hand positions).

When you are modeling and explaining a skill, there are ways of describing the behavior that will help your athletes clearly understand what you want. Keep it clear, and be specific. For example, if you are modeling a component of freestyle arm pull, you might say: "Your hand should enter the water *in front of your shoulder*, with your fingers and thumb like this," or "During the first part of your pull, keep your elbow *high* and *bend your arm* so that *your hand curves underneath* your stomach, like this," or "Your fingertips should pass under *the center of your stomach, or your belly button*," or "As you complete your stroke, push your hand *past the bottom part of your bathing suit at your side*, to get a full stroke. You can hold your thumb out to see if you can feel the skin below your suit."

Thus, instead of simply saying, "Do it like this," you give your athletes very specific prompts: "in front of your shoulder," "elbow high," "fingertips near your belly button," "hand pushed past bathing suit," and so forth, depending on the component being modeled. Your athletes will not only better understand what you are saying, they will attend more closely to the key movements if you identify those movements as you demonstrate the skill. It is also important to keep in mind that young athletes cannot remember many things at once. Although you might model the whole skill once or twice at the start, you should then emphasize one or two of the components that the learner should concentrate on while practicing. After those are mastered, you can point out one or two additional components to add to the skill, and so on until the entire skill is mastered.

When you model incorrect movements, exaggerate the error and describe what you know to be common mistakes with respect to that particular skill. It's also a good idea to explain "why" the behavior is incorrect. For example, if you are modeling the arm pull for the freestyle stroke, you might emphasize common errors such as reaching over in front of the head (wrong because it causes the body to twist), pulling with a low or dropped elbow (decreases speed), pulling with a straight, rather than bent arm (makes a swimmer tire quickly), or pulling in a straight line (not as effective as pulling in an S pattern). For each error that you describe, model and exaggerate the incorrect performance, then perform the stroke correctly.

2. Describe positive consequences of successful performance. Sometimes athletes are not sure why they are performing particular drills. Sometimes the coach doesn't take the trouble to explain the positive results that can occur from consistently following certain practice routines. For example, a coach might tell a lineman on a certain play to partially block a hard-charging defensive lineman, then go down for the secondary. If the coach further explains that the play is designed to trap the defensive lineman, then the offensive lineman is more apt to maneuver the defensive lineman into a position vulnerable to the trap. If the coach takes the time to point out the natural rewards that accrue to those who follow certain practice strategies, the chances are increased that the athletes will in fact practice various exercises and routines diligently.

3. **Ask questions to test for understanding.** After you have explained your expectations, check the athlete's knowledge by asking specific questions. To continue with our example of teaching the hand pull for freestyle swimming, the coach might ask, "Where does the hand enter the water?" or "Where should your elbow be during the first part of the pull?" If you get wrong answers or faulty demonstrations, assume that the beginners haven't quite understood the correct way of performing the skill. Repeat the modeling and instruction phase. One more consideration: In a situation like this where a teacher is asking questions, silence very often means "I don't know."

4. **Ask athletes to role-play skills.** A swimming coach might ask athletes to role-play the freestyle stroke while standing beside the pool. A golf instructor might ask the student to role-play the motion of a golf stroke without actually requiring him or her to hit a golf ball. A basketball coach might ask an athlete to role-play dribbling by showing the appropriate arm movements, the crouch of the legs, the bent position of the body, the head and finger positions, all of which can be role-played without using a basketball. This type of role-playing allows the athlete to concentrate solely on practicing the correct form or movements of a skill without worrying about the end result. If the athletes perform incorrectly, the coach can provide immediate corrective feedback and ask the athlete to repeat the role-playing.

GUIDELINES FOR REWARDING DESIRABLE BEHAVIORS

Now that your athletes know what is expected of them, you have to require actual performance and reward the features that are correctly done. This is one of the most critical parts of the teaching process. Often at this point (where the athlete has to perform the actual skill) there is a strong tendency for the coach to begin pointing out mistakes. That tendency must be resisted. This is *not* the best time to issue excessive corrective feedback. During the first few tries, athletes should be made to feel a sense of accomplishment and should experience positive rewards for *attempting* the skill. The following guidelines will help you to effectively use rewards to strengthen and improve desirable behaviors and new skills.

1. **Frequently reward athlete's desirable behaviors.** Coaches are important to an athlete. It is a fact, however, that some coaches are more effective when dealing with their athletes than others are. What makes one coach more effective than another? In their research at the

University of Washington, Smith and co-workers (1979) investigated the differences between coaches to whom young baseball players responded favorably and those to whom they responded less favorably. Their research showed that an important factor was the frequency with which the coaches rewarded desirable behaviors. The young ball players they observed responded most favorably to the coach who dispensed frequent rewards. (Interestingly, they also found that young athletes preferred coaches who gave more technical instruction.)

How often should a coach provide rewards? To begin with, most coaches do not provide rewards as often as they could. Research in physical education classes has shown that a student teacher can easily provide rewards at a rate of four or five per minute during class (Siedentop, 1976). A reward, remember, can be a simple thing such as praise. Indeed, praise can be an extremely effective reward when used properly. Regardless of the type of reward you use, however, there is no doubt that the presentation of frequent rewards for desirable behavior is an effective coaching technique. The rule is simple and straightforward: If you want your athletes to repeat a particular behavior, reward instances of that behavior when you see them.

2. Make sure rewards are rewards from athlete's point of view and not just from coach's point of view. Technically, a reward or positive reinforcer is something that, when presented after a behavior, causes that behavior to be strengthened. In a practical sense, a reward is anything the athlete likes, wants, or enjoys. The key phrase here is "the athlete." Some coaches forget that it is the athlete who is to be rewarded, not the coach. "O.K., team!," said one football coach, "if y'all run the next play perfectly, I'll let you come into the coach's dressing room and watch some films of me when I played ball." Wow! That's really exciting! For the coach. It is less clear that this "privilege" would be a reward for the players. Do you think that all of the players would have tried to run the plays perfectly? Some might. Some probably wouldn't. How do you know what each athlete prefers? There are several ways to determine which rewards are good for individual athletes. One simple way is to let the athletes choose their own rewards.

The questionnaire shown in Fig. 4-3 is designed to help coaches identify specific people, objects, events, or activities that can be used as rewards in the coaching situation. To administer the questionnaire, coaches should either interview each player individually or give the questionnaire to the players and allow them to write in their responses to the questions.

Another way to determine if something is a reward is to observe its effect on athlete's behavior. If an athlete tries harder or performs the

behavior better or more often in order to earn a particular consequence, then you have a clear indication that the consequence is indeed a reward. Let's listen in on Coach Liskevych talking to the
Women's Varsity volleyball team at the University of the Pacific: "I've
worked out a new drill. The receivers could be doing a better job of
passing the ball. So here's the deal. You must be wondering about that
big box over there by the net [a sturdy cardboard box about 51 inches
high, with an opening 29 inches square at the top, placed along the net
about 20 inches from the center line of the court]. I'm going to feed you
some off-speed floating serves from just behind the 10 foot line over
there to either a right or left service reception spot. Your job is to
receive the serve and pass the ball into the 'setter box'." "Piece of cake,
Coach," said one of the players. "Each of you will get 30 serves, 15 from
the left position and 15 from the right position. If you put more than
25% of them into the setter box, you can each earn a dollar." The
players scrambled to get into line. Surprisingly, an average of only 20%
of their serves went into the setter box. The setter box made them
realize just how small the target area was and how much they had
previously relied on the mobility of the setter to save bad passes during
a game. At the next practice the coach said, "Today, with our setter box
drill, you can earn an hour of private instruction with me if you serve
nine of your 30 shots into the box." This time, the players averaged
30% accuracy. Over the next several practices the coach alternated the
money reward condition with the private instruction reward condition, and also with a condition during which no additional rewards
were attained for showing a criterion number of serves into the setter
box. Of surprise to Coach Liskevych, average accuracy of the passes
was 33.8% during the private instruction reward condition, whereas it
was only 26.6% during the money reward condition. The study very
nicely demonstrated the value of examining rewards in terms of
whether they increase the behavior that they follow. (For more information on this study, *see* McKenzie and Liskevych, 1983.)

It is appropriate at this point to comment on a frequently cited
distinction between intrinsic and extrinsic reinforcement. Some people criticize recommendations to deliberately use material reinforcers
to strengthen behavior. They argue that extrinsic reinforcement for a
behavior that a person finds (or should find) intrinsically reinforcing
will undermine his or her motivation to engage in that behavior when
the extrinsic reinforcement is no longer provided. An alternative
phrasing of the criticism is that too many material rewards will undermine intrinsic motivation of young athletes so that they are less
likely to perform for the intrinsic value of the activity itself. We have

Rewards Survey

Please answer the following questions, and return the questionnaire to the coach.

Social Rewards

Place a check mark beside the kinds of approval that you like others to show.

____ Facial signs (e.g., smiles, nods, winks)

____ Hand and body signs (e.g., clapping hands, holding thumbs up, clasping hands overhead)

____ Physical contact (e.g., a pat on the back, a hand shake, a hug)

____ Praise about yourself (e.g., you're smart, very helpful, a nice person)

____ Praise about your athletic skills (e.g., you have a great throwing arm, backhand, jumpshot)

Activity Rewards

What are some of the activities that you would like to do more often during practice sessions?

1. _____   3. _____

2. _____   4. _____

(EXAMPLES: Have a free swim time; shoot baskets for fun; help the coach set up equipment; help the coach score time trials; be the leader of the group for awhile; be the first to demonstrate skills; change playing positions for fun, i.e., be the catcher or pitcher or quarterback, for a change)

Equipment Rewards

Which pieces of sports equipment would you like to be allowed to use more often during practice?

1. _____   3. _____

2. _____   4. _____

(EXAMPLES: Paddleboards, tumbling mats, diving board, tires or tackle machine for football, ball machines for tennis or golf, a stop watch to time your own trials, an exercise bike, a pulse meter)

FIGURE 4-3

Outings as Rewards

Place a check mark beside the things you would like to do with the whole team.

_____ See a film about a favorite sports celebrity or a special sports event

_____ Tour a sports museum or hall of fame in your local area

_____ Hear a lecture or have a visit from a local professional athlete

_____ Go to a competition or sports event. such as a game or track meet. where professionals or high-ranking amateurs are competing

_____ Visit a practice session for professional athletes

_____ Have a team party or dance

_____ Other events or activities _____
_____

Possessional Rewards

Place a check mark beside the things you would like to have or own.

_____ Team sweater

_____ Team crest

_____ Team uniform

_____ Personal chart that shows your progress from week to week

_____ Particular piece of sports equipment that you could borrow for 1 week

_____ Other _____

Unique Opportunity Rewards

Place a check mark beside the unique opportunities that you would like to have.

_____ Opportunity to be an usher or helper at a special professional sports event

_____ Opportunity to be a bat boy or water girl or scorekeeper for one game with the local professional team

_____ Opportunity to play an exhibition game or play one inning. one set of tennis. one end in curling. with or against a local pro team or professional

_____ Other _____

several reactions to that criticism. First, as recommended earlier in this chapter, we agree that coaches should try to arrange conditions so that athletes experience naturally rewarding consequences for participation in sport. If young athletes frequently encounter natural reinforcers for participation in sport, their behavior is more likely to be described as intrinsically motivated. The problem is that not all young athletes experience natural reinforcers for sport participation. A low level of entry skills, a high level of competition, a coach who emphasizes the negative approach, and several other factors can all contribute to a situation that initially contains little or no reinforcement for a beginner. Our second point, therefore, is that deliberately managed material reinforcers are better than no reinforcers at all. If reinforcers introduced by a coach can increase the chances of a beginner acquiring skills and experiencing some of the natural rewards for sport participation, then the coach should not hesitate to use deliberately managed material rewards. Third, experimental evidence indicates that deliberately reinforcing individuals for particular behaviors in a given situation rarely leads to deterioration of those behaviors in other situations (Martin and Pear, 1983).

3. Use prescriptive praise. Praise is often a powerful reward. If an athlete performs well, a simple positive comment from the coach can be very rewarding: "Good!" "Well done!" "All right!" "Super!" "Terrific!" "Way to go!" "You're doing a lot better!" "That was great!" However, another type of praise can be especially effective when you are trying to get a particular behavior to occur more often. It is called prescriptive praise. When using prescriptive praise, the coach identifies that aspect of the athlete's performance that was desirable or that indicated improvement. In other words, you don't just tell them that they "did good." You tell them *what* they did. A basketball coach, for example, could say something like, "Nice follow-through on your foul shot! You pointed your index finger at the basket, and you didn't pull the string!" This coach has identified for the shooter the exact behavior that was performed well. This is an example of prescriptive praise. It is especially useful when a coach wants to encourage the athlete to concentrate on a particular component of a skill.

4. Present rewards immediately after desirable performance. For maximum effectiveness, a reward should be given immediately after the desired behavior occurs. Timing is important. Not only is delayed reinforcement (a delayed reward) much less effective, but when there is a delay between the desired behavior and the presentation of the reward, you run the risk of accidently rewarding and therefore strengthening some *other* behavior. The implication of this guideline, then, is that a coach should be constantly on the alert for desirable behaviors and reward them as soon as possible after they occur. Remember, in some cases 10 minutes later may be 10 minutes too late—if you are seeking to be maximally effective.

5. Reward correct approximations of desired behavior. Have you ever met a beginner who executed a skill perfectly the very first time he or she tried? It's a rare occurrence. Most beginners' skills are imperfect, to say the least. If you want to improve their skills, you must first be aware of their present level of skill and reward small improvements. This technique is sometimes called shaping. It's a bit like building a bridge. You start with one brick, lay it in the correct place, and then move on to the next brick. It takes time before those bricks begin to actually look like a bridge. It works the same way with behavior. You reward approximations of correct execution, one small behavior at a time, until you have the desired response. If you wait for the "perfect" skill to occur before you start rewarding, you'll still be waiting at the end of the season, with athletes who haven't learned very much.

Reprinted with special permission of King Features Syndicate. Inc.

Shaping can be used to modify the form of a behavior, the force of a behavior, the amount of a behavior, and the speed with which a behavior is performed. For example, suppose a hockey coach has a young defenseman who continually plays the puck rather than taking the man on a one-on-one basis, even though he has been told frequently to play the man. Through a series of one-on-one drills, the coach might start out by saying to the defenseman, "When he's coming down on you, keep your eyes on his chest. I'm not asking you to throw a crunching body check. I just want you to keep your eyes on his chest and move in the same direction that he does." The coach could praise the young defenseman for moving with the oncoming player on the next few opportunities, independent of whether body contact is made. Over the next few trials the coach might then request of the young defenseman, "In addition to keeping your eyes on his chest and moving in the direction that he does, try to make some body contact before he gets by you." This new level might then be praised on the next few one-on-one drills. Finally, the coach might withhold praise on subsequent one-on-one drills until the young defenseman not only makes body contact but makes contact sufficiently to take the oncoming forward out of the play. Note the differences between shaping in this instance and alternative strategies that the coach might have followed. The coach could have told the young player, "Take the body or you'll sit on the bench" (control by threat), or that the other defensemen take the man, and "If you're as good as they are, you should be able to also!" (threat by guilt-tripping), or perhaps some other strategy. With shaping, the coach simply reinforced successive approximations to the final desired behavior. No aversive control was used. You can provide your athletes with the same positive learning experience by rewarding close approximations to the final skill you've aimed for.

6. **When teaching new skill, require several repetitions in a row, and reward each instance.** Often when a coach must work with a group of athletes, the coach will provide positive feedback to one person who has correctly performed a skill, and then move on to another athlete immediately. Although this strategy allows the coach to interact with a number of athletes, it is not the most effective way to strengthen skills in an individual player. One-trial learning is expecting a lot of your athletes, especially beginners. It is much more effective to observe the athlete execute the skill several times and to present a reward for each correct try. After the beginner has tried several times and has been rewarded for each execution, the coach can ask the athlete to practice alone for awhile, and move on to the next athlete. After several minutes the coach should return to the first athlete and provide a few additional rewards for maintaining the correct performance (if you don't leave them alone *too* long, chances are the beginning athlete will still be doing it correctly). This strategy is important to remember when you are teaching a new skill. The time you spend strengthening that new skill when it is first being learned is time you won't have to spend later—correcting errors in execution. The rule is simple. In the beginning, lots of rewards for correct behaviors. The behavior/reward ratio can be decreased later. It won't be necessary to keep up the high rate forever. Once the new skill is learned, it can be maintained by less frequent rewards or by natural rewards, the natural consequences of executing well in the competitive environment.

7. Reward desirable performance when it occurs to correct stimulus or signal in environment. As athletes begin to acquire the correct skills, encourage them to practice under closer approximations of game conditions. For example, it is one thing for a beginning basketball player to shoot baskets when he or she is all alone with nothing between him or her and the basket. It's something else again to shoot a basket when an opposing player is standing in front waving his or her arms in the air. Obviously, learning to shoot over an opposing player is an important skill for playing under game conditions. It makes sense, then, to arrange practice situations that approximate the "real" game situations along various dimensions. For example, junior high and high school basketball players spend a lot of time shooting baskets, from 2 feet, 4 feet, 6 feet, a standing shot, a jump shot, a hook shot, and so on. But how many times in a game do they get to shoot a basket like that with no one in front of them trying to block the shot? Not often. At the junior high and high school level, coaches are better off to enforce the rule "With the exception of foul shots, you should practice shooting baskets with someone or something in front of you about 90% of the time." The players could shoot, for example, over coat racks, over coat racks with coats on them, over a player standing with arms at his or her side, over cheerleaders, over cheerleaders waving their hands, over cheerleaders jumping up and down. The obstacles that the players have to shoot over could be gradually changed to more closely approximate an opposition player trying to block the shot (Fig. 4-4).

8. After behavior has been well-developed, wean individual from initial schedule of rewards. Although behavior is learned most effectively when it is rewarded often during the initial trials, it is *not* necessary to maintain a high frequency of rewards. At the point where a new skill is properly learned, other rewards begin to naturally support the maintenance of the skill. A swimmer with a more efficient form is more likely to swim faster races. A basketball player with good shooting form is more likely to score baskets. These are natural rewards that can help to maintain a learned behavior. And an important goal of any training program is for athletes to perform effectively in sports for the natural consequences of doing so. This does not mean, however, that you as a coach can stop dispensing rewards to individual athletes. Rewards from the coach are necessary to encourage sustained effort and performance at repetitive practice (more about this in Chapter 6, on motivation). The frequency with which rewards are dispensed can be decreased, however, and new skills maintained on the lower ratio of rewards.

One very good reason that you can never eliminate altogether the provision of rewards to your athletes is that competitive situations contain punishers as well as natural rewards. Good performance or perfectly executed skills by members of the losing team are not necessarily natural rewards. Sometimes in this situation, even the coach begins to punish or criticize the athletes, hoping to spur the team to try harder and perform at a higher level. A losing situation, however, is precisely the type in which the coach should increase the output of rewards for skilled play. In short, don't dump water on a dying fire; feed it to bring it back to full flame! It is also necessary for coaches to continue to provide some level of reward for their athletes simply because an athlete rarely approaches a point where there is nothing left to learn. The coach therefore should continue to provide rewards for slight improvements by individual players to encourage the athletes to continually improve and refine their skills and to maintain skills at a high level.

FIGURE 4-4
In basketball you often must shoot over opponents (A), so shoot over obstacles when practicing (B through D).

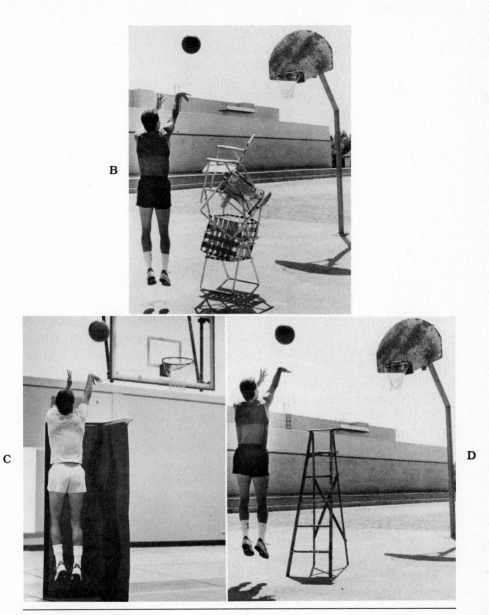

FIGURE 4-4, cont'd
For legend see opposite page.

SUMMARY

Successful teaching of new skills to athletes requires that coaches attend to several preliminary considerations. First, as emphasized in Chapter 3, behavioral assessment of an athlete's current level of performance is one of the first steps in effective instruction. An important second step is to prepare task analyses of the skills to be taught. Armed with task analyses and behavioral progressions, a coach is ready to proceed with instructing the athletes about the skills to be mastered. Effective instructional tools include modeling, descriptions of correct performance, descriptions of potential problems with incorrect alternative performances, asking questions to test athlete's understanding, and opportunities to role-play skills. When the instructional sequence reaches the point at which the athletes are ready to practice the components being taught, effective reward systems for the athletes are critical. Coaches should ensure that (1) rewards are effective from the athletes' point of view, (2) rewards are dispensed according to a number of guidelines that maximize their effectiveness, and (3) the athletes are weaned from the initial schedule of rewards so that natural rewards will support skill maintenance. The final step in effective instruction is to ensure that the newly acquired skills are transferred to the competitive environment. Additional strategies for this final step are described in Chapter 9.

Coach's Checklist

The guidelines for teaching new skills are shown in the checklist in Fig. 4-5. We suggest that you use this checklist as a convenient reminder sheet, and that you ask a volunteer to question you on the details of the guidelines. You might also ask an assistant coach or volunteer to study this chapter and to use the checklist to assess your performance during practices and games. Improvements in your behavioral coaching skills as revealed on the checklist will reward your efforts at applying behavioral coaching.

Review Questions

1. Briefly describe three preliminary considerations to strengthening desirable behaviors.
2. Describe, with examples, the distinction between natural, or intrinsic, rewards and extra, or extrinsic, rewards. Describe an example of each.
3. Briefly describe four guidelines for instructing athletes about skills to be mastered.

C O A C H ' S   C H E C K L I S T

Teaching New Skills _____

	Date						
SCORING KEY: √ = *Satisfactory (performed by coach each time new skills are taught)* X = *Less than satisfactory*							
Preliminary Considerations							
1. Conduct behavioral assessments to determine athletes' current level of skills							
2. Prepare task analyses of skills to be taught							
3. Arrange practice conditions so that athletes will experience naturally rewarding consequences							
Guidelines for Instructing Athletes About Skills To Be Mastered							
1. Combine modeling with instruction							
2. Describe positive consequences of successful performance							
3. Ask questions to test for understanding							
4. Ask athletes to role-play skills							
Guidelines for Rewarding Desirable Behaviors							
1. Frequently reward athletes for desirable behaviors							
2. Make sure rewards are rewards from athlete's point of view (i.e., do reward survey)							
3. Use prescriptive praise							
4. Reward immediately after desirable performance							
5. Reward correct approximations of desired behavior							
6. When teaching new skill, require several repetitions in a row and reward each instance.							
7. Reward desirable performance when it occurs to correct stimulus in environment							
8. After behavior has been well developed, wean individual off initial schedule of rewards							

FIGURE 4-5

4. Describe two strategies for ensuring that your athletes understand what it is that you want them to do.
5. According to the authors, what is one of the most critical parts of the teaching process, and what is the strong tendency that the coach must avoid during that part?
6. Briefly list the eight guidelines for rewarding desirable behaviors.
7. Describe the difference between regular praise and prescriptive praise. Explain with examples.
8. Briefly describe two ways to determine which rewards are good for individual athletes.
9. What is meant by the term "shaping"? Describe an example.
10. What are two reasons why, as a coach, you should never eliminate altogether the provision of rewards for specific skills of your athletes, even though those skills may be well developed?

Mini-Lab Exercises

1. Consider a sport that you have played or would like to coach. List some simple behaviors and some complex behaviors for that sport. List some of the behaviors that you would like to see in athletes that you consider highly coachable.
2. Ask a young athlete that you know to complete the Reward Survey in Fig. 4-3. Make sure that you explain to the athlete that you will be using the results of the survey only to complete an assignment and that results will remain confidential. Examine the completed survey and identify three effective reinforcers that you could conveniently use in coaching that individual.
3. Pick a skill of a sport that you have played or would like to coach. Describe in detail how you might go about shaping that skill in a young athlete. If possible, try to arrange an opportunity to apply your procedures, and take data on the results.
4. Consider the behavioral progression and mastery criteria for teaching golf shown in Fig. 4-2. Now consider a sport that you have played or would like to coach. Choose a skill in that sport and describe a behavioral progression and mastery criteria that might be used to teach that skill.
5. List 10 different phrases that you might use to express enthusiastic approval to a young athlete. Practice varying these phrases until they come naturally.
6. Take a close look at one of your own sport behaviors. Describe how that specific behavior was probably shaped by the natural environment. Put your example in sentence form, for example, "I was probably shaped to hit a Ping-Pong ball with a good chop stroke. That is,

after learning basic Ping-Pong skills, each time I tried a bit of a chop, the ball would fly off the table. Eventually a slight chop was rewarded by the ball landing on the table and the other person hitting the ball into the net. As the other person learned to return my chops, I was rewarded for putting slightly increasing amounts of chop on the ball. In all cases, the reward was returning the ball to the other side of the table, and an even greater reward was returning it to the other side of the table so that the other person missed."

References

Martin, G.L., and Pear, J.J. (1983). Behavior modification: What it is and how to do it. 2nd ed. Englewood Cliffs, N.J.: Prentice-Hall.

McKenzie, T.L., and Liskevych, T.N. (1983). Using the multi-element baseline design to examine motivation in volleyball training. In G.L. Martin and D. Hrycaiko, eds., Behavior modification and coaching: Principles, procedures and research. Springfield, Ill.: Charles C Thomas.

Siedentop, D. (1976). Developing teaching skills in physical education. Boston: Houghton Mifflin.

Simek, T.C., and O'Brien, R.M. (1981). Total golf: A behavioral approach to lowering your score and getting more out of your game. Huntington, N.Y.: B-Mod Associates.

Smith, R.E., Smoll, F.L., and Curtis, B. (1979). Coaching effectiveness training: A cognitive behavioral approach to enhancing relationship skills in youth sport coaches. Journal of Sport Psychology 1:39-73.

Selected Readings

Chelladura, P., and Stothart, C. (1978). Backward chaining: A method of teaching motor skills. Canadian Association for Health, Physical Education and Recreation Journal 45(1):26-29, 36-37.

Darst, P.W. (1979). Contingency management learning system. AAHPER Research Consortium Symposium Papers, vol. 2, book 1, pp. 81-85.

Darst, P.W., and Steeves, D. (1980). A competency-based approach to secondary student teaching in physical education. Research Quarterly 51(2):274-285.

Dodds, P. (1976). Love and joy in the gymnasium. Quest 26:109-116.

Fueyo, U., Saudergas, R.A., and Bushall, D., Jr. (1975). Two types of feedback in teaching swimming skills to handicapped children. Perceptual and Motor Skills 40:963-966.

Johnston-O'Connor, E.J., and Kirschenbaum, D.S. (in press). Something succeeds like success: Positive self-monitoring for unskilled golfers. Cognitive Therapy and Research

Komaki, J., and Barnett, F.T. (1977). A behavioral approach to coaching football: Improving the play execution of the offensive backfield on a youth football team. Journal of Applied Behavior Analysis 10:657-664.

McKenzie, T.L. (1982). Research on modeling: Implications for physical educators. Journal of Teaching in Physical Education 1(3):23-30.

McKenzie, T.L., Clark, E.K., and McKenzie, R.E. (1984). Instructional strategies: Influence on teacher and student behavior. Journal of Teaching in Physical Education 3(2):20-28.

Rushall, B.S. (1975). Applied behavior analysis for sports and physical education. International Journal of Sports Psychology 6:75-88.

Rushall. B.S.. and Ford. D. (1982). Teaching backwards: An alternative skill instruction progression. Canadian Association for Health. Physical Education and Recreation Journal **48**(5):16-20.

Simek. T.C.. and O'Brien. R.M. (1978). Immediate auditory feedback to improve putting quickly. Perceptual and Motor Skills **47**:1133-1134.

Smoll. F.L.. Smith. R.E.. and Curtis. B. (1978). Behavioral guidelines for youth sport coaches. Journal of Physical Education and Recreation **49**:46-47.

Valeriote. T. (1984). Childrens' sport programs: The coach. Ottawa. Ontario: New Traditions.

Westcott. W. (1979). Physical educators and coaches as models of behavior. Journal of Physical Education and Recreation **50**:31-32.

Westcott. W. (1980). Effects of teacher modeling on children's peer encouragement behavior. Research Quarterly **51**(3):585-587.

Yamamoto. L.. and Inomata. K. (1982). Effect of mental rehearsal with part and whole demonstration models on acquisition of backstroke swimming skills. Perceptual and Motor Skills **54**:1067-1070.

5

Decreasing Errors

In Chapter 1, we discussed several situations in which beginners were making errors. We talked about Charlie Jones, the coach of the Pop Warner football team. The statistics that Michael Appelbaum's father had gathered clearly showed that the team's backfield correctly executed, on average, only about 60% of their plays; the other 40% were persistent errors. And don't forget Mary Henderson's tennis classes and her problem of repeatedly serving into the net. Coach Hill had frequently pointed out Mary's mistakes, but the errors were still there. These are the types of situations that we discuss in this chapter.

When you coach beginners, you know that a major portion of practice time will be spent helping your players to acquire new athletic skills. Over time, you will no doubt notice considerable improvement in the beginners that you are coaching. You will probably also notice that some of your athletes are still making errors. Consistent application of the guidelines for teaching the fundamentals described in Chapter 4 will yield positive results in most cases. Errors, however, sometimes require special attention. In this chapter we describe some behavioral strategies that have been used successfully to decrease several types of *persistent* errors made by beginners.

The reasons why errors are repeated are numerous. Consequently, an error correction strategy that can be adopted by a coach should depend, in part, on discovering the reasons behind the error. Remember, even a beginner knows the goal: "I have to run (jump, throw) better." It is the coach who gets stuck with figuring out the problem: "Why doesn't that beginner run faster (jump higher, throw harder)?" It is also the coach who is challenged to solve the problem.

Reprinted with special permission of King Features Syndicate. Inc.

DECREASING ERRORS WHEN BEGINNERS ARE JUST LEARNING TO PERFORM A SKILL

> To err is human, but when the eraser runs out ahead of the pencil, you're overdoing it. —*J. Jenkins*

This quote is a fairly accurate description of Mary Henderson's problem with her tennis game. When it came to her ability to serve, Mary was making far more errors than aces. Hillory Buzas, a doctoral candidate in clinical psychology at Georgia State University, was interested in just the sort of situation that Mary Henderson found herself in. Hillory had been observing a 14- to 15-year-old girls' tennis class at a local high school. The students had by then participated in several tennis classes. They could perform the forehand and the backhand and serve correctly on occasion. However, the girls were still making numerous errors.

Hillory observed that, as a general rule, the coach first discussed and demonstrated correct performance of a skill. After instructions, the students were given an opportunity to practice the skill, while the coach pointed out any errors of execution. Most often, the coach commented on those things that the players were doing incorrectly. Rarely did the coach point out correct or nearly correct components of the skill. Under the supervision of her faculty advisor, Dr. Teodore Ayllon, and with the cooperation of the team coach, Hillory began a study of a strategy for decreasing student errors (Buzas and Ayllon, 1981).

The first step in the study was to assess the specific components of each skill the students had to perform. The methods used to assess these skills were similar to those we recommended in Chapter 3. The tennis coach helped Hillory to prepare task analyses of the components of the forehand, backhand, and serve. For example, the specific components that were assessed for the serve are listed in Fig. 5-1.

Observations of the students' performance on the components on the checklists revealed that, under the standard coaching procedure, students performed the three skills with errors on an average of 87% of the trials. After discussion of these results, the coach agreed to try a behavioral coaching program.

The behavioral coaching strategy in this case was simple and straightforward. The coach agreed to concentrate solely on rewarding correct or nearly correct behavior and to pay absolutely no attention to errors. This meant that when an error occurred, the coach did not comment in any way. Instead, the coach watched for and praised components (those listed on the checklists) that were performed correctly or nearly correctly. As recommended in Chapter 4, the coach applied both general praise and prescriptive praise (e.g., "Good! That was much better. You transferred your weight from your back foot to your front foot at just the right time."). The behavioral coaching program showed quick and powerful effects. Students who were averaging ap-

Components of Serve _____

1. For a right-handed player, the left foot should be positioned just behind the baseline at a 45-degree angle to it, and the right foot a comfortable distance behind the left and parallel to the baseline.

2. The player should use either a Continental or an Eastern forehand grip.

3. The swing should begin with both hands and racket in front of the player; then the hands come down past the body, with the right hand (for the right-handed player, left for a left-handed player) continuing on back until arm and racket shaft are out parallel to the ground in back of the player. Next the elbow is bent and the racket head drops behind the neck, and then [the player] releases and swings forward to hit the ball with the racket (following through until face down by the player's opposite shin).

4. As the hand with the racket swings back, the other hand goes up to toss the ball.

5. The ball should go over the net without touching the net, and land inside or on the lines of the service court on the other side of the net.

From Buzas. H.P.. and Ayllon. T.

FIGURE 5-1

proximately 13% correct performance under the traditional program shot up to almost 50% correct performance in only a few sessions. Not only did they perform better, but there were many signs that they also enjoyed it more: they smiled, they made positive comments about their tennis abilities, and they were eager to practice their skills. By concentrating on rewarding correct behavior, the coach had helped the students to zero in on their best skills. By removing the element of negative feedback, the coach had stopped attending to errors and had, in a sense, allowed some of the mistakes to die a natural death.

We want to make it clear that we're not suggesting that simply attending to correct responses and ignoring errors will decrease those errors in all situations. If you try this approach, there are several points to keep in mind. First, a detailed checklist, such as that for the components of the serve or for assessing foul shooting in basketball (Fig. 5-2) will help you to easily and quickly identify correct or incorrect components of skills.

If volunteers with minimal experience are helping you to monitor the performance of the athletes, you may want to add pictures to the checklists to help prompt the observers about the correct components (for example, *see* Fig. 2-1 for scoring the backstroke in swimming, and Fig. 3-3 for scoring the drive block in football).

Second, your athletes should be in the process of *learning* the new skills. We're not talking about players who have been performing for 2 or 3 years and who have developed persistent bad habits or mistakes. Eliminating mistakes that have such a long history usually requires special procedures, such as those described later in this chapter. Another prerequisite to the procedure of praising correct responses and ignoring errors is that your coaching situation allows repeated opportunities for the athlete to practice. It is also necessary for you to have opportunities to provide *frequent* and *immediate* general praise and prescriptive praise after correct performance. Finally, the beginners must perform the skills correctly at least once in a while before you initiate your praise procedure.

DECREASING ERRORS WHEN MOTIVATION IS THE PROBLEM

> Personally, I'm always ready to learn, although I do not always like being taught.—*Winston Churchill*

Sometimes a beginner knows how to perform the skill, and has done so with minimal errors during several practices or games. For some reason, however, errors are now observed to occur frequently. From the way the player is performing, it might seem to the coach that

C H E C K L I S T

Assessing Foul Shooting in Basketball _____

SCORING KEY: G = *Good* I = *Needs improvement*	Date						
1. Foot position: Shoulder width apart, parallel and pointed toward hoop							
2. Centering and mental rehearsal: Shooter appears to mentally rehearse while standing erect and holding ball in both hands at about waist level (*See* Chapter 9 for more discussion of this component.)							
3. Preshot pattern: Shooter always follows same procedure (e.g., dribbling ball three times, then positioning seams for grip)							
4. Grip: Same for every shot, fingers and thumb spread, ball not touching palm							
5. Set to shoot: Knees bent for power (approximately 45-degree angle), back straight, head up							
6. Set to shoot: Elbow under ball, bent to approximately 90-degree angle and pointing at basket							
7. Follow through: Shooter finishes up on toes, snaps wrist, points index finger at basket, and does not "pull the string"							
8. Shooter appears to be looking at basket throughout shot (not looking at ball)							

Guidelines for Recording

It is impossible to observe all of the above points on one shot. It is necessary to monitor different shots and score different components at different times. We recommend scoring components as follows:

First shot: record components 1, 2, 3
Second shot: record component 4
Third shot: record component 5
Fourth shot: record component 6
Fifth shot: record component 7
Sixth shot: record component 8

Prepared by Scott Martin.

FIGURE 5-2

the player just isn't trying, that there is an apparent lack of effort. What is the common reaction of a coach in this situation? "Move it, Johnson! Whaddya think this is, a walk in the park? Hustle! Hustle! Hustle!" Hollering. That's what many coaches do in such situations. Unfortunately, excessive hollering and reprimands have all of the negative side effects that we talked about in Chapter 2. Fortunately, there's an alternative.

Remember Coach Keedwell and the problem of improper turns and unscheduled swimmer stops during sets? The swimmers knew how to perform racing turns, but often didn't. They were physically fit to swim the sets without stopping in the middle, but they often stopped. Sometimes beginners make errors simply because it's not worth their while to perform without errors. What happened when Coach Keedwell's swimmers executed a proper racing turn? They had to hold their breath for much longer than if they didn't. What happened if they swam a set without stopping in the middle? They became more tired. Now let's consider the opposite. What happened when they swam up to the end of the lane, touched, looked around, and then started swimming again? They got a bit of a rest and got to see what the other swimmers were doing. Maybe they even got to wave or shout at their friend in the next lane. Now what happened if they touched down in the middle of a set? Again, they got to look around, wave at someone, rest. When beginners make errors simply because it's not worth their while to perform without errors, one possible strategy is for the coach to make available extra rewards for improved performance by that beginner. That is exactly what happened when Coach Keedwell required the swimmers to swim sets with a minimal number of unscheduled stops and missed turns in order to earn relays. When motivation seems to be the problem, check to see if you are using available rewards effectively. If error-free performance is observed during several practices when extra rewards are available for improved performance, it's possible that the natural rewards for good performance will begin to take over. At that point, the athlete can gradually be weaned from the extra rewards.

DECREASING PERSISTENT, WELL-LEARNED ERRORS

Beginners sometimes experience a good deal of success in a sport despite the fact that they may be making one or two fundamental errors in performing their skills. Some athletes learn to compensate for the errors and, initially, manage to do well in spite of them. For example, the star high jumper at the local high school might experience a great deal of success at that level. Despite the fact that this athlete's technique may be flawed, for example, by a habit of trailing the back leg, he or she is still the best high jumper the school has. As they say, nothing succeeds like success. At least it might work at the junior high or high school level. Later, when the athlete reaches the college level, the same flaw might get in the way. But eliminating the error is much harder to do then, thanks to all those years during which the error was practiced, was not corrected, and indeed was actually rewarded by the experience of success. When a skill results in early success, all of the components of that skill are strengthened, including the components that are actually errors. The more an athlete practices with a defective component, and the more that athlete achieves success in spite of it, the more difficult it will be to eliminate the error later on. The task of eliminating such an error inevitably falls to the coach. The athlete, in this situation, is usually too busy riding the crest of the wave of early success. When the coach points out the problem, the athlete might respond, "But back in highschool, I was the best high jumper they had! My style isn't wrong coach, it's just unique!" Or the athlete might try a new approach while the coach is watching, but return to the old, incorrect form when the coach moves on. Roger LePage found himself faced with that type of situation.

Roger was one of the coaches of the Manitoba Marlin swim club. Roger had identified several swimmers who had two or more persistent basic flaws in their strokes. Although the usual coaching techniques had helped many of the swimmers to show considerable improvement, these particular swimmers tended to make the same errors in practice after practice. With the help of Sandra Koop, a doctoral student in psychology at the University of Manitoba, a behavioral coaching program was designed to deal with this problem (Koop and Martin, 1983).

Each of the students who participated in the behavioral coaching program had been in age-group competitive swimming for a full year. The swimmers had practiced for 1 hour approximately three times a week, and swam in a meet about once a month. During practice they swam approximately 2000 meters, approximately one quarter freestyle. Five hundred meters freestyle is 20 lengths in a 25-meter pool. Thus, if the swimmers averaged 25 strokes per length, they swam approximately 500 freestyle strokes during each practice. If there was an error in the stroke, that swimmer was repeating the error 500 times during each practice. If you multiply 500 by the number of practices, you discover that the error was being repeated many thousands of times in a year. Good grief! No wonder it's so hard to get rid of a bad habit!

This problem of errors while swimming was considerably different from the problem Hillory Buzas studied when she observed the beginner's tennis class, described earlier in this chapter. In that situation the coaching strategy was to reward correct components of the skill and to ignore the errors. In Hillory's study, that method probably worked, in part, because the errors had not been occurring for a long time. The same strategy, however, is less likely to work when a coach wants to correct an error that has occurred on several thousand trials. That type of error is persistent, and very resistant to change. For that reason, Sandi and Dr. Martin theorized that a behavioral coaching procedure with a number of components was needed—a procedure that was different and "special" in comparison with the less complicated approach that Hillory used. The error correction package they used effectively combined most of the guidelines for teaching fundamentals (*see* Chapter 4).

Part of the program included training sessions in a small pool near the Marlin's regular practice pool. The training program in the small pool was designed to decrease errors to near zero. The program in the larger, regular practice pool was designed to ensure the maintenance of correct performance. The entire program was implemented by Coach LePage. As outlined in Fig. 5-3, Roger provided extensive instruction and modeling before the swimmer entered the small pool. As the swimmer swam six consecutive laps, Roger provided *praise for correct performance and immediate feedback for errors.* Specifically, he walked along the edge of the pool, carrying a long stick with a soft pad on one end. If an error occurred, he immediately tapped the swimmer lightly on the shoulder to indicate that a mistake had been made. If the swimmer completed a lap with two or fewer errors, Roger provided praise at the end of the lap. When a swimmer reached criterion (three consecutive practices with two or fewer errors on each of the six required laps), he or she graduated to the maintenance program in the practice pool. For a period of three practices in the practice pool, the coach provided a reminder, something like, "Remember what we were working on in the small pool? That's right, the way you lift your arms in freestyle. What were you doing wrong? What *should* you do? Right. And what do you say to yourself each stroke? Right. Good for you. Now, I want to see nice high elbows during practice in the big pool. OK? Good for you!" Roger also provided two instances of praise for correct performance of the target behaviors during each of the first three practices in the practice pool. During maintenance practice sessions 4 to 6 in the larger pool, the swimmer received a reminder only.

Error Correction Package

Training *(in small pool)*

1. While coach and swimmer were standing on deck, the coach:
   a. Identified target component and described correct performance
   b. Modeled incorrect way that swimmer was doing target component, then modeled correct behavior
   c. Asked swimmer to imitate incorrect and correct ways of performing target component
   d. Asked swimmer if he/she could feel the difference between incorrect and correct behaviors
   e. Had swimmer role-play correct behavior several times.
   f. Instructed swimmer to swim six laps in small pool while attempting to perform target behavior correctly.
2. While swimmer was swimming six laps, the coach:
   a. Provided positive verbal feedback immediately after each correctly swum lap
   b. Tapped swimmer on shoulder for each occurrence of error on target behavior
   c. Stopped swimmer and gave corrective feedback if three consecutive errors occurred
3. After swimmer had completed six laps, the coach:
   a. Provided social approval and feedback regarding swimmer's performance
   b. Reminded swimmer to practice correct behavior during remainder of practice in regular practice pool

Maintenance (M) *(two phases, in regular practice pool)*

1. M1 (three practice sessions), the coach:
   a. Gave reminder to perform target behavior correctly before practice
   b. Provided at least two instances of feedback or reinforcement to swimmer for correctly practicing target stroke
2. M2 (three practice sessions), the coach:
   a. Gave reminder to perform target behavior correctly

FIGURE 5-3

Guidelines for Skill Development and Motivation

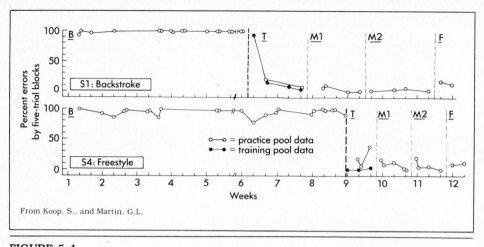

From Koop. S.. and Martin. G.L.

FIGURE 5-4

Percentage of errors in five-trial blocks made by swimmers 1 and 4 during all phases of experiment. B. baseline; T. training; M1. first maintenance phase; M2. second maintenance phase; F. follow-up.

The program worked well. All of the swimmers showed rapid improvement in the small pool when the "heavyweight" error correction procedure was used. All of the swimmers transferred their improved performance to the regular practice sessions in the larger pool. Finally, all of the swimmers managed to maintain their improved skills for at least 2 weeks after the training program ended. At that point, some of the swimmers needed an extra reminder. When the reminder was provided, however, the swimmers showed immediate improvement.

Detailed data for two of the swimmers is shown in Fig. 5-4. We present these data to emphasize once more the first characteristic of effective behavioral coaching, namely, that it emphasizes specific measurement of athletic behaviors and the use of these measures as the primary means for evaluating the effectiveness of specific coaching techniques. The data clearly demonstrate that, for each of the two swimmers, improvement occurred only at the point where the behavioral coaching procedure was used. You will also notice the staggered presentation of the treatment. That is, swimmer 1 received the treatment for the backstroke during weeks 6 and 7; swimmer 4, however, did not receive any treatment during that time. That swimmer 1 improved during weeks 6 and 7 when the treatment was applied, and swimmer 4 did not improve under normal coaching conditions, provides convincing evidence that the improvement was attributable to the treatment and not the result of some chance factor. When the treatment was applied to swimmer 4 during week 9, that swimmer also improved. This type of research design, called delayed treatment or multiple baseline design, is common in behavior modification research (for a detailed description, *see* Martin and Pear, 1983).

DECREASING ERRORS WITH THE "FREEZE" TECHNIQUE

Mary Allison, a doctoral student from Georgia State University, and her supervisor, Dr. Teodore Ayllon, devised and researched a behavioral error correction program that required minimal time to implement and could be used in normal practice sessions by the regular coaching staff (Allison and Ayllon, 1980). Their program combined several behavioral procedures with the "freeze" technique. One of their studies examined the possibility of decreasing errors made by 11- and 12-year-old football players during blocking drills.

The behavioral coaching program proceeded as follows: The coach took a group of players and had them run a series of plays. During each play one player was instructed to block. If the block was thrown correctly, the coach let the players complete the play. On completion, the coach blew a whistle and praised the player who blocked correctly. However, if the coach noticed that some part of the block was incorrect, he immediately blew his whistle and yelled, "Freeze!" The player who had blocked incorrectly would freeze, that is, stop moving and hold his physical position exactly. The coach would first describe, in detail, the incorrect aspects of the player's physical position. Then the coach would describe, in detail, the correct position. Finally, the coach would model the correct position. The player would then imitate the correct physical position. During this imitation, the coach would encourage the player to notice various aspects of his body position. For example, the coach might say, "O.K., now, see how your leg is bent? Your arm is pointing down? Your head is thrown way back?" The coach would encourage the player to "feel" the difference between the correct and the incorrect body position. To help the player feel the difference more precisely, the coach would also encourage the player to notice how his muscles felt: "Can you feel how tense your calf muscle is now? When you're doing it correctly, the muscle should be tensed, ready to drive forward. See how it feels? Good!" The players were then allowed to complete the play. Overall, one application of the continued error correction procedure and freeze technique took about 50 or 60 seconds of the coach's and the player's time. One minute. Enough time to provide the feedback to improve the skill. Not enough time to interfere seriously with getting on with the practice. Rather a classic case of "It's not the quantity of time you spend with a child, it's the quality." The Allison-Ayllon procedure makes the most of a relatively small amount of time.

The results of the Allison and Ayllon study proved the point. The procedure was researched with five different players. Each player had been averaging less than 10% correct blocks in practice. When the error correction plus the freeze technique was used, the five players showed an immediate improvement, to approximately 50% to 60% correct execution of the block. Research has demonstrated the effectiveness of behavioral coaching with the freeze technique for decreasing errors in football, gymnastics, and tennis (Allison and Ayllon, 1980), soccer (Rush and Ayllon, 1984), sprinting in track (Shapiro and Shapiro, 1985), and classical ballet (Fitterling and Ayllon, 1983). The freeze technique for correcting a golf swing and for correcting an error in blocking in football is illustrated in Fig. 5-5.

This technique, then, might be considered when a coach is teaching an individual or a group of athletes. With a group, when the coach yells, "Freeze," only one player goes through the correction procedure. But the other players can also freeze and watch and learn from the instructions and discussion between the coach and the athlete who is trying to correct a skill. In a sense, everyone on the team can benefit from these 60-second interactions. The choice of procedures is up to the coach. If time during practice sessions is limited, the error correction plus freeze technique might work best. If a coach has adequate time, or if the freeze technique is inappropriate (such as when teaching swimming), then the procedure of choice might be the multiple component procedure used by Koop and Martin (1983) with its one-on-one instruction over several successive practices.

Let us hasten to point out that we are not suggesting that the individual components of these techniques are particularly new. For years, many coaches have used instructions, modeling, guidance, rewards, even the freeze technique. We are suggesting, however, that there is room for improvement in the consistency with which combinations of these techniques are used. Moreover, greater use should be made of regular data collection to verify the effectiveness of specific coaching programs.

DECREASING ERRORS USING VIDEOTAPED REPLAY

We're all aware of the frequent use of videotapes and game films in professional sports to help players to improve their skills. With modern advances in microelectronics, use of videotaped feedback is also becoming increasingly common in grade school, junior high, high

FIGURE 5-5
Behavioral coaching package. 1. Athlete uses incorrect technique.
*Coach yells, "Freeze!" (**A** and **B**).*   Continued.

FIGURE 5-5, cont'd
*Behavioral coaching package. 2. Athlete observes correct model from "freeze" position (**C** and **D**).*

FIGURE 5-5, cont'd
Behavioral coaching package. 3. Athlete performs with correct technique. Coach praises, "Now you've got it!" (E and F).

school, college, and in various community organizations involving competitive sports with kids. Coaches of beginners have used video-taped feedback to try to improve performance in team sports such as football and basketball and in individual sports such as gymnastics, swimming, and karate. It may come as a surprise that not all uses of videotaped replay for improving athletic skills are helpful. In fact, more than 50 experiments have been conducted to study the value of video-taped feedback as a learning aid. Surprisingly, more than half of the studies found no significant differences between videotaped feedback conditions and other experimental or control conditions (Rothstein, 1980). This means that a coach cannot expect a player to improve simply on the basis of seeing one or two videotapes showing his or her errors.

Are there conditions under which videotaped replay can be helpful for decreasing errors? Yes. Rothstein (1980) reviewed the many stud-ies that had examined videotaped replay in skill development. She then summarized the conditions under which videotaped replay might be expected to be maximally helpful:

1. Advanced beginners (players of the sport for 2 to 3 years) benefit more from the use of videotaped replay than do players just learning a skill.
2. Coaches should show videotaped feedback on a skill on several separate occasions, with multiple replays on each occasion, be-fore expecting lasting improvements from the athletes.
3. When showing videotaped replays of a skill, performers should be prompted about specific body positions to attend to while observing the replay.
4. Immediately after observing a videotaped replay depicting an error, an athlete should be given an opportunity to practice the correct form of the behavior and to receive praise for executing it correctly. The correctly executed behavior should be video-taped immediately and observed by the athlete. Then the ath-lete should be given another opportunity to practice the correct form of the behavior and to receive positive praise for executing it correctly. This should be followed by a third videotaping, a third observation, and a third practice opportunity. This repe-tition of performing, videotaping, observing on videotape, per-forming again, receiving praise, and so on, is what's meant by multiple replays on each occasion.

Receiving praise may be the most important. As we mentioned in earlier chapters, positive reinforcement is an extremely important aspect of the learning process. Observing an error on videotape replay and discussing and role-playing correct performance is one thing, but correct execution with praise is something else again. Repeated praise may do more to strengthen correct performance and decrease errors than any other single factor.

SUMMARY

The strategy selected by a coach for decreasing persistent errors made by young athletes will depend to some extent on the reason(s) for the error in the first place. In this chapter we reviewed five behavioral strategies for decreasing persistent errors. If beginners just learning a skill perform some components correctly but frequently make errors on other components, the coach might simply praise correct or near correct components of the skill and ignore the errors. If a beginner knows how to perform a skill correctly but appears to make errors because of "lack of effort," the coach might try adding new rewards to improve the athlete's motivation. In a third situation, a young athlete with several years of success may have a long-standing bad habit in technique or form. In such cases a multiple-component error correction package applied over several consecutive practices may be necessary to eliminate the error. An alternative in dealing with this type of problem is to use videotape feedback. In such cases a coach should plan to provide videotape feedback several times during a practice, and repeat it across several practices, in order to have a significant effect on reducing the frequency of the error. In another situation described, errors are often made by one or more individuals in a group of beginners learning a skill. The coach might consider a behavioral programming package with the "freeze" technique. When the coach yells, "Freeze!," all the players stop and hold their positions. The coach goes through an error correction procedure with one of the players while the others watch and learn from the instructions and discussion from the coach.

There is nothing especially new about individual components of any of the above techniques. What is new are the research demonstrations that have verified the effectiveness of these strategies when they are consistently applied.

Coach's Checklist

Fig. 5-6 presents a summary checklist to remind you to choose and carry out the behavioral error correction package most suited to your particular situation. We encourage you to review this checklist before individual practices.

Decreasing Errors

Determine which of the following situations you are dealing with. Implement steps for decreasing errors appropriate to that situation.

Name	Date of Completion									

Situation 1 *One or more beginners are just learning a skill. They occasionally perform correctly, but errors are more common than correct performance. Also, the skills can be practiced repeatedly within a session. Try praising correct or near correct components of skills and ignoring errors.*

1. Prepare checklist of correct components of skills, and monitor performance.
2. Provide immediate, general praise and prescriptive praise when skill is performed correctly or near correctly.
3. If entire skill is not performed correctly, praise specific components that are performed correctly.
4. When skill is performed at satisfactory level, gradually withdraw your praise over several sessions.

Situation 2 *A beginner knows how to perform a skill, and has done so with minimal errors in several situations, but now makes many errors because of an apparent lack of effort. Try "managing motivation."*

1. Monitor performance with checklist.
2. Observe and talk with performer to ensure that other causes of errors (e.g., anxiety, fatigue) can be ruled out.
3. Select an effective reinforcer, and instruct him/her how reward can be earned for performance with minimal errors.
4. Continue program for several sessions or practices or games to ensure that strategy has effectively decreased errors.
5. Wean athlete of extra reward by gradually withdrawing it over several practices or sessions or games.

FIGURE 5-6

Name _____

Date of Completion

Situation 3 *A beginner has been performing a particular skill or activity for a year or more, and has developed a persistent bad habit or error. The error has been repeated hundreds of times. However, the individual has probably achieved some overall success in spite of the error. Try a multiple-component error correction package.*

1. Monitor performance with a checklist.
2. Provide many cues and instructions for correct performance.
    a. Instructions
    b. Modeling
    c. Ask beginner to role-play both correct and incorrect form.
    d. Ask beginner if he/she can feel difference between correct and incorrect form.
    e. Explain consequences of correct and incorrect forms on subsequent trials.
3. Provide immediate consequences for correct performance and for each instance of error.
    a. Praise instances of correct performance.
    b. Provide immediate reminder after each instance of error, either by touching beginner or verbally calling out "Error."
4. Transfer improved performance to regular practices or games.
    a. Move to regular practice or game area if special practice or game area has been used.
    b. Provide reminders at start of practice or game and two or three instances of praise during practice or game, for correct performance.
    c. Over several practices or games, withdraw reminders and praise for correct performance.

Continued.

COACH'S CHECKLIST

Decreasing Errors—cont'd

Name	Date of Completion

Situation 4 *A group of beginners are learning a skill or a play while performing as a team, such as blocking on a play in football. They occasionally perform correctly, but errors by one or more individuals are more common than correct performance. Also, the skills can be practiced repeatedly within a session. Try a behavioral programming package with the "freeze" technique.*

1. Monitor performance with checklist.
2. Describe correct and incorrect behaviors to group, and explain "freeze" technique.
3. Have players execute a play. When an error is observed by an individual:
   a. Yell "Freeze."
   b. Describe details of incorrect position to "frozen" individual.
   c. Describe and model details of correct position.
   d. Ask individual to imitate correct position and to notice details of placement of arms, legs, body.
   e. Ask players to continue to play.
4. At end of each play, praise individuals who perform components correctly.
5. Continue repetitions of plays during practices until acceptable level of performance is attained.

FIGURE 5-6, cont'd

Name _____	Date of Completion								

Situation 5 *Your athletes have been performing relatively well at various skills for 2 or 3 years. One or more athletes have persistent flaws that you would like to correct. using videotaped feedback.*

1. Videotape athlete performing skill in practice.

2. Have athlete observe videotape immediately after performing skill (taped), and point out specific body positions and correct and incorrect behaviors.

3. Have athlete perform skill several times more in that same practice, and videotape performance.

4. Once again, have athlete observe videotaped performance immediately after videotaping, and point out correct and incorrect behaviors.

5. For third time in that practice, have athlete perform again, and videotape performance. By this time, athlete should be performing correctly or with considerable improvement.

6. Once again, have athlete observe videotaped performance in that same practice, and discuss correct and incorrect behaviors. Provide praise for executing correctly.

7. At minimum of two additional practices in close succession after practice in which multiple videotapings were completed, as described above, conduct multiple videotaped feedback sessions. Multiple replays within practice, repeated over three practices in a row, can be expected to have significant effect on correcting error performance.

Review Questions

1. Drawing on your experience, and thinking about the material in Chapter 4, describe at least three reasons why beginners make errors or mistakes when executing a new skill.
2. When working with beginners, under what conditions might you, as coach, concentrate solely on rewarding correct behavior and paying no attention to errors as a strategy for decreasing errors?
3. What might lead you to suspect that a particular individual is making errors simply because of lack of effort, or lack of motivation?
4. If you think that an individual is making errors because of lack of motivation, what error correction strategy might you follow? Outline the steps.
5. When might it be necessary to use a multiple-component error correction program such as that researched by Koop and Martin with swimmers?
6. Consider the summary guidelines for teaching new skills (Fig. 4-5). Now consider the training program implemented by Roger LePage to correct the persistent flaws in the strokes of some of his beginning swimmers. Which of the guidelines for instructing athletes about skills to be mastered did Roger apply? Which of the guidelines for rewarding desirable behaviors did he apply?
7. What appear to be the main characteristics of the delayed treatment or multiple baseline research design? Why could Koop and Martin convincingly say that improvement in the swimmers was the result of their behavioral coaching package and not attributable to some chance variable?
8. Briefly list four rules that should be applied to effectively use videotaped replays for improving skilled motor performance.

Mini-Lab Exercises

1. Consider a sport that you have played. Try to remember a persistent error that you made when performing one of the skills appropriate for that sport.
   a. Name what you would consider to be the best error correction strategy, on the basis of material in this chapter.
   b. Justify your choice of error correction strategy.
   c. Outline in detail the steps you would follow if you coached an athlete who showed that particular error.
2. Contact a coach that you know who coaches a youth sport. Volunteer to conduct a project to help eliminate an error often repeated by one of the athletes. On the basis of information in this chapter, and with the coach's supervision and support, implement the error cor-

rection strategy that you consider will work best with the young athlete. Be sure to use behavioral checklists to take data to evaluate the success of your approach. Also, be sure that you follow the ethical guidelines from Chapter 3 for explaining to the young athletes the purpose of your efforts.

References

Allison. M.G.. and Ayllon. T. (1980). Behavioral coaching in the development of skills in football. gymnastics. and tennis. Journal of Applied Behavior Analysis **13**:297-314.

Buzas. H.P.. and Ayllon. T. (1981). Differential reinforcement in coaching skills. Behavior Modification **5**:372-385.

Fitterling. J.M.. and Ayllon. T. (1983). Behavioral coaching in classical ballet: Enhancing skill development. Behavior Modification **7**:345-368.

Koop. S.. and Martin. G.L. (1983). A coaching strategy to reduce swimming stroke errors with beginning age-group swimmers. Journal of Applied Behavior Analysis **16**:447-460.

Martin. G.L.. and Pear. J.J. (1983). Behavior modification: What it is and how to do it. 2nd ed. Englewood Cliffs. N.J.: Prentice-Hall.

Rothstein. A.L. (1980). Effective use of videotape replay in learning motor skills. Journal of Physical Education and Recreation **51**:59-60.

Rush. D.B.. and Ayllon. T. (1984). Peer behavioral coaching: Soccer. Journal of Sport Psychology **6**:325-334.

Shapiro. E.S.. and Shapiro. S. (1985). Behavioral coaching in the development of skills in track. Behavior Modification **9**:211-224.

Selected Readings

Kirschenbaum. D.S. (1984). Self-regulation and sport psychology: Nurturing an emerging symbiosis. Journal of Sport Psychology **6**:159-183.

Kirschenbaum. D.S.. Ordman. A.M.. Tomarken. A.J.. and Holtzbauer. R. (1982). Effects of differential self-monitoring and level of mastery on sports performance: Brain power bowling. Cognitive Therapy and Research **6**:335-342.

Silva T.M. III. and Weinberg. R.S.. eds. (1984). Psychological foundations of sport. Champaign. Ill.: Human Kinetics Publishers.

Motivating Practice and Endurance Training

The problem of motivation can be difficult and sometimes confusing. Let's assume that you coach a group of young athletes. Each has participated in their sport for at least 2 or 3 years. All of them have made considerable progress at learning the fundamentals. If your sport is a team sport, your team is probably in a league, plays a game at least once a week, and has from three to five practices per week. If your sport is a single-player sport, such as swimming, your athletes probably attend at least one competition per month and practice from five to eight times a week. In other words, you are in a coaching situation in which the beginning athletes are really "into" their sport. To improve, these athletes must work hard at practice to increase their endurance and to improve their level of skill. Most of these beginners want to improve, and know that they have to work hard to improve. They may not, however, be motivated to consistently work hard at practices. Often it is the coach who must come up with strategies for encouraging the beginner to work at improving his or her fitness level. It is often the coach who must encourage the persistent practice of reverse kips in gymnastics or the repetitive practice of hundreds of foul shots in basketball. The coach must also find ways to make practices fun as well as useful for the young athlete. How might a coach go about encouraging hard work, persistent practice, and skill and fitness development *and* maintain the athlete's enjoyment of the sport? This chapter will provide some answers to this question.

PRELIMINARY CONSIDERATIONS

1. What are the characteristics of the sport? Techniques for motivating athletes depend to some extent on the nature of the sport itself. For example, some sports, such as swimming and distance running, are based largely on endurance training. Other sports, such as gymnastics or figure skating, require additional emphasis on repetitive practice for controlled motor movement and for timing, rhythm, and balance. Sports such as table tennis require the development of fine motor skills and excellent eye-hand coordination. Many sports require aspects of all of these. The degree of importance of any one characteristic varies from sport to sport. One characteristic, however, remains constant in all sports: to be skillful and successful, considerable time must be spent practicing repetitive (and sometimes boring) activities.

One type of motivational factor related to the nature of the sport is the frequency of competition. For comparison purposes, consider a typical hockey team of 9- and 10-year-old players. They probably participate in a minimum of three to five practice sessions and one real game per week. This means that they must put in an average of 4 hours of practice time for each 1 hour of competition. A group of 9- and 10-year-old figure skaters, on the other hand, is more likely to participate in four to six competitions during the entire year. The beginning figure skaters, then, must put in many hours of practice before they have an opportunity to perform in a competitive situation.

The point here is that the hockey coach is in a position to use frequent reminders of the upcoming weekly game as a motivator for these beginners. The figure skating coach, however, faces a more difficult situation. Reminders of a competition that is going to happen 3 or 4 months in the future are less likely to motivate beginners to work hard *now*. The figure skating coach, therefore, would probably find it necessary to spend more time planning and implementing effective motivation strategies during weekly practice sessions.

A second important motivational factor related to the type of sport you coach is whether it's a team sport or a single-player sport. If, for example, a batter hits a home run during a baseball game, that player's achievement benefits the entire team, and all of the players will probably feel good about it. One player's behavior can provide rewards for everyone. The same is true when a hockey player scores a goal, when a football player makes a touchdown, or when a basketball player sinks a shot. Single-player sports are somewhat different. Although a junior high or high school may have a golf team, each player who belongs to that team is an athlete who competes alone. The golfer who sinks a hole in one is likely to feel terrific, but his or her performance on the links will mainly provide personal motivation. The same is true of sports, such as swimming, gymnastics, distance running, or weight lifting. We do not mean to imply that an outstanding performance of an athlete in an individual sport is of benefit only to that athlete. A great routine in gymnastics, for example, might set the rest of the gymnasts up to achieve higher scores. An outstanding swim early in a meet might give the rest of the swimmers on the team a big lift. Nevertheless, a member of a team in an individual sport is also likely to be competing against other members of that team. Thus the single-player sport can present a problem for coaches: how to increase the rewards that are provided through a sense of team spirit and cooperation. The coach who works at training athletes in a single-player sport should be prepared to develop motivational techniques that will provide the athletes with those "missing rewards."

2. Why do beginners participate? Techniques for motivating athletes also depend on the nature of the individual. Beginners get involved in sports for many different reasons (Gould, Feltz, Weiss, and Petlichkoff, 1982; Wankel and Kreisel, 1985). Coaches must not make the mistake of assuming that every beginner is keen to develop his or her abilities. It's not true that everyone wants to be a superstar. From the viewpoint of behavioral psychology, we know that many people participate in sports because past participation provided rewards. However, the aspects of the sport that prove rewarding will differ from person to person.

First, some people enjoy competition because winners get lots of attention. Ribbons, medals, congratulations from friends, or praise from the coach are all rewards that result when an athlete wins. These types of rewards can have a powerful effect on some athletes.

Second, some people participate because it's "the thing to do." Often the operative factor here is peer group influence. Approval, praise and attention from peers for being one of the gang, for attending practices faithfully, and for participating can function as major motivational factors for some persons.

Third, some people participate mainly because of the consequences that result from self-improvement. For them it is rewarding to be able to swim faster this month than they did last month, or to make progress in lifting heavier weights, increasing muscle size, or toning up flabby muscles, or simply to experience the satisfaction of mastering a new skill (*see* Dickinson, 1977, for a discussion of how self-improvement acquires reward value).

A fourth kind of reward derives from the sensory stimulation that is experienced while participating in a given sport. Many sports provide participants with visual, tactile, and auditory sensations, which can be rewarding to some athletes. For the early morning jogger it might be the quiet beauty of a sunlit wood or the smell of wood smoke on a crisp fall day. For a cyclist it might be the feeling of a summer breeze ruffling through one's hair or the sensation of speed and movement as he or she cycles at an ever-increasing pace. Or it may be the exhilarating sensations of "floating" or "flying" that a sky diver experiences while free-falling from thousands of feet above the earth. It's all a matter of individual preference. Any one of these types of sensory experiences can be rewarding to a particular individual and may, as a result, go a long way toward influencing the athlete to persist in practicing his or her chosen sport.

Now that we've discussed some of the rewards that motivate athletes to participate in a sport, let's look for a moment at the opposite side of the coin. Every experienced coach who has spent time working with beginners is painfully aware that not all beginners participate because of the rewards that the sport may provide. We cannot ignore the fact that some kids play a sport because their parents want them to. Most coaches have met Michael, the hockey player whose dad always wanted to play hockey but never got the chance. Or perhaps you know Melissa, whose mother once almost made it to Wimbledon. Some beginners are on your team because of parental pressure, not personal desire. And in some cases, although a beginner may not be trying to please Mom or Dad, he or she may be trying to impress a peer group. Bobby's buddies all play football. So Bobby, who doesn't particularly like contact sports but does want to be accepted by his friends, is trying out for the football team. And then, of course, there's Lorinda. Her parents taught her that geting all sweaty and huffing and puffing is kind of unladylike. But all the girls in Lorinda's peer group are sports-minded "80s ladies," so Lorinda is trying to gain a spot on the racquetball team. Unfortunately, these and other gender role dilemmas still exist in our society. Ridicule or rejection by peers is an adverse consequence that may be escaped or avoided by a person's participation in sports.

It is necessary to try to gain some understanding of the reasons why beginners are participating in the first place. Such understanding can be crucial when a coach is trying to motivate beginners for practice and endurance training. If the coach and the parents are keen, but the beginner is not, an unfortunate situation can occur. The less than enthusiastic beginner may simply refuse to practice. Then the coach and the parents may resort to nagging and hollering, to "encourage" the beginner to improve. The resulting scenes are not only unpleasant and unfair to the beginner, but they are likely to produce the very opposite effect to the one desired by the coach and the parents.

All beginners should be encouraged to sample different sports and to participate in those that will provide maximum rewards and minimal aversive feelings. Motivating practice and endurance training will show better results in the long run if the strategies used are reward strategies rather than aversive consequences (Dickinson, 1977; Martin and Pear, 1983). Taking the time to get to know your athletes at the start of the season can be time well spent. Many coaches sit down with their athletes and talk about their reasons for coming out for that sport. As an aid to getting to know your beginners, you might want to make use of the questionnaire shown in Fig. 6-1. Ask your athletes to fill out the form provided, and talk to each of them about the answers they have given.

3. **What is the developmental level of the beginners?** A final preliminary consideration in the selection of motivational techniques is the developmental level of your beginners.

"On my team, we don't pussyfoot around. When I talk, you listen. I'm only going to tell you once, so listen carefully. I believe that if you treat kids like adults they act like adults. OK, now, let's get started." Have you ever heard a coach talk to a group of kids that way? Chances are that you have. Although there may be an element of truth to the notion that if you treat kids like adults they will act like adults, the fact is that kids are not adults. Developmental psychologists have been studying children and teenagers for many, many years. Although there are individual exceptions, we can now provide some guidelines as to realistic expectations for the majority of kids at various age levels. Drawing on this information, a group of psychologists and physical educators developed a section of *Coaching Theory Level 3* (1980) of the National Coaching Certification Program in Canada. They prepared a detailed list of the kinds of things that coaches might expect from young athletes in three age groups: 6 to 11 years old, 11 to 15 years, and 15 to 18 years. We summarize some of these guidelines for you here. We refer to the three groups as the younger group, the middle group, and the older group.

In the younger group, physical development places certain restrictions on athletic activities. At the 6- to 8-year-old level, reaction time is slow, hand-eye coordination is poor, and muscle and connective tissue

Pre-Season Questionnaire _____

I will be able to do a better job as a coach if I know some of the reasons why you want to participate in this sport. Please take a few minutes to write your answers to the following questions. The answers that you give will be seen only by the coaches. Later we'll get together and talk about your answers. Thank you. — *The Coach*

1. Why do you think you came out for the team this year?

2. What do you expect to get out of being involved with the team?

3. What do you expect to have to put into it?

4. What do you like best about this sport?

5. What do you like least about it?

From the National Coaching Certification Manual.

FIGURE 6-1

6. Do you have any specific goals or objectives that you would like to accomplish this year? If yes, what are they?

7. Do you have any long-range goals that you are aiming at? If yes, what are they?

8. Is there anything in particular that you find really exciting about participating (i.e., motivates you)? If yes, what?

9. Is there anything in particular that you find really gets you down or makes you feel like quitting?

10. Is there anything that coaches, other athletes, or other people do that really bugs you?

Continued.

Pre-Season Questionnaire—cont'd _____

11. When you participated last year, was there anything you would like to have had changed? If yes, what?

12. When you do something really well, how do you like others to respond?

13. When you do something poorly, how do you like others to respond?

14. How important is this sport at this time in your life?

    Not very   1   2   3   4   5   6   7   8   9   10   Extremely
    important   important

    Comments:

If you have any suggestions during the course of the season, or if something is getting to you, be sure to come and talk to one of the coaches. We're all on the same team!

FIGURE 6-1, cont'd

are quite susceptible to injury from excessive stress (such as heavy weight lifting). However, these kids are capable of considerable aerobic endurance activities. With regard to physical differences, coaches must be sensitive to the differential growth rate of children in this age group. Toward the end of the young period (i.e., at 10 or 11 years of age), some kids have sudden growth spurts; others will not experience this stage of growth until later. It is important for a coach to encourage the "late" growers to continue to participate. When these kids catch up in size in their later years, they may do quite well.

What about the behavior patterns of this age group? In general, these children have a relatively short attention span. Complex, detailed instructions or complicated game strategies simply go over their heads. Simple, brief instructions coupled with frequent positive reinforcement is the most effective teaching strategy. With respect to this age group in particular, coaches must resist tendencies to over-emphasize winning or to holler at or chastise kids for mistakes. Each of these young athletes should receive a fair share of the coach's praise and attention. The emphasis should be on fun, fitness, and realistic skill development. (An excellent set of manuals for parents, coaches, and administrators for instructing this age group are those by Valeriote, 1984a, b, and c.)

In the middle age group, physical growth still varies quite a bit from one individual to the next. In competitive sports, especially body contact sports, the coach must be careful not to put a 120-pound youngster who has not yet had a growth spurt in competition with a youth of the same age who may be close to 6 feet in height and 180 pounds in weight. Athletes in this age group are susceptible to muscle and connective tissue injuries (such as might occur, for example, from pushing too hard too soon in weight training). Some athletes in this age group will be the size of an adult but not have the strength. Finally, coaches must be especially sensitive to the fact that this age group is in its prime years of early sexual development. Puberty can be a trying time, and both early and late developers may experience problems in adjustment to the social, psychological, and physiological changes that are occurring in their young lives.

In terms of the behavioral characteristics of the middle age group, these young people can be challenged by more detailed instructional techniques and more complex game and team strategies. It is important, though, that coaches put emphasis on positive reinforcement for skill development and improvement, as opposed to emphasizing winning at all costs. Finally, although it is important for a coach to be a good listener at all levels, it is perhaps most important when dealing with the middle age group. Adults are often unaware as to where adolescents are coming from. At least part of being an adolescent is having a new and stronger desire to be taken seriously by adults. Genuine and attentive listening on the part of the coach can be a helpful response to the teenage athlete's needs. Remember that, although adolescents often spend their energy engaged in battle with the adult population, the most frequent target of adolescent confusion is "the parent." No matter which psychological development theory you advocate, it is all part of learning to grow up, and away from the dependence of childhood. At any rate, consideration of the developmental level of the athletes is important in the selection of appropriate motivational techniques.

Reprinted with special permission of King Features Syndicate, Inc.

In the older group, physical growth stabilizes. Muscles grow to maturity by approximately age 17 years, whereas muscular strength continues to increase on into the twenties. Moreover, although girls reach full growth by the age of 15 or 16 years, it is not until age 18 or 19 in boys that the epiphyses (growth centers of the long bones, that is, legs and arms) solidify. Although young people in this group are capable of safely pursuing a variety of weight training and cardiovascular fitness activities, caution must still be used with 16- and 17-year-old boys in heavy resistance training and in contact sports such as football. In terms of social and emotional characteristics, athletes at this level can and should become more involved than ever in goal setting, decision making, self-monitoring of progress, and personal selection of rewards for their participation in sports.

GUIDELINES FOR MOTIVATING BEGINNERS AT PRACTICES

As we mentioned in previous chapters, there are many natural motivators associated with sports activities. By natural, we mean that the coach does not deliberately plan and distribute these types of rewards; they occur as a natural consequence of participation. For example, self-improvement is a natural reward for most people. In this section, however, we are not talking about natural motivators. In the preceding section we talked about some preliminary considerations; now we will discuss deliberate things that a coach can do to help motivate young athletes to practice skills and improve endurance.

1. **Praise.** Remembering to watch for and praise athletes' desirable behaviors requires reminders and practice. One useful method is for a coach to write out a list of the athletes' names on a 3 × 5 index card and carry the card (and a pencil) around during the practice session. Each time the coach praises a skill demonstrated by one of the athletes, he or she puts a checkmark beside that athlete's name. The coach's goals are to try to praise each athlete several times during each practice, and to ensure that the praise/reprimand ratio favors praise. The benefits here are twofold. The athletes each get to experience the rewards of the coach's praise, and the coach can make sure that no athlete has been forgotten. Fig. 6-2 shows a sample of the reminder sheet used by some coaches of the Manitoba Marlins. The sheet is kept on a clipboard and used throughout each practice. Whenever a coach interacts with a swimmer, she or he places a checkmark in the appropriate column beside that swimmer's name.

Coaches should also try to be sensitive to factors such as work volume. Be aware of and praise the athlete who does a little more in this practice than in the last practice. Noticing and praising the increase in output can provide athletes with the motivation to continue to improve their output.

Finally, coaches should be sensitive to and praise effort. The *Coaching Theory Level 3* manual of the Canadian National Coaching Certification Program states: "There is a common conflict exhibited in many sport situations: athletes are satisfied with their effort levels and coaches are dissatisfied with them." Because of this, it is possible to visit almost any practice session of any sport and see a coach urging beginners to "Try harder," "Dig, dig, dig," or "Pour it on." Athletes who believe they are already trying their hardest—and the coach starts yelling, "Try harder"—may be discouraged enough to decide they simply cannot do better. It is usually more effective to pick out the ones showing behaviors characteristic of digging or pouring it on and to praise them. Sooner or later, the others who only thought that they were pouring it on will probably reach the genuine digging level, and the coach can then praise them for their effort as well. (A system for evaluating effort is described later in this chapter.)

Marlin Practice _____

Date_____

Set	Time	Prompt	Total Distance

Swimmers in Lane 6	Praise	Corrective Feedback	"Let's Go" Prompt	Reprimand	Swimmers in Lane 5	Praise	Corrective Feedback	"Let's Go" Prompt	Reprimand	Swimmers in Lane 4	Praise	Corrective Feedback	"Let's Go" Prompt	Reprimand
1														
2														
3														
4														
5														
6														
7														

From Martin, G.L., LePage, R., and Koop, S.

FIGURE 6-2
Reminder sheet for swim coach to give frequent praise to beginning swimmers during practice.

Remember, the positive approach can save wear and tear on the coach by eliminating the ineffective hollering that may lead to nothing more than frustration for coach and athletes alike. The positive approach can also save wear and tear on a beginning athlete's morale and self-confidence. In the end, everyone benefits.

2. Use fun activities as rewards for specific practice behaviors. Many sports provide coaches with the chance to have some sort of activity, such as a scrimmage session in hockey or basketball or a water polo match for the members of a swim team, at the end of most practice sessions. These activities are often considered fun times by the athletes. Because they are fun activities, they have potential as rewards. If, however, an activity is scheduled to occur at a set time, it is not, by behavioral definitions, a reward for certain practice behaviors. For example, if the water polo match is scheduled for Friday afternoons each week, then the match may reward the swimmers for showing up on Fridays. It does not, however, have much effect on the work or effort the athletes may put out during the practice itself. Coaches should try to set clear practice goals for every practice session, and use the scrimmages, relays, or other fun activities as rewards for achieving those goals (Fig. 6-3). If the goals are not met, then the reward should not be presented. If the coach sets up reasonable practice goals, the athletes will have just about as many opportunities to scrimmage or to have relays. The possibility of having a fun time at practice will act as a motivator to achieve the practice goals only if the fun time occurs as a consequence of the practice goals being met (Cracklen and Martin, 1983).

3. Encourage positive peer interaction. Peer approval and attention can be a powerful motivator. Unfortunately, peer power often encourages undesirable practice behaviors. It is possible, however, for a coach to increase the chances of positive peer interaction by discussing with the athletes ways in which they can cooperate with and help each other.

One such example was described in Chapter 1, and involved Jim Dawson, the coach of the Clifton Junior High School basketball team, in Columbus. You may recall that Coach Dawson was concerned about the kind of practice effort that he was getting from his players at practices. In particular, he expressed concerns about the degree of support and encouragement among teammates in the practice setting. He was also concerned about a series of lay-up drills and jump shooting drills that he used to open each practice, and the team's free throw shooting during practice. The motivational system he decided on included a point system and public recording of those points by volunteer stu-

Guidelines for Skill Development and Motivation

FIGURE 6-3
Schedule "fun" scrimmages as reward for meeting practice goals.

dents who served as managers for the team. Players could earn points for performance in lay-up drills, jump shooting drills, and free throw drills at daily practice. In addition, they could earn points by being a team player and encouraging their teammates. Points were deducted if Coach Dawson saw an instance of lack of hustle or of bad attitude. All of this was explained to the players in detail. In addition to recording the points at each practice, players who earned a sufficient number of points were rewarded with an "Eagle Effort" award at a post-season banquet, and had their names posted on the "eagle effort board" in a conspicuous place in the hall leading to the gymnasium.

As described in Chapter 1, the system was highly effective. Performance improved in lay-up drills, jump shooting performance, and free throw shooting at practices. What about the peer encouragement part of it? In Siedentop's words:

> But the most dramatic improvement was in the "team player" category. Before implementation, four to six instances of criticism were detected during each practice session. Approximately 10 to 12 instances of peer encouragement were detected. The management system "required" that players encourage one another in order to win their points. During the first practice session after implementation, the managers recorded over 80 statements of encouragement among teammates and also reported that they probably didn't record more than one third of what actually happened. There were simply too many supporting comments to monitor them all. Coach Dawson reported that for several days the supporting comments were "pretty phony." There was much laughter following comments and it all seemed pretty much "put on." But then a funny thing happened. The laughter slowly subsided. The boys got more comfortable saying nice things to one another. The comments got more genuine. At one point, according to Coach Dawson, the mood of his practices changed dramatically. He calls it the most amazing transformation he has seen in his coaching career. "By the end of the season," said Jim, "we were more together than I ever could have imagined." Teachers would stop Jim and ask him, "What in the world is going on in your practices?" He could reply in all honesty, "We have started to really help each other." (1980, p. 53)

STEPS IN DEVELOPING AND MAINTAINING A MOTIVATIONAL SYSTEM: PUTTING IT ALL TOGETHER

The task of motivating a group of athletes in practice is difficult. As mentioned, the coach must consider the nature of the sport, the various and different reasons that athletes are participating, the developmental level of the individuals involved, and a host of other things. Is there a general motivational system that has widespread applicability to a number of different sports and a number of different individuals? Yes. However, the coach must devote care and attention to the details of the components of such a system in order to maximize its potential applicability to as many athletes as possible. The components of such a system include behavior recording (either self-recording or recording by observers), display of results (either publicly or privately for each individual), providing frequent and immediate feedback concerning behavior recorded, setting performance goals, and finally, rewarding goal attainment.

1. Identify behaviors that you wish to motivate. The first step is to identify the behaviors that you wish to increase, for example, the number of laps swum per hour, the total distance run each day, the number of correct jumps performed in a figure skating practice, the time required to complete a set exercise routine, the number of correct executions of backfield plays, percentage of correct blocks by linemen, percentage of aces served in tennis.

Sometimes it might be helpful to assign points to particular behaviors so that each individual can be given a total score at the end of practice. For example, a point system for evaluating player performance during ice hockey scrimmages is shown in Fig. 6-4. Other performance indicators have been described for high school basketball and football practices (Siedentop, 1980), age-group swimming prac-

Ice Hockey Behaviors and Assigned Points per Instance _____

Goals for	+4	Goals scored against	−2
Assists	+4	Losing turnover	−1
Goals scored for (but didn't get goal or assist)	+2	Penalty in offensive zone	−1
		Penalty when on power play	−1
Shots on goal	+2	Face-off lost	−1
Shots at goal	+1		
Going to aid of teammate	+1		
Headmanning puck to open player	+1		
Forcing turnover	+3		
Finishing check	+2		
Face-off won	+1		

Prepared by Paul Milton.

FIGURE 6-4

tices (Cracklen and Martin, 1983; Martin et al., 1983; McKenzie and Rushall, 1974), and exhibition games for a barnstorming baseball team (Heward, 1978).

2. Arrange for the behaviors to be recorded. In order for an individual to know that he or she has done more of something, that something has to be recorded. Earlier in this chapter we described how Coach Dawson and Daryl Siedentop taught student managers to record various statistics at practices of the Clifton Junior High basketball team. Parents or other volunteers might also be enlisted to record behavior during repeated practices and to make that information available to the participants, as requested by the coach.

Another possibility is for the athletes to self-record. For example, McKenzie and Rushall (1974) designed a self-recording system to motivate age-group competitive swimmers to swim faster over longer periods during practice. A program board like that shown in Fig. 6-5 was placed at the end of each of the lanes of the pool.

A transparent pocket along the top edge of each board enabled the coaches to write the practice requirements on program unit cards. The cards, indicating a set of repeats, were then inserted along the top of the board. The coaches were able to insert any training program they wished, and could easily alter the training program content between sessions by changing the work unit cards. At a given practice, the names of swimmers in a lane were written along the left side with a grease pencil. As a swimmer completed a work unit (e.g., a 400-yard freestyle swim consisting of 16 lengths), that swimmer placed a check beside his or her name with the grease pencil. After each practice, the check marks and swimmers' names were erased from the boards with a solvent. The swimmers took turns assuming the responsibility of caring for and preparing the board for practice.

Why should a program board of this sort exert a motivational influence on the swimmers? In theory, there are several reasons. As soon as a swimmer completed a set, there was a clear stimulus to perform the next set. Also, because the swimmers finished sets at different times, reinforcement for fooling around at the end of the lane was no longer present because other swimmers were not there. Self-recording provides positive reinforcement for swimmers for appropriate behaviors. Moreover, public recognition, attention and praise, and approval from coaches and peers occurred intermittently as the swimmer posted a checkmark. Finally, the program board may have exerted an element of public commitment to the training task.

How effective were the program boards as motivational devices? When the distances swum before the program boards were compared with the distances swum after the program boards were introduced,

Guidelines for Skill Development and Motivation

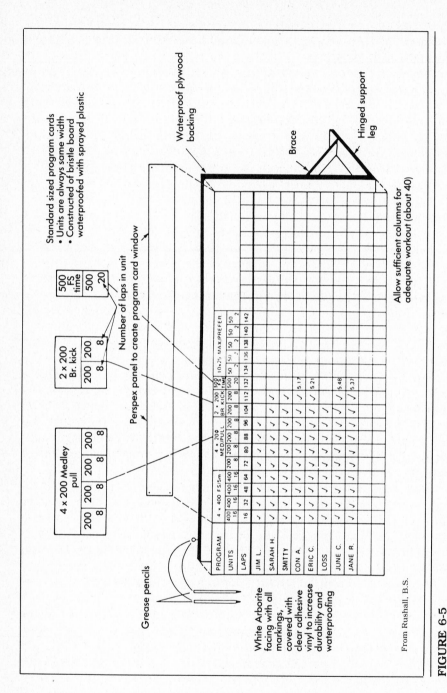

FIGURE 6-5

Suggested structure for program boards and program unit cards.

there was an average increase for all swimmers of 27%. This represented an additional 619 yards per practice for each swimmer. In addition, use of the program boards allowed swimmers to continue with repetitive activities on an independent basis; they did not have to wait at the end of the pool for instructions from coaches. Moreover, inasmuch as all of the swimmers rarely completed an activity at the same time, they tended not to congregate at the end of the pool. Thus there were far fewer disruptive behaviors. The coaches were freer to monitor swimming skills and provide feedback on individual strokes and to praise swimmers for stroke performance and for completing activities. In other words, coaches were better able to function as effective behavioral coaches. Finally, most of the swimmers preferred to use the program boards. There were one or two exceptions, however. One girl was overheard saying, "I don't like them. They make me work too hard" (McKenzie and Rushall, 1974, p. 205). For the majority of the swimmers, who preferred using the boards, different aspects of their use appeared to be reinforcing. Some swimmers enjoyed having the opportunity of working at their own pace. Some enjoyed working with others, and teamed up with a partner to monitor each others' performance. Still others obviously enjoyed the attention and praise that came from the coach when they completed an activity and checked that activity off beside their names.

The program boards used by McKenzie and Rushall required that the swimmers self-monitor their performance during practice. Another possibility is to have athletes complete self-evaluation checklists after practices. For example, Randy Ambrosie, all-Canadian offensive tackle with the University of Manitoba Bisons, with the help of Jody Young, a graduate student in physical education, developed the checklist shown in Fig. 6-6.

Randy recorded self-evaluations after practices during the week before an important game with the University of Calgary. He found the checklist to be very helpful in maintaining his concentration on various aspects of technique. Such a checklist can also help a coach to focus feedback on specifics of practice performance, as opposed to just making vague, general comments.

3. **Display the behaviors in a way that provides meaningful feedback.** "Detailed feedback is a necessary characteristic in order that goal setting may affect performance" (Rushall, 1979). This is a critical component of a motivational system. If an athlete can see a simple set of check marks on a graph that is easy to interpret and that clearly displays progress, then opportunities arise for factors such as self-praise, attention, coach's praise, and knowledge of improvement to

Self-Evaluation Form

Date *OCT. 29 - NOV. 2, 84*

	M	T	W	Th	F
Skill Evaluation					
Assess each on a scale of 1 to 5. where 1 = less than 50% of opportunities. 3 = 50% to 70% of opportunities. and 5 = almost all the time.					
1. Pass blocking					
a. Butt down	4	3	3	4	3
b. Back straight	4	3	3	4	3
c. Hands out in front	4	4	4	4	4
d. Foot movement. lead steps	4	4	4	4	4
e. Contact on chest	NA	3	3	4	4
2. Run blocking					
a. Lead steps	4	4	4	4	4
b. Quickness off ball	3	3	3	3	3
c. Explosion into man	NA	3	3	3	3
d. Extension and hip thrust through man	NA	3	3	4	4
e. Contact on body. not outside	NA	3	3	4	4
3. Blocking success					
a. One-on-one	NA	3	NA	NA	NA
b. Team situations	NA	3	4	5	5
Contributing Factors					
Rate each subjectively on a scale of 1 to 5. where 1 = very poor. and 5 = super or great.					
1. Effort	4	3	4	4	4
2. Concentration	3	2	3	4	5
3. Physical well-being	3	3	3	4	4
4. Sleeping habits (minus [−] = too little. too tired; checkmark [√] = about right. 7 1/2 to 8 hours; plus [+] means too much. too sluggish.)	−	−	−	√	√
5. Eating habits	Not great	OK	OK	OK	OK

FIGURE 6-6

Self-evaluation form allows offensive tackle of football team to self-monitor practice performance during week before game.

Comments:

Monday - Late class, did not get a proper warm-up, missed contact drills. Worked on technique during offensive team time.

Tuesday - Pass blocking wasn't great; run blocking, have to get better hand placement and use upper body. Neck was sore. Didn't have a great practice.

Game Saturday - Very cold. Pass blocking was good except butt could have been lower.

Run Blocking - Could have been more explosive. Butt positioning could have been better on a few occasions in the game.

play a role in motivating that athlete. Providing information about some aspect of behavior just after the behavior has occurred is what we mean by feedback. However, the feedback has to be meaningful. Beginners are unlikely to respond to feedback concerning their performance based on complex mathematical equations or delayed computer printouts. A simple system of check marks or a simple graph that can be displayed immediately is more likely to be effective.

Frequently, feedback can be enhanced if the measure of behavior is publicly displayed on a chart. In fact, Van Houten (1980) suggests that public posting is by far the most important rule when using feedback to motivate others. There is little doubt that public posting can be effective in stimulating peer interactions that might reinforce increased output. Public posting can also serve as an important reminder to coaches to provide praise for progress. However, the coach must not lose sight of the fact that public posting might be embarrassing and aversive to some people. If public posting is to be used, it should be designed so that it encourages teammates to praise each other or to compete against themselves. It should never be used to encourage unhealthy competition among young athletes. Care should be taken to ensure that the public posting procedure does not bring positive attention to some at the cost of embarrassment and aversive feelings in others. Often, the manner in which the procedure is introduced can be critical.

An example of the use of posted charts to motivate practice performance was described by Daniels (1983). As coach of a junior girls gymnastics team in Lethbridge, Alberta, she decided that the team members needed a motivational system to help them recognize intermediate accomplishments and successes in developing parts of skills and combinations. As expressed by Coach Daniels, "The joy a gymnast feels once finally mastering a new skill is often darkened by such statements from the coach as: 'Your lay-out is great! Now we can start on twisting,' or 'That aerial is really solid! Let's start working it on the beam.' Although the prospect of attaining even higher goals probably excites a gymnast, sometimes more emphasis should be placed on recognizing the time and effort spent acquiring the newest skill."

Coach Daniels designed charts for each apparatus and hung them on the wall in the gymnasium. A sample chart is shown in Fig. 6-7. Stars were used to indicate success at various stages of skill development. When a gymnast began working on a skill, she was given a green star (for GO). A red star indicated that active spotting aides were no longer necessary; and a gold star meant that the skill was competition

Unevens

SCORING KEY: ◯   = Go (Begin practice)

◻   = Stop (No spotting aids)

☆   = Meet ready

Name	Skill/Combination	Starting (Date)	No Active Spotting (Date)	Competition Ready (Date)
Lynne	Straddle cut catch	◯ 9/15	◻ 11/4	☆ 12/5
Andie	Inside salto	◯ 9/15		
Sue	Uprise to handstand			
Mary	Cast handstand ½T (HB)	◯ 9/15	◻ 12/23	☆ 1/26
Wendy	Giant	◯ 9/15	◻ 1/6	
Gail	Hecht dismount	◯ 9/20	◻ 10/30	☆ 1/15
Liz	Straddle cut catch	◯ 9/20		
Patti	Cast handstand	◯ 9/20		
Tracey	Cast handstand			
Sue	Beat full	◯ 9/20	◻ 10/24	☆ 12/12
Andie	Uprise	◯ 9/20	◻ 11/16	

From Daniels. D.B.

FIGURE 6-7
Wall chart for marking progress of young gymnasts.

ready. When a gymnast received a gold star, she was awarded a teddy bear (the team mascot) button to sew on the collar of her warm-up suit. As described by Dr. Daniels (1983), the system served a number of valuable motivational purposes:

> The charts were a constant visual reminder to the team of individual progress. If a gymnast wasn't working hard enough or had taken a long time to acquire a red star, the other team members began to help and encourage her. The gymnasts never questioned the vast differences in the difficulty levels of some skills.
>
> This system also helped the gymnast tell the coach which skills she really wanted to learn and kept the coach informed about the progress of team members in their individual training programs.

4. Ensure that the coach's praise or feedback is immediate and frequent. As soon as possible after a behavior has occurred, the coach should praise and post feedback for desirable performance. In many situations, self-recording seems to be an effective strategy for ensuring immediate feedback. The feedback and praise should also occur frequently, especially at the beginning of a season. By frequently, we mean that beginners should receive feedback or praise several times during a practice.

5. Set performance goals. In this section, we're not talking about general goal setting in terms of the accomplishments that an athlete may wish to achieve over a season or over several years. Rather, we're talking about a goal-setting procedure relative to the specific performances that are being monitored for motivating practice and endurance training. Obviously, coaches might want to encourage athletes to set goals in a variety of areas, for example, skill development, cooperation with team members, cooperation with officials, long-term results achieved (*see* Chapter 10). Within our motivation system for motivating practice and endurance training, however, we're only concerned about the specific practice behaviors that we want to increase in frequency and quality.

> The scientific research involved with goal-setting indicates that performances are better when individuals strive for a number of goals in a single performance than when striving for a single goal. (Rushall, 1979)

One goal might be set that requires a fair bit of improvement before it can be attained. If there is a reasonable probability that the goal will not be reached in a practice, there should be a second-level goal, and perhaps a third-level goal, that requires less improvement on the part of the athlete. Because rewards are typically associated with achieving goals, it is important to structure goal setting so that at least one goal will be achieved within a practice session. Also, it is important to be very specific in the content of the goal setting. Indicate the exact behaviors that make up the goal rather than using vague terms such as "Loosen up," "Hustle," "Stick it to them."

Goals might be set for effort as well as for results, although assessment of effort is obviously much more subjective. One possible strategy is for the coach and the athletes to independently assess effort and then compare their assessments at the end of practice. For example, while coaching a group of beginners in the Manitoba Marlin Swim Club, Coach Martin assessed effort at the end of each practice. Swimmers were encouraged to assess themselves on a scale of 1 to 10. A 10 meant "You have worked hard to swim each of the sets without resting during the set; you started each of the sets when I asked you to, without wasting time adjusting your goggles or fooling around; you practiced your racing turns; and you completed all of your sets within the times." A 5 meant "You fooled around a lot, skipped some laps on three or more sets, stopped at the end of the lane at least five or six times during practice, and took two or three bathroom breaks. If you give yourself a score of 6, 7, 8, or 9, then you are somewhere in between." At the end of each practice the swimmers and the coach sat down as a group, and the coach asked, "OK, how many would rate yourselves as at least a 5? How about a 6?," and so on. By a show of hands, each swimmer indicated their self-rating. The coach then indicated what he considered the overall team rating to be. If the swimmers wanted the coach to indicate his or her assessment of their individual ratings, this was done privately. In general, there was considerable agreement between the ratings assigned by the coach and the ratings assigned by the swimmers. Before implementing this system, the coach had subjectively rated approximately one fourth of the swimmers as showing an effort of approximately 7 or less. After the rating system was implemented, most of the swimmers both swam (according to the coach's ratings) and self-rated somewhere in the neighborhood of 8, 9, or 10.

6. Reward goal attainment. In addition to self-praise and peer attention when goals are attained, coaches should use every opportunity to publicly praise goal attainment by beginners. To avoid setting up a situation that creates negative peer interaction, encourage everyone on the team to reach their own personal goals.

Another effective way to reward goal attainment is to identify a group goal toward which everyone on the team can earn points. The possible ways to provide a special group reward for the team are endless. All that is required is a sense of fun and perhaps a little imagination. For example:

1. Throw a party for the team. Make it a masquerade party (everybody comes as their favorite football player, tennis pro, or fish— if it's a swim club).
2. Organize a weekend camp-out at the coach's cabin or summer cottage; have a weiner roast, corn roast, clam dig.
3. Ask a farmer to take the gang on a sleigh ride, or a rancher to provide horseback riding.
4. Ask a sporting goods store to donate some inexpensive T-shirts or pennants and get them printed with phrases such as "We've got a goal in life." Hand out the shirts or flags at the end of the practice during which the team goal is met.
5. Take a team picture with one person holding up a sign that says "We did it!," and get it blown up to giant poster size. Hang the poster in the gym or at the pool during practices.

As we said, the choices are endless. If some of our suggestions sound outlandish, remember that there are lots of sports fans in your community who would be more than willing to help a bunch of young athletes. Explain your reasons for wanting a special reward for the gang. You may be surprised at the positive response you get. Who knows? You may even find a new volunteer to help you at practices!

SUMMARY

Is it possible for coaches to hold attention, gain respect, encourage athletes to consistently practice repetitive activities, and at the same time make the practices fun? We believe the answer is yes. One preliminary step to motivating athletes is to consider the nature of the sport itself. If it's an individual sport, a coach may have to introduce specific activities to develop team spirit. If it's a team sport, coaches may have to ensure that athletes practice individual skills rather than relying on other members of the team to cover their weaknesses. A second preliminary step is to examine the reasons the athletes are participating. A useful tactic is for coaches to ask athletes to fill out a pre-season questionnaire in which they are encouraged to describe what they like about the sport, what they hope to get out of it, and what they're willing to put into it. A final preliminary consideration is the developmental level of the athletes. This chapter reviewed some of the things that coaches might expect from young athletes in three different age groups: 6 to 11 years, 11 to 15 years, and 15 to 18 years.

Guidelines that coaches can follow to help motivate young athletes to practice skills and improve endurance include (1) introducing a system to ensure that coach's praise is used as an effective motivator, (2) scheduling fun activities as rewards for specific practice behaviors, and (3) introducing a deliberate strategy for encouraging positive peer interaction at practices. A specific motivational system that can be applied to a number of different sports and for a number of different individuals requires that a coach (1) clearly identify the behaviors to be motivated, (2) arrange for the behaviors to be recorded, (3) display the behaviors on a chart or graph that provides meaningful feedback to the athletes, (4) ensure that coaches' praise or feedback is immediate and frequent during practice, (5) set specific performance goals for practices, and (6) introduce a deliberate reward system for the team and for individuals for goal attainment.

Coach's Checklist

General guidelines for improving your management of practice and endurance training are summarized in the checklist in Fig. 6-8. We suggest you use the checklist as a convenient reminder sheet to ensure that you follow all of the guidelines.

Review Questions

1. Describe several ways in which the nature of the sport has implications for the necessity of extra motivational techniques for athletes' practice behaviors.
2. Briefly describe at least four reasons why beginners participate in sports.
3. Describe at least two physical characteristics and two behavioral characteristics that a coach must keep in mind with respect to the developmental level of a younger group, a middle group, and an older group.
4. Consider the reminder sheet for the swim coach shown in Fig. 6-2. Outline three rules that a coach of age-group competitive swimmers should follow at practices with respect to praise, corrective feedback, and reprimands.
5. What is the common conflict exhibited in many sports situations concerning effort? How do we recommend that this conflict be resolved?
6. Explain what we mean by using available rewards as rewards. In other words, from a practical perspective, what does this mean for coaches?

C O A C H ' S   C H E C K L I S T

Motivating Practice and Endurance Training ____

	Date Completed					
1. Administer pre-season questionnaire (see Fig. 6-1) and discuss results individually with athletes.						
2. Review characteristics that might be expected for developmental level of your athletes.						
3. Choose best performance indicators of behaviors that you wish to motivate.						
4. Arrange for performance indicators to be recorded.						
5. Prepare graph or display that conveniently and simply displays behaviors to be recorded.						
6. Use coach's prompt sheet (see Fig. 6-2) to ensure that you praise each athlete in every practice and that you dispense more praise than reprimands.						
7. Set performance goals for practices with team, and encourage individuals to set personal practice goals.						
8. Arrange to reward goal attainment.						

FIGURE 6-8

7. How did Coach Jim Dawson go about encouraging his high school basketball players to be team players?
8. Why do you suppose that the program boards used by McKenzie and Rushall had the effect that was observed with members of the swim team?
9. What are some practical limitations of the program board procedures that might limit their applicability to sports other than swimming?
10. In a sentence each, list six steps in developing a motivational system to improve athletes' practice behaviors.

Mini-Lab Exercises

1. Describe the details of how you might use a program board procedure in a different sport.
2. Identify a sport that you have played or hope to coach. Consider six desirable practice behaviors in that sport that you would like to motivate athletes to do. List a plausible practice performance goal for each of the six behaviors.
3. Prepare a description of each of the behaviors that you listed in question 2 so that observers (student managers or parent volunteers) can reliably record those behaviors as they occur during practices.
4. Design and describe a public display or graph that could be used to plot the practice behaviors that student managers will record so that the athletes can clearly see progress across practices.
5. Some coaches suggest that athletes should have patience, dedication, desire, determination, and a positive attitude. Although these terms are somewhat vague, it should be possible to identify specific behaviors or quantitative indicators for each of them. Identify three quantitative indicators for each term. (Hint: Try to remember what it was that you did, when you played a sport, when the coach said that you had a positive attitude. Also, try to remember specific things other athletes did when coaches were likely to use the other terms listed above.)

References

Bradshaw, D. (1984). Motivation through basketball statistics. Coaching Review **7** (May/June):52-54.

Coaching theory level 3 (1981). Ottawa, Ontario: Coaching Association of Canada.

Cracklen, C., and Martin, G.L. (1983). Earning fun with correct techniques. Swimming Technique **20**:29-32.

Daniels, D.B. (1983). Keeping high. Coaching Review 6 (May/June):16-17.

Dickinson, J. (1977). A behavior analysis of sport. Princeton, N.J.: Princeton Book Co.

Gould, D., Feltz, D., Weiss, M., and Petlichkoff, L. (1982). Participation motives in competitive youth swimmers. In T. Orlick, J. Partington, and J. Salmela, eds., Mental training for coaches and athletes. Ottawa, Ontario: Coaching Association of Canada, pp. 57-59.

Heward, W.L. (1978). Operant conditioning of a .300 hitter? The effects of reinforcement on the offensive efficiency of a barnstorming baseball team. Behavior Modification 2(1):25-40.

Martin, G.L., LePage, R., and Koop, S. (1983). Applications of behavior modification for coaching age-group competitive swimmers. In G.L. Martin and D. Hrycaiko, eds., Behavior modification and coaching: Principles, procedures, and research. Springfield, Ill.: Charles C Thomas.

Martin, G.L., and Pear, J.J. (1983). Behavior modification: What it is and how to do it. 2nd ed. Englewood Cliffs, N.J.: Prentice-Hall.

McKenzie, T.L., and Rushall, B.S. (1974). Effects of self-recording on attendance and performance in a competitive swimming training environment. Journal of Applied Behavior Analysis 7:199-206.

Rushall, B.S. (1975). A motivational device for competitive swimming training. Swimming Technique 11:103-106.

Rushall, B.S. (1979). Psyching in sports. London: Pelham.

Siedentop, D. (1980). The management of practice behavior. In W.F. Straub, ed., Sports psychology: An analysis of athletic behavior. Ithaca, N.Y.: Mouvement Publications.

Valeriote, T. (1984a). Children's sport programs: The administrator. Ottawa, Ontario: New Traditions.

Valeriote, T. (1984b). Children's sport programs: The coach. Ottawa, Ontario: New Traditions.

Valeriote, T. (1984c). Children's sport programs: The parent. Ottawa, Ontario: New Traditions.

Van Houten, R. (1980). How to motivate others through feedback. Lawrence, Kansas: H & H Enterprises.

Wankel, L.M., and Kreisel, P.S.J. (1985). Factors underlying enjoyment of youth sports: Sport and age-group comparisons. Journal of Sport Psychology 7:51-64.

Selected Readings

Allen, L.D., and Iwata, B.A. (1980). Reinforcing exercise maintenance using existing high-rate activities. Behavior Modification 4:337-354.

Bell, K.F., and Patterson, M.R. (1978). A self-monitoring technique for enhancement of swimming performance. Swimming Technique 14:103-106.

Epstein, L.H., Wing, R.R., Thompson, J.K., and Griffin, W. (1980). Attendance and fitness in aerobic exercise: The effects of contract and lottery procedures. Behavior Modification 4:465-479.

Hume, K.M., Martin, G.L., Gonzalez, P., Cracklen, C., and Genthon, S. (1985). A self-monitoring feedback package for improving freestyle figure skating practice behaviors. Journal of Sport Psychology 7:333-345.

Howard, F.R., Figlerski, F.W., and O'Brien, R.M. (1982). The performance of major league baseball pitchers on long-term guaranteed contracts. In R.M. O'Brien, A.M. Dickinson, and M.P. Rosow, eds., Industrial behavior modification: A management handbook. New York: Pergamon.

Kau, M.L., and Fischer, J. (1974). Self-modification of exercise behavior. Journal of Behavior Therapy and Experimental Psychiatry 5:213-214.

Keefe, F.J., and Blumenthal, J.A. (1980). The life fitness program: A behavioral approach to making exercise a habit. Journal of Behavior Therapy and Experimental Psychiatry 11:31-34.

King, A.C., and Frederiksen, L.W. (1984). Low-cost strategies for increasing exercise behavior: Relapse preparation training and social support. Behavior Modification 8: 3-21.

McKenzie, T.L., and Liskevych, T.N. (1983). Using the multielement baseline design to examine motivation in volleyball training. In G.L. Martin and D. Hrycaiko, eds., Behavior modification and coaching: Principles, procedures, and research. Springfield, Ill.: Charles C Thomas.

Oldridge, N.B., and Jones, N.L. (1981). Contracting as a strategy to reduce drop-out in exercise rehabilitation. Medicine and Science in Sports and Exercise 13:125-126.

Decreasing Problem Behaviors

Problem behaviors in athletic environments occur for a wide variety of reasons. By problem behaviors, we do not mean skill deficiencies. Those should be dealt with according to the techniques described in Chapter 5 for decreasing errors. Rather, in this chapter we're concerned with such things as athletes putting down other athletes, destroying or failing to put equipment away in its proper place, annoying and disruptive behaviors while the coach is talking to the team, off-task behaviors during practices, excessive socializing or fooling around during drills, inappropriate aggressive behaviors, temper tantrums, and so forth.

Is it possible for a coach to control annoying and disruptive behaviors of some athletes in sports settings, and still maintain the positive approach advocated in this book? In most cases, yes. This chapter describes several strategies that can be used to prevent certain behavior problems from occurring in the first place, and to quickly decrease those problems that do occur. Occasionally, however, the positive approach alone is not sufficient. Sometimes the problem behavior causes problems for the whole team, problems that a coach can't ignore. In addition to describing positive procedures for decreasing problem behaviors, this chapter also presents two procedures involving mildly aversive components—procedures that can be used in conjunction with the positive approach, and that have a strong research base to demonstrate their effectiveness (Axelrod and Apsche, 1983).

135

IT HELPS TO CONSIDER THE CAUSE

Some consideration of the causes of problem behaviors may help you to prevent them before they occur. Alternatively, if problems are already ongoing, some consideration of the cause of the problem will likely help you to select the best treatment strategy.

Some problems can stem from a lack of understanding by your athletes as to what you expect of them at practices. Some of your athletes may have worked with a previous coach who allowed athletes to do things that you consider problematic. A previous coach may even have encouraged behaviors that you find annoying. As described below, many problem behaviors can be prevented simply by clarifying rules and expectations up front at the start of a season. If you don't clarify your expectations, you can be assured that at least some of your athletes will show what you consider to be problem behaviors.

Reprinted with special permission of King Features Syndicate, Inc.

Other athletes may show problem behaviors at practices simply because it is not worth their while to perform in desirable ways. The case of the swimmers described in Chapter 3, who stopped in the middle of sets and failed to practice tumble turns, is just such an example. If nothing much by way of positive consequences happens when athletes perform well, and if they get attention (usually from peers) for showing problem behaviors, then problem behaviors will occur. Such situations can usually be dealt with rather easily by carefully restructuring the rewards in your practice environments to follow desirable athletic behaviors as described in Chapter 6.

In still other cases, athletes may show problem behaviors because they don't have the skills to earn rewards for skilled athletic performance. In such cases, it's not that there are no rewards available for desirable behaviors; rather, there are no skills in the individual's repertoire that enable him or her to earn those rewards. A hockey player who has poor skating skills, poor passing skills, and poor stick-handling skills, for example, might show excessive roughhousing and other problem behaviors during practices simply as a way of getting at least some attention in an athletic environment. In such cases you must carefully design a structured training program appropriate for the skill level of the individual so that rewards and recognition can be earned for showing steady improvement rather than problem behaviors.

Still other problem behaviors may stem from the process of extinction. In behavioral science, when the usual rewards are withheld after a previously rewarded behavior, that behavior is likely to decrease in frequency. This is called extinction. In a simplified sense, if a particular behavior is ignored, it will eventually go away. However, that's the long-term effect. In the short term, withholding rewards following previously rewarded behaviors may cause emotional behavior as a side effect. Consider, for example, what happens when your favorite vending machine takes your money but doesn't deliver the goods. You're likely to aggressively push the buttons several times, bang the side of the machine, and utter a few choice words under your breath. You're showing the short-term effects of extinction: emotional behavior. This might be seen on a team when a new kid moves to town. Let's suppose the new kid, Charlie, is a superstar. Until Charlie came to town, Freddie was Number 1. Freddie got lots of rewards for his athletic performance on the team. Now, for approximately the same behaviors, Freddie no longer gets much attention. Most of it now goes to Charlie. It may seem to the coach that Freddie has a problem. During the past week, he has shown temper tantrums, sulking and pouting, unprovoked aggression toward his teammates, and a variety of other emotional behaviors. Like your behavior toward the vending machine, Freddie is showing the short-term effects of extinction. In such situations the coach must be careful not to inadvertently provide a great deal of attention to someone like Freddie *only* following emotional outbursts. That will worsen the problem. Also, the coach must refrain from labeling Freddie a poor sport and blaming him for his burst of problem behaviors. What the coach must do is to talk the situation over with Freddie away from the athletic environment, have Freddie set personal goals, encourage him to work for improvement against himself, and deliberately provide a little extra feedback for Freddie contingent on self-improvement. In this type of situation it's important for a coach to change his or her behavior from only rewarding winning athletic peformance to also rewarding the achievement of personal goals, efforts, and desirable social behaviors of someone like Freddie. At all costs, the coach must avoid ignoring Freddie and concentrating solely on the new superstar.

Still other problem behaviors stem from the dynamics of interpersonal interactions for the athletes away from the athletic environment. Susie wasn't invited to the sleepover that most of the other girls on the team will be attending on Friday night. Scott just broke up with his girlfriend. Mary's parents are about to divorce. Alex is on the verge of failing tenth grade. Michael doesn't want to be in athletics at all; he's on the team only because his dad keeps pushing him to play. His dad also bought the team new sweaters. All kinds of interpersonal interactions away from the athletic environment can cause problem behaviors for athletes that spill over into the practices and games. Moreover, extreme anxiety, phobias, inadequate social skills, complete absence of functional problem-solving skills, sexual hang-ups, drug and alcohol dependencies, and a myriad of other problems present in many young individuals will also be present in athletes. The coach, although not expected to treat such problems, must be constantly sensitive to their existence and be ever ready to refer athletes to other professionals who can help in such cases.

STRATEGIES FOR DEALING WITH PROBLEM BEHAVIORS

1. **Involve the athletes in identifying reasonable rules and expectations, and clear consequences for rule violations.** Remember Fred Thister from Chapter 1? Fred was the volunteer coach of the Shaftsbury Sharks, the age-group competitive swim club. As you may recall, Fred knew a lot about swimming, but he had difficulty managing the kids in practice. Now, Fred Thister is a fictitious character. But the problems alluded to in Chapter 1 are real. Young swimmers at an age-group practice are likely to show such behaviors as pushing other swimmers into the pool, grabbing the feet of a swimmer swimming ahead of them, filling their bathing caps full of water and throwing them at other swimmers, failing to swim up to and touch the pool lane wall, and performing a variety of uncooperative and disruptive behaviors. Anticipating such difficulties, the coaches of the Manitoba Marlins prepared a list of "Good News and Bad News" behaviors for swimmers at practice (see Fig. 7-1).

At the start of the season, each of the swimmers was given a copy of the "good news" and "bad news" behaviors of swimmers at practices. They had fun talking about the behaviors at the team meeting. "OK," said Coach Rod Small, "Let's go over the list. The first bad news behavior is delaying getting into the pool until the coach yells at least three

Bad News and Good News Behaviors

Some of the things that swimmers do at practices do not help them to become better swimmers. Other things that you can do at practices will definitely help you to improve so that you can swim to the best of your ability. We've made a list of the "bad news behaviors" that will prevent you from becoming better swimmers, and "good news behaviors" that will help you to become better swimmers if you practice them. We hope that you will study these lists and that you will encourage each other to practice the "good news behaviors."

Bad News Behaviors
practice behaviors that won't help you improve, and they may interfere with others

1. Delay getting into the pool until the coach yells at least three times.
2. Complain loudly when the coach asks you to do certain exercises.
3. Swim hard only when the coach yells at you.
4. Fail to swim up to and touch the pool walls on each lap.
5. Never practice tumble turns on laps.
6. Hit other kids by flipping your goggles at them.
7. Skip as many laps as you can without the coach noticing.
8. Stand up at every end on backstroke so that you don't improve your turns.
9. Stop and adjust your goggles and bathing suit more often than anyone else in the club.
10. Ask the coach lots of irrelevant questions to waste time.
11. Grab the feet of the swimmer swimming in front of you.
12. Pull yourself along by grabbing the lane marker.

Good News Behaviors
practice behaviors that will help you improve so that you get better times and swim to the best of your ability

1. Consistently arrive on deck 10 minutes before practice and do warm-up exercises on your own.
2. Make sure your goggles are adjusted *before* practice begins.
3. Be in the pool right at the start of practice in order to get the most out of practice time.
4. Push hard even when the coach is not looking, especially near the end of practice.
5. Practice correct form of strokes, even though it may seem strange or difficult at first.
6. Encourage your teammates to work hard so that they will improve and so that you will have better competition.
7. Practice your worst stroke when the coach says you can swim any stroke you want.
8. Use every opportunity at both ends to practice and improve turns.
9. Get all of your repeats under the time suggested by the coach.
10. Be one of the first to start when the coach gives you something challenging and difficult to swim.

From Martin, G.L., LePage, R., and Koop, S.

FIGURE 7-1

times. Everybody who did that at least once a week last year raise your hands." The swimmers looked at each other and grinned and giggled. No hands were raised. "Come on now, let's be honest," said Coach Small. Up went two or three hands, then another two or three. Before long, everybody got into the swing of things and honestly self-evaluated whether they showed good news or bad news behaviors. At the team meeting, the swimmers agreed that they would much rather practice with people who mostly showed good news behaviors. The good news and bad news behaviors were reviewed several times by the coaches and the swimmers throughout the season. Clearly identifying and discussing expectations at the start of the season is an important first step.

Clarifying expectations should not be left just to specific practice behaviors. Attitudinal behaviors away from practices are also important. For example, at the start of a season, team members might be prompted as follows:

1. Encourage your team captains to assume positive leadership. This can include such things as presenting a list of concerns to the coaches, collecting ideas from other team members to deal with concerns, arranging to see some films, organizing team activities away from the athletic environment, being positive at practices.

2. If you genuinely want help with your technique, sport psyching, team-building group sessions, or anything else, ask the coaches. Assume initiative in letting coaches know what you want.

3. If different coaches give you conflicting suggestions, ask for a meeting with all of them to discuss them.

4. Set a personal goal for each practice (e.g., total distance, making certain sets, concentrating on technique). Tell at least one other team member about your goal at the start of practice.

5. Tell the coach when you feel you have had a good practice. Coaches like feedback, too.

6. If you see other team members working hard in practice, compliment them.

7. Pair up with another team member in a buddy system. Take turns assuming responsibility for pushing each other in practice.

8. Self-evaluate your performance at practices regularly. Go for several perfect 10's each week.

9. Set up personal contracts with coaches (e.g., "Coach, if I have eight really good practices this week, will you arrange for me to get some videotaped feedback on Saturday?").

All of these are examples of positive steps that you can take *now*. There are also negative behaviors to avoid:

1. Complaining. It's contagious. ("I'm tired." "You can't be serious." "It's boring.") Don't be a follower and join in such griping and moaning.
2. Stopping others from working hard. Getting in the way of other athletes, telling them not to work so hard, and causing lots of distractions are destructive to good training and team development.
3. Talking about problems without doing anything about them. If you're dissatisfied with some aspect of a coach's program, and you complain about it to other athletes without approaching the coach, that's also destructive.
4. Putting down positive suggestions and efforts by others ("We can't do that." "That's dumb." "No way." "Who cares?"). Put-downs, like complaints, are contagious and destructive to a positive training environment.

In any sport, there have to be some dos and don'ts at practices and competitions. Allowing young people to run free and do the things that may be acceptable at the beach or a public park does not make for effective learning in a practice session. There have to be some rules. Moreover, we know that individuals are more willing to accept rules and consequences for rule violations when they have had input into their development, and if they have publicly committed themselves to following the rules. When formulating rules and consequences for rule violations, ask yourself several questions. Are the rules fair? How well do particular rules contribute to the effectiveness of your practice organization? How well do they contribute to the instruction of the athletes? Are the consequences for rule violations fair to the individuals involved, and to the rest of the team? Once you have set rules that you believe will contribute to making a better team and helping the individual athletes to improve, you should then discuss them with the athletes, even if they are young children. After the players have had a chance to make suggestions and express their ideas concerning your rules, and after you have had a chance to incorporate those suggestions that appear to be helpful, then you should encourage the athletes to make a commitment to follow the rules. In this way the rules become theirs as well as yours. With respect to consequences, ask the athletes up front, "Do you think they're fair? If you don't think they're fair, say why." If you present your rules up front, ensure that they're fair and acceptable to your athletes, ensure that the athletes agree with the consequences for rule violations, and get a commitment from the athletes to follow the rules, then you have minimized the chances of problem behaviors occurring in the first place.

2. Help athletes self-monitor desirable alternative behaviors. When a problem behavior persists, one strategy is to use self-monitoring to increase a desirable competing behavior. Let's look in on a practice of the St. Anne's Figure Skating Club. Michelle Hume, the professional instructor and coach of the club, is in the middle of a half-hour lesson with Sally. Heather, Claudia, and Cathy are supposed to be practicing their routines and spending extra time on the difficult jumps and spins. For the last 3 minutes, however, Heather and Claudia have been standing along the boards, talking excitedly about the upcoming school dance. Cathy had just completed her fifth loop in a row. Coach Hume looks away from Sally and says, "Heather and Claudia, you're supposed to be practicing your routines, not standing around talking. Let's get at it." Then, "Cathy," Coach Hume hollers, "You've done a loop five times in a row. What you really have trouble with is the double loop, the double axle, and the double Salchow. Why aren't you practicing those?"

Off-task behavior, excessive socializing, and failure to practice the really difficult routines are not uncommon problems facing coaches of various sports. Coach Hume, who was also a graduate student in sport psychology at the University of Manitoba, decided to tackle the problem head on. Rather than continuing to nag about the off-task behavior, she set out to investigate a self-monitoring feedback system for improving desirable alternative behaviors of the skaters. Her first step was to prepare a checklist of the jumps and spins that Heather, Claudia, and Cathy were expected to practice for 45 minutes per day while she gave lessons to other skaters. In addition to listing them all individually, she also listed the specific combination of jumps and spins that constituted each skater's individual program (Fig. 7-2).

Over the next several practices, appropriately trained university students kept track of the frequency of jumps and spins attempted and the number of times a skater practiced her program, and the amount of time spent off-task. The initial observations confirmed Michelle's suspicions. The three skaters averaged a little more than 10 minutes of off-task behavior in each 45-minute session. They averaged approximately 60 spins or jumps attempted per session, most of which were of the "easy" variety. Michelle thought they should be averaging at least 100 per session, and should be working more on the difficult jumps and spins.

A big chart was prepared for each skater, containing the checklist shown in Fig. 7-2, a graph, and appropriate instructions (Fig. 7-3).

Coach Hume explained the charts to the skaters: "Each practice session. I want you to do the first three elements on your chart, and then come and record them here. Then practice the next three elements, and come and record them. Continue in this way until you've practiced all of the elements, which should take approximately 15 minutes. Then go through the whole routine again. After all of the elements have been checked twice, then do your program, and record it over on this side. After doing your program, record the elements in the appropriate column and assess their quality. Thereafter, continue practicing on those elements that you rated as poor when you were doing your program." After some discussion and an initial practice session, the skaters began using the charts. At the end of each practice, their performance was added to the graphs so that they could clearly see their progress.

The results can be seen in Fig. 7-4. During sessions when the charts were in use, the skaters averaged more than a hundred elements per practice and from 2 to 3 minutes of off-task behavior. In other words, they improved by approximately 90% with this self-monitoring system. Once the system was implemented, the only additional time required of Coach Hume was a few minutes at the end of each practice session to review the results with the skaters, update their graphs, and praise their performance.

The basic strategy illustrated by Coach Hume's study (Hume et al., 1985) is quite straightforward. Coaches should identify desirable practice behaviors, and should add some kind of a system to keep track of whether such behaviors occur. Hume emphasized self-monitoring. In the studies described by Siedentop (1980) to improve practice behaviors of high school football and basketball teams, team managers monitored the desirable behaviors. When there is a clear focus on improving a variety of desirable practice behaviors, problem behaviors are likely to be minimized.

Once again, the data presented in Fig. 7-4 illustrate the first characteristic of effective behavioral coaching: frequent measurement of athletic performance and use of these measures as a primary means for evaluating the effectiveness of specific coaching techniques. These data also illustrate one of the most common of the behavioral research designs, the ABAB or replication-reversal design. With this design, each subject serves as his or her own control in the sense that behavior during treatment is compared with the individual's behavior during the phase before treatment. The treatment phase is usually introduced at least twice (followng the first baseline, and then following a reversal to baseline) so that the experimenter may be certain that the behavior change is in fact the result of the particular treatment used and not

Text continued on p. 149.

Guidelines for Skill Development and Motivation

Practice Elements

Practice Elements	F	F	F	F	F	F	F	F	F	F	F	Total
SPINS												
Scratch												
Sit												
Camel												
Layback												
Flying camel												
Flying sit												
Flying back-sit												
Sit-change-sit												
Back one foot												
Combinations												
JUMPS												
Waltz												
Salchow												
Toe loop												
Toe walley												
Loop												
Flip												

Program Content in Order	g-try 1	g-try 2	g-try 3	Total
1. Double flip				
2. Combo spin (camel-sit, back-sit, one-foot spin)				
3. Double axel				
4. Double toe loop				
5. Layback to back-sit				
6. Double loop				
7. Footwork				
8. Double Salchow				
9. Footwork				

Lutz																		
½-Flip, 1½-flip, flip																		
Axel																		
Inside axel																		
Double Salchow																		
Double toe loop																		
Double toe walley																		
Double loop																		
Double flip																		
Double Lutz																		
Double axel																		
Split jump																		
Stag																		
Walley																		
Combinations																		
Butterfly																		
TOTAL JUMPS																		

10. Axel–double toe combo								
11. Circular footwork								
12. Flying camel								
13. Double loop								
14. Footwork								
15. ½-Flip, 1½-flip, fly								
16. Double Lutz								
17. Sit spin								
18. Russian split jump								
19. One-foot spin								
20. Illusion								
TOTAL								

From Hume. K.M.. Martin. G.L.. Gonzalez. P.. et al.

FIGURE 7-2
Practice elements for figure skating program.

Guidelines for Skill Development and Motivation

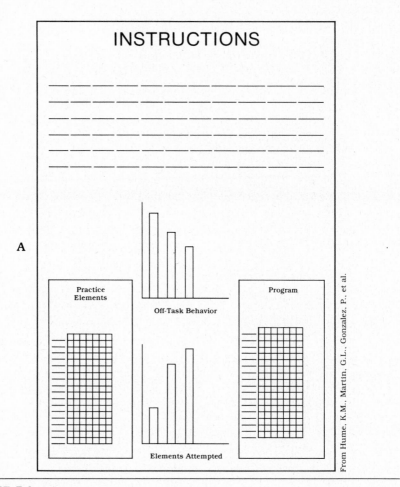

FIGURE 7-3
Self-monitoring program for improving figure skating performance.
A, Self-monitoring chart.

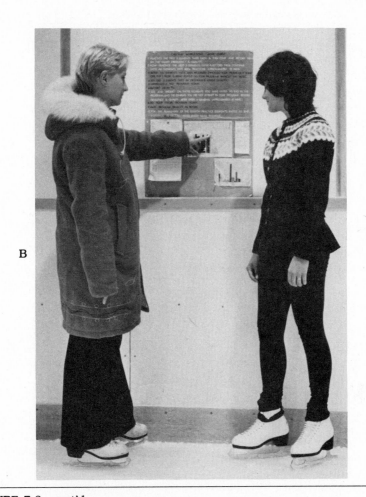

B

FIGURE 7-3, cont'd
*B, Michelle compliments Cathy for increasing number of elements
(spins, jumps) attempted during session.*

Guidelines for Skill Development and Motivation

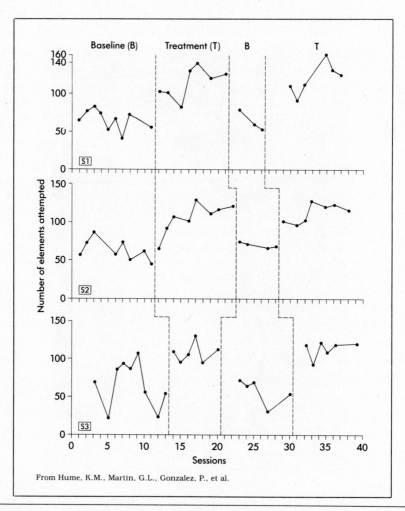

From Hume, K.M., Martin, G.L., Gonzalez, P., et al.

FIGURE 7-4

Number of elements attempted per 45-minute session by subjects (S1, S2, S3) during all experimental phases.

due to some chance variable that happens to coincide with the introduction of treatment. With a successful replication of treatment effects, it becomes much less plausible to suppose that the effects were caused by some uncontrolled variable. This design is described in more detail in Martin and Pear (1983).

3. **Have paper-and-pencil practices during the season.** Jean Leathers coached the high school girl's volleyball team in Fairview, Ohio. After 9 years in athletics as a coach and player, she had frequently experienced the frustration that stemmed from a common problem among coaches: a communication gap between coach and players. Coach Leathers reported that the traditional methods of solving the communications gap—team meetings and individual conferences—had helped; but the gap still existed. In 1983 Coach Leathers came up with a method of dealing with this problem that was so effective that she had her most successful coaching season ever (Leathers, 1984). Midway through the 1983 season she held a "paper-and-pencil-practice." She asked the team three questions:

1. What do you like/dislike so far about the season?
2. What are our strengths/weaknesses?
3. What do we need to improve on, and how can we do it?

The players were asked not to discuss the questions; rather, each girl was asked to write down her own answers to the questions. They were also asked not to sign their names, because Coach Leathers wanted to promote total honesty. The answers included such things as, "I like the perfection drill." "I hate it when people tell me how to stand or how to hit the ball." "No real dislikes, except not putting people in the front row when they should be there."

Coach Leathers learned many things that had not surfaced in previous open discussions. She stopped doing some of the drills that the players disliked and designed some new drills. The players' perceptions of who was most valuable and who wasn't had an effect on game plans. Surprisingly, this did not lead to more time for players whom the coach saw as better players. Rather, it led to playing a particular player more whom the other players thought should have been given more playing time. By the season's end, the girl had earned a starting position. The week after the paper-and-pencil practice, Coach Leathers held another team meeting, during which she summarized everyone's answers. In the weeks that followed, several of the players approached her to work out various misunderstandings. Finally, Coach Leathers felt that it proved to her players that she really did care about their feelings, opinions, and attitudes, and that this reflected strongly on the way they performed during the remainder of the season.

You will recall that in Chapter 2 we outlined six characteristics of effective behavioral coaching. The sixth characteristic was that it emphasizes the need for continually including the views of the athlete in evaluating goals, the acceptability of coaching procedures used to achieve these goals, and the desirability of the results obtained. This is exactly what Coach Leathers' paper-and-pencil practice accomplished. A paper-and-pencil practice has the obvious benefit of encouraging the athletes to give some thought to their concerns, and expressing them anonymously in a nonpunitive environment. Equally important is the necessity for the coach to accept and respond to the feedback as potentially valuable constructive criticism. A highly defensive coach must not organize such sessions. The "I'm going to find out who said that and really make him pay" attitude must be avoided.

4. **When the positive approach doesn't work, then what?** Throughout this book, we have emphasized the positive approach to coaching. If a coach provides lots of rewards for desirable behaviors of athletes, those behaviors will occur more often. But occasionally you will encounter well-established oppositional behavior in an athlete that appears to be "out of control." That is, the individual does not appear to respond to systematic attention and approval for desirable behaviors. Attempts by the coach to continue to ignore the problem behavior may be unfair to the rest of the team. A coach can't allow one individual to ignore team rules or disrupt practices for all of the other persons. Two procedures that have worked effectively in many such cases are reprimands and time-out.

Reprimands. It was the eighth practice of the season for the Mayville High football team. Coach Johnson watched the scrimmage from the sidelines. The offensive team clapped their hands in unison, broke the huddle, and hustled toward their positions. One of the things stressed by Coach Johnson, again and again and again, was hustle. He wanted the players to move through the drills speedily, and with enthusiasm. He wanted the players to move quickly before and after each play was run during a scrimmage, and to provide a lot of effort during each play. Suddenly Coach Johnson blew his whistle and walked briskly toward Billy Hansen, the wide receiver. As soon as Billy saw the coach approaching, he knew what was coming: one of Coach Johnson's reprimands. Coach Johnson stopped about a foot away from Billy. Looking Billy sternly in the eye, almost nose-to-nose, Coach Johnson said in a firm (but not loud) tone of voice, "I don't like it when you walk slowly to your position after the huddle! If you do that in practice, you'll do it in a game. If you do it in a game, it might cause a delay-of-game penalty, and it gives the defense that much more time to look at our setup. I want you to *hustle!* I get really upset when a player doesn't care enough to hustle! It makes me feel like that player doesn't care about the team!" Coach Johnson continued to stare sternly at Billy. Ten seconds went by. Fifteen seconds. Billy was starting to squirm. Twenty seconds of silence passed. Coach Johnson relaxed, stepped back a bit, and put his hand on Billy's shoulder. "Billy," Coach Johnson said softly, "I think you're a valuable member of this team. You've already improved a lot as a wide receiver, and I think you've got the potential to improve even more. Let's remember to hustle!" Coach Johnson walked back to the sidelines, and the team picked up the scrimmage where they left off. During the next practice, the team hustled from start to finish. Coach Johnson singled out several players and complimented them for their exceptional hustle. Billy Hansen was one of them.

Reprimands may be the most common form of punishment applied by coaches, parents, teachers, and others. Only recently, however, has research identified the importance of several steps that should be followed to ensure the effectiveness of reprimands for decreasing behavior (Blanchard and Johnson, 1982; Van Houten, 1980; Van Houten and Doleys, 1983). What are those steps? Let's reexamine the interaction between Coach Johnson and Billy Hansen.

First, athletes should understand what's expected and have the skills to do something right. Coach Johnson had discussed hustling at several team meetings. Billy knew what was expected of him. If a player knows what's expected, has been reminded several times, and still behaves inappropriately, then a reprimand might be appropriate. Second, the reprimand should immediately follow the problem behavior. Note that Coach Johnson did not wait for the team to complete the play. He blew the whistle and immediately walked over to Billy and delivered the reprimand for lack of hustle. Third, the reprimand identified three specific things: the undesirable behavior, the reason why the behavior was undesirable, and the desirable alternative behavior. Note that Coach Johnson did not attack Billy as a person, only his behavior. Coach Johnson did not blurt out something like, "What's wrong with you Dummy? Are you lazy or stupid or both?" Coach Johnson did not holler, swear, or call Billy names. Rather, he sternly identified the undesirable behavior, the reason it was undesirable, and the desirable alternative. Fourth, after telling Billy what he did wrong, the coach expressed how angry and frustrated he felt about it. Fifth, the reprimand was accompanied by a stern look and a firm voice, and it was delivered when the coach was almost nose-to-nose with Billy. Coach Johnson didn't holler from across the field. He invaded Billy's personal space and delivered the reprimand. Sixth, the coach maintained his "reprimand stare" during approximately 15 to 20 seconds of silence to accentuate the aversiveness of the situation. Seventh, during the second half of the reprimand, the coach kindly reminded Billy how valuable he was to the team and encouraged him to try harder to remember to hustle. As expressed by Blanchard and Johnson, the goal of a reprimand is to "eliminate the behavior and keep the person" (1982, p. 88). Eighth, in the very next practice, the coach capitalized on an opportunity to publicly praise Billy for his hustle, the desirable alternative. Finally, Coach Johnson did not lose control of his emotions when delivering the reprimand. When the reprimand was over, it was over. He did not hound Billy for the rest of the practice. He did not snarl and scream and holler at everybody in sight for the next 15 to 20 minutes. The reprimand was not an uncontrolled expression of anger from the coach; it was a deliberate behavior management strategy used in a consistent and effective manner.

Time-out. The full term for time-out is time out from positive reinforcement. It is a procedure for decreasing a specific undesirable behavior by eliminating, for a brief period of time, opportunities for that person to receive attention or other rewards after an undesirable behavior occurs. Time-out is a mild punishment procedure. In a general sense, sending a child to his or her room after bad behavior is a form of time-out. However, the child may be able to play with toys and do other things while in his room, which would decrease the effectiveness of such a time-out. When a coach requires an athlete to sit at the edge of the field or court for a brief period of time following undesirable behavior, that is also a form of time-out. While time-out has been used by humans since early times, behavioral psychologists have recently experimentally examined the steps that can make time-out an effective procedure for decreasing unwanted behavior (Brantner and Doherty, 1983).

First, let's clarify some misconceptions and no-no's. Requiring a child in a classroom to sit on a stool in a corner and wear a dunce cap may be a form of time-out. It is also ridicule and degradation. Although removing the child from a room may be an acceptable and necessary procedure to decrease certain unwanted behaviors, ridiculing or degrading a child is never acceptable. The same is true for athletics. Another no-no is pairing punishment with exercise. Requiring a football player to leave the field and run up and down the bleachers 50 times may involve a component of time-out. It also involves pairing exercise with punishment, and that, in the long term, is highly undesirable (Dickinson, 1977). If a coach yells, hollers, screams, and perhaps swears at an athlete while in the process of requiring the athlete to sit alone for the next half hour, that process may involve an element of time-out. Nevertheless, the yelling, hollering, screaming, and duration of time-out are both unwarranted and undesirable.

How should time-out be used to effectively treat behavior? Vance and Marilyn Hall, noted behavioral psychologists, have outlined several steps to ensure the effectiveness of time-out procedures (Hall and Hall, 1980):

1. *Selecting candidates for using time-out.* While time-out has been effectively used with a wide range of persons, including adults, it has been most widely and effectively used with children from approximately 2 to 12 years of age.

2. *Defining or pinpointing the behavior you want to change.* The specific behavior to be decreased must be defined clearly enough that all concerned know exactly when the behavior has or hasn't occurred.

3. *Measuring the behavior selected.* After the behavior has been defined, it should be recorded and charted for several sessions or days or practices. This phase is important to prove at a later date that the time-out procedure has indeed been effective.

4. *Setting a goal for the target behavior.* What is an accepted level of the undesirable behavior? In some cases, it may be zero. In other cases, you may be willing to put up with a certain frequency of the behavior so long as it is reasonable. Your goal should be clearly identified.

5. *Making sure the environment is rewarding.* Time-out from positive reinforcement will decrease behavior only if there is positive reinforcement in that particular environment for the individual. You must ensure that when the individual is behaving *appropriately* at practices or competitions, you or others are providing appropriate and frequent rewards.

6. *Deciding how long each time-out will last.* Research suggests that each time-out period should last from 2 to 5 minutes. Longer time-outs do not add appreciably to the effect of time-out as a decelerator of problem behavior.

7. *Explaining time-out to the person.* It is important that you sit down with the athlete and explain your concern and that it is to the athlete's and the rest of the team's benefit if the undesirable behavior decreases. Further explain that, from now on, each time the undesirable behavior occurs, you will place that person in time-out for the designated period.

8. *Beginning to use time-out.* Let's suppose that one of your athletes excessively puts down another athlete. After trying several things, you have decided to try a time-out procedure. You have gone through all of the previous steps and are ready to start. Now, when the athlete puts someone else down, you simple say, in a matter-of-fact tone of voice, "That's a put-down. Go to time-out." Check your watch and make sure that the person goes to the time-out area and stays there for the designated period.

9. *Continuing to concentrate on maintaining good behavior.* If you have used time-out properly, the problem behavior should begin to decrease in frequency within a few applications of the time-out procedure. When the problem behavior decreases, be careful to avoid decreasing your attention for desirable behavior. If the environment is no longer rewarding, the individual may again show disruptive behavior as an attention-getting device.

When you feel that the program is no longer warranted, explain to the individual that it is no longer necessary, and also instruct him or her as to your expectations for continued desirable behavior.

5. Sometimes special problems require special procedures. Sometimes you may encounter an athlete who shows a problem that you haven't been able to deal with. You've tried various things, and nothing seems to work. Let's suppose that, for whatever reasons, you don't want to simply get rid of the problem by getting rid of the individual. In such cases, we suggest that you contact the closest university and inquire about people in their psychology department who have expertise in behavior modification. Experts in behavior modification have successfully designed programs to decrease a variety of problem behaviors of persons ranging in age from the very young to the very old, of normal persons and of severely disturbed individuals, and in a wide variety of situations and settings (Martin and Pear, 1983). Examples in physical education and sport environments include reducing disruptive behavior of youths at an urban recreation center (Pearce and Risley, 1974), decreasing a variety of aggressive behaviors in physical education classes (McKenzie, 1980), decreasing off-task behavior and increasing on-task behavior of a class of behaviorally disordered students in physical education (Vogler and French, 1983), decreasing the number of absentees, number of late arrivals, and number of swimmers leaving early at swimming practices (McKenzie and Rushall, 1974), decreasing the number of weights left on the floor by college weight lifters (Darden and Madsen, 1972), decreasing various inappropriate behaviors, such as changing stroke, stopping, not swimming in, and not pushing off in a swimming environment (McKenzie and Rushall, 1980), and decreasing a variety of personal behavior problems of individuals in a sophomore physical education class (Hall, 1979). If you have such problems, chances are that a psychology professor who teaches behavior modification at a university will have students who can help you design a program and collect the data to evaluate its results. In such cases, you should also expect the professor to provide supervision of the students to ensure that the program meets acceptable ethical standards.

SUMMARY

This chapter describes strategies for decreasing a variety of undesirable problem behaviors in athletic environments. Consideration of the causes of problem behaviors might help a coach prevent problems in the first place, or in designing effective treatment programs after they occur. Problem behaviors might occur because athletes do not know or understand what the coach expects from them at practices; because they don't have the skills to earn rewards for skilled performance and therefore show problem behaviors to get attention; because it is a natural reaction for people to show emotional behavior when previously earned rewards are no longer forthcoming for behavior that was effective in the past; or for a variety of other reasons.

At the start of the season, the coach and team members together should agree on unacceptable (as well as desirable) behaviors of team members at practices and competitions. The coach should also ask the players for a commitment to follow the rules, and everyone should clearly understand consequences for rule violations. During the season, an effective strategy for minimizing problem behaviors is for the coach to praise and attend to desirable alternative behaviors. If problem behaviors persist, a coach could consider a more explicit self-monitoring and feedback system. Specifically, athletes might self-monitor the occurrence of desirable alternative behaviors, graph their performance, set goals, and be rewarded for goal attainment. A coach might also consider having a paper-and-pencil practice during the season, in which the athletes are encouraged to write down their likes and dislikes about the season and to identify things that need to be improved. If an individual athlete does not appear to respond to the positive approach by itself, then the coach may feel that it is necessary to supplement the positive approach with either a reprimand or a time-out procedure. With the reprimand procedure, the coach approaches the offending athlete, sternly identifies the undesirable behavior, the reason it was undesirable, and the desirable alternative behavior, maintains eye contact with the athlete for a few seconds, and ends with a positive statement about some of the athlete's strengths. With the time-out procedure, the athlete is required to sit along the sidelines for a few minutes immediately after each instance of the undesirable behavior. If it appears that outside expertise is needed to deal with a problem behavior, the coach is encouraged to seek assistance from a behavior therapist at a nearby university.

Coach's Checklist

Guidelines for decreasing problem behaviors have been summarized in the form of a checklist in Fig. 7-5. We suggest that you use the checklist as a convenient reminder sheet for selecting and following the guidelines for the appropriate procedure.

Review Questions

1. What are the authors referring to when they talk about problem behaviors?
2. Briefly describe several different possible causes of problem behaviors.
3. List four specific steps that a coach might take at the beginning of the season to minimize chances of problem behaviors occurring in the first place (see Fig. 7-5).
4. Sometimes a coach will say about an athlete, "So-and-so really has a bad attitude." Drawing from information in the first part of this chapter, describe behaviors characteristic of a bad attitude.
5. In two or three sentences, explain why you think the replication-reversal design is so called.
6. In the replication-reversal design, in what sense does the subject serve as her or his own control?
7. Why were Hume and co-workers confident that the improvement in the performance of the figure skaters was in fact the result of the treatment?
8. What is a paper-and-pencil practice?
9. Why do you suppose that athletes might provide information in a paper-and-pencil practice that would not surface in an open discussion?
10. Briefly list the nine steps that Coach Johnson followed in delivering a reprimand to Billy Hansen.
11. Outline several reasons why you think the reprimand procedure might be fair or unfair to the athlete involved.

C O A C H ' S   C H E C K L I S T

Decreasing Problem Behaviors

SCORING KEY: √ = *Satisfactory (performed by coach at appropriate times)*

X = *Less than satisfactory*

Date

Start of Season

1. At a team meeting at beginning of season, present, in writing, lists of appropriate and unacceptable behaviors at practices and at competitions.
2. Discuss unacceptable and acceptable behaviors with team members, and revise lists according to their input.
3. Discuss with team members acceptable consequences for rule violations.
4. Ask team members for commitment to follow the rules.

During Season

1. When problem behaviors occur, consider possible causes. Provide feedback to individual and/or take appropriate action.
2. If problem behavior is repeated across practices, consider implementing self-monitoring system of desirable alternative behaviors.
   a. Monitor frequency of undesirable behavior.
   b. Design self-monitoring sheet of desirable alternative behaviors.
   c. Explain system to athletes.
   d. Implement system and graph results across several practices.
   e. If results are positive, show graphs to athletes and encourage them to continue to self-monitor.

FIGURE 7-5

Continued.

C O A C H ' S   C H E C K L I S T

Decreasing Problem Behaviors—cont'd _____

	Date							
During Season—cont'd								
3. If problem behavior is repeated across several practices and positive procedures do not appear to work, consider using reprimands.								
a. Athlete should understand what is expected and be able to behave appropriately.								
b. Reprimand should immediately follow problem behavior.								
c. Reprimand should be delivered in a firm voice, with a stern look, and while standing immediately in front of the individual.								
d. Reprimand should identify desirable behavior, reason that behavior is undesirable, and desirable alternative behavior.								
e. Reprimand should be followed by 15 to 20 seconds of silent "reprimand stare."								
f. Reprimand should be concluded by explaining that individual is valuable to team and by encouraging the individual to try to remember to perform appropriate behavior in the future.								
g. Coach should look for and praise appropriate alternative behavior of that individual during next few practices.								
4. If a problem behavior is repeated across several practices, and if positive procedures and reprimand procedures have not worked, then coach should consider time-out procedure.								
a. Problem behavior should be clearly identified and monitored over several practices.								
b. Coach should set clear goal with respect to problem behavior.								

FIGURE 7-5, cont'd

	Date						

c. Coach should make sure environment provides rewards for desirable behaviors.

d. Time-out program should be explained to the individual.

e. Time-out program should be implemented, used consistently following undesirable behavior, and include time-outs that last from 2 to 5 minutes.

f. Coach should monitor progress and continue to concentrate on maintaining good behavior across several practices.

g. Coach should explain when he or she feels program is no longer necessary, and outline expectations for continued desirable behavior.

5. Have paper and pencil practice in middle of season to get feedback from your athletes.

6. If you think that outside expertise is necessary to deal with problem, consider contacting a behavior therapist at a nearby university.

Guidelines for Skill Development and Motivation

12. Define what is meant by time-out, and give an example. Explain how time-out differs from more common punishment procedures.
13. List the nine steps involved in administering a time-out procedure.

Mini-Lab Exercises

1. Arrange to attend two or three practices of a youth sport. Observe the young athletes for instances of problem behaviors that occur at practices. Choose one of the undesirable behaviors and clearly define it. For that behavior, try to identify the probable causes (i.e., try to identify the controlling stimuli as well as possible reinforcing consequences for instances of that behavior).
2. Suppose that you were given the task of designing procedures to decrease the problem behavior that you identified in question 1. Describe the details of a self-monitoring system (similar to that used with figure skaters in this chapter) that a coach might implement to increase desirable alternative behaviors to displace the problem behavior of the athlete.
3. Consider a sport that you have played or would like to coach. For that sport, and following the example in Fig. 7-1, prepare a list of "good news" and "bad news" behaviors of young athletes who typically attend practices for that sport.

References

Axelrod. S.. and Apsche. J.. eds. (1983). The effects of punishment on human behavior. New York: Academic Press.

Blanchard. K.. and Johnson. S. (1982). The One Minute Manager. New York: William Morrow & Co.

Brantner. J.P.. and Doherty. M.A. (1983). A review of time-out: A conceptual and methodological analysis. In S. Axelrod and J. Apsche. eds.. The effects of punishment on human behavior. New York: Academic Press.

Darden. E.. and Madsen. C.H. (1972). Behavior modification for weight-lifting room problems. College Student Journal 6:95-99.

Dickinson. J. (1977). A behavior analysis of sport. Princeton. N.J.: Princeton Book Co.

Hall. R.V.. and Hall. M.C. (1980). How to use time-out. Lawrence. Kans.: H & H Enterprises.

Hall. W.D. (1979). Behavioral self-modification in teacher education. AAHPER research consortium symposium papers. vol. 2. book 1. pp. 70-74.

Hume. K.M.. Martin. G.L.. Gonzalez. P.. Cracklen. C.. and Genthon. S. (1985). A self-monitoring feedback package for improving freestyle figure skating practice behaviors. Journal of Sport Psychology 7:333-345.

Leathers. J. (1984). The paper and pencil practice. Coaching Review 7:39-42.

Martin. G.L.. and Pear. J.J. (1983). Behavior modification: What it is and how to do it. 2nd ed. Englewood Cliffs. N.J.: Prentice-Hall.

McKenzie. T.L. (1980). Behavioral engineering in elementary school physical education. In P. Klavora and K. Whipper. eds. Psychological and sociological factors in sport. Toronto: University of Toronto Press. pp. 194-203.

McKenzie. T.L.. and Rushall. B.S. (1974). Effects of self-recording on attendance and performance in a competitive swimming training environment. Journal of Applied Behavior Analysis 7:199-206.

McKenzie. T.L.. and Rushall. B.S. (1980). Controlling inappropriate behaviors in a competitive swimming environment. Education and Treatment of children 3:205-216.

Pierce. C.H.. and Risley. T.R. (1974). Improving job performance of neighbourhood youth corps aides in an urban recreation centre. Journal of Applied Behavior Analysis 7:207-215.

Siedentop. D. (1980). The management of practice behavior. In W.F. Straub. ed.. Sport psychology: An analysis of athletic behavior. Ithaca. N.Y.: Mouvement Publications.

Van Houten. R. (1980). How to use reprimands. Lawrence. Kans. H & H Enterprises.

Van Houten. R.. and Doleys. D.M. (1983). Are social reprimands effective? In S. Axelrod and J. Apsche. eds.. The effects of punishment on human behavior. New York: Academic Press. pp. 45-70.

Vogler. E.W.. and French. R.W. (1983). The effects of a group contingency strategy on behaviorally disordered students in physical education. Research Quarterly 53(3): 273-277.

Selected Readings

Franks. C.M. (1984). New developments in behavior therapy: From research to clinical application. New York: Haworth Press.

Graziano. A.M.. and Mooney. K.C. (1984). Children and behavior therapy. New York: Aldine Publishing Co.

Turner. S.M.. Calhoon. K.S.. and Adams. H.E.. eds. (1981). Handbook of clinical behavior therapy. New York: John Wiley & Sons.

Watson. D.L.. and Tharp. R.G. (1985). Self-directed behavior: Self-modification for personal adjustment. Monterey. Calif.: Brooks-Cole.

PART

III

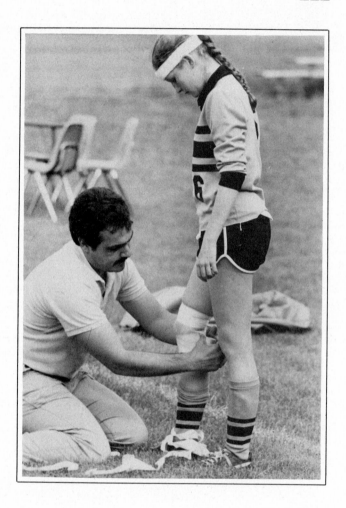

"EXTRAS"
THAT MAKE
A BETTER COACH

Planning a Conditioning and Nutrition Program

As athletes progress in their sport, physical conditioning, balanced nutrition, and plenty of rest become increasingly important as foundations of top-level performance. To develop training programs with maximum potential for helping athletes, coaches must understand the different types and amount of muscle activity required for their sport, the energy systems that serve that muscular activity, and the types of training programs that are most likely to develop the specific energy systems demanded. In addition, coaches of young people can never lose sight of requirements of the particular age group with which they are dealing. That is, the young athlete is somewhere between the ages of 8 and 18 years, attends school for most of the day, plays games, requires a lot of energy for daily functioning, consumes in varying degrees whatever food is placed on the table, and inevitably indulges in soft drinks and all kinds of junk foods. Athletes at the younger end of the continuum should be exposed to general conditioning programs. As athletes move up the age continuum, more specificity in training programs is acceptable. With these considerations in mind, in this chapter we consider how different sports demand different types of muscular and aerobic fitness. We outline strategies that get and keep athletes in good physical condition. We also discuss the importance of nutrition for athletes, and present some nutritional guidelines that all athletes should understand and be encouraged to follow.

THE THREE ENERGY SYSTEMS

As can be seen in Table 8-1, different sports have different fitness demands and draw on different energy systems. To understand how different training programs meet the different fitness requirements, it is necessary for coaches to have some understanding of the three basic energy systems. A useful way of conceptualizing muscle activity in the three energy systems is to imagine the muscles working like engines. Muscle movement requires fuel. Muscle movement also produces waste products. The waste products must be cleared in a way that's satisfactory to the whole system.

Anaerobic Alactic

Anaerobic means without oxygen. Alactic means that the muscle activity does not produce lactic acid (a waste product). The anaerobic alactic system is a stored-energy system. The chemical energy in food is converted to a substance called adenosine triphosphate (ATP) and is stored in muscles. When an athlete puts on a burst of speed or performs a high resistance movement lasting up to 10 seconds, the energy for the muscles is provided mainly by the anaerobic alactic system in that oxygen is not required and lactic acid is not produced. Unfortunately, this small store of energy is depleted very quickly, and if exercise is to continue, another energy system must be used.

Anaerobic Lactic

For all-out intense efforts (muscular activity) lasting longer than a few seconds, the energy is provided by carbohydrate fuel. The fuel is stored as a sugar (glucose) in the body's extracellular water (mainly in the blood) and as glycogen in the muscles and liver. The carbohydrate fuel can be used to quickly provide energy without oxygen. Through a process called glycolysis, the muscle uses carbohydrate fuel to quickly produce and restore supplies of ATP to sustain high-intensity short activity. However, this process also leads to a rapid build-up of lactic acid, which results in decreased muscle performance and fatigue. This energy system produces up to 75% of the energy required for intense efforts lasting 30 to 50 seconds. Beyond that time, the anaerobic lactic energy system continues to participate in the energy supply to an ever-decreasing extent. At approximately 10 minutes of continuous all-out activity, it contributes less than 10% of the energy required.

Aerobic

Beyond 2 minutes of sustained exercise, the majority of energy is supplied by the aerobic energy system. Aerobic means with oxygen. In the aerobic energy system, fuel is provided by both carbohydrates and fats stored in the body, and oxygen is used in the energy conversion process. The oxygen contributes to the oxidation of fat and carbohydrate. When the carbohydrate is burned aerobically, it provides a much more efficient use of energy. Also, providing that the pace is not too great, lactic acid is not built up.

The approximate contributions of the three energy systems as fuel for maximal effort during 2 minutes of intense exercise are summarized in the graph in Fig. 8-1.

T A B L E   8 - 1

Sports, Fitness Demands, and Energy Systems ⎯⎯⎯⎯⎯⎯⎯⎯⎯

Sport	Muscular and Cardiovascular Fitness Demands	Energy Systems Used*
Weight lifting Shot putting	Strength for short intense effort (up to 10 sec.)	Mainly anaerobic alactic
Blocking in football Serving in tennis Hitting in baseball	Strength plus speed for short intense effort (up to 10 sec.)	Mainly anaerobic alactic
400-Meter running sprint 50-Meter swim Some aspects of hockey, basketball, soccer	All-out speed for 25-50 sec.	Mainly anaerobic lactic, some anaerobic alactic and some aerobic
Wrestling, gymnastics Some aspects of basketball	Strength and speed for intense, longer efforts (1-3 min.)	Some anaerobic lactic, some aerobic
400-Meter swim 3000-Meter running race	Speed and endurance for middle-distance races (3-10 min.)	Some anaerobic lactic, mainly aerobic
Marathon running Cross-country skiing	Endurance for longer events (beyond 10 min.)	Mainly aerobic, with anaerobic lactic during sprints at beginning or end of race

*Does not include repetitions or recovery.

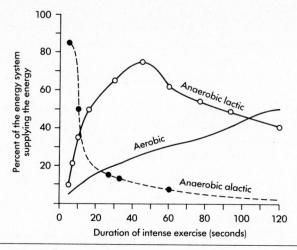

FIGURE 8-1

Approximate percent of energy provided by three energy systems for different durations of intense exercise.

IMPLICATIONS OF THE THREE ENERGY SYSTEMS FOR TRAINING

1. Build an aerobic base. Aerobic fitness refers to the ability of the body to take, transport, and use oxygen. The more aerobically fit you are, the more oxygen your body can process in a given period of time. Obviously, aerobic fitness is essential for sports involving muscular activity in excess of 2 minutes duration. For all sports, however, athletes should be encouraged to develop their aerobic fitness levels as a foundation for further training. There are several reasons for this. First, studies have shown that people who do various aerobic exercises regularly are less susceptible to heart attack later in life (Farquhar, 1978). Second, even in sports where the average play lasts for just a few seconds (and is therefore fueled by anaerobic energy), such as in football, the aerobic energy system will still contribute approximately 10% to 20% of the energy that is used. Moreover, athletes are able to recover faster between plays if they have a higher level of aerobic fitness. It is no accident that professional football teams that have incorporated aerobic fitness into their training programs, such as the Dallas Cowboys, have achieved considerable success and are typically strong in the second half of the game (Cooper, 1982). Third, because it involves the burning of fat, aerobic training is beneficial in reducing excess body fat and excess body weight. Fourth, there is evidence that aerobic fitness helps athletes to avoid injuries (Cooper).

Effective aerobic training requires that moderately intense activity (such as distance running, bicycling, or swimming) occur for a minimum period of time. Although young individuals are capable of considerable aerobic training, intense aerobic training should not be introduced until puberty.

How intense should the aerobic activity be? There are several rules of thumb that can be used to help your athletes monitor whether their aerobic exercise activity is sufficiently vigorous to produce a training effect. A strategy described by Cooper (1982) requires athletes to determined predicted maximum heart rate (PMHR). For men, PMHR equals 205 minus half of age; for women, PMHR equals 220 minus age. An aerobic training effect is achieved if the exercise routine causes heart rate to exceed 80% of the PMHR for 20 minutes. A second rule of thumb is that your athletes should be aerobically exercising vigorously enough to feel "almost tired" during the last half of the aerobic exercise session (Farquhar, 1978). A third rule of thumb is that the athletes should be breathing heavily but still able to talk while exercising (Farquhar).

If you have access to an appropriate fitness laboratory, then you may have the luxury of having your athletes assessed as to their maximum oxygen uptake ($Vo_{2\ max}$), or "maximal aerobic power." This is the amount of oxygen that can be consumed per minute during maximal exercise. Stated differently, it is the highest attainable rate of aerobic metabolism during performance of rhythmic, dynamic exercise involving large muscle groups. A preliminary test of cardiorespiratory fitness in terms of $Vo_{2\ max}$ can be used to set a training program that would start at an intensity of 65% to 70% of $Vo_{2\ max}$. More specific recommendations on this approach are recommended in *Coaching theory level 3* (1981).

How long should the aerobic workout last? This depends in part on the level of fitness of the athletes at the beginning of the program. In general, many authorities recommend that minimal training effects require continuous activity of at least 20 minutes that produces an elevated heart rate and also causes the athlete to sweat. Many reports also recommend aiming for or building to a continuous aerobic workout that lasts up to 30 minutes. This would provide a reasonable base for athletes who are simply trying to build their aerobic capabilities for most sports. Sports such as distance running, cross-country skiing, or speed swimming require more advanced goals (Fox and Mathews, 1981). Another consideration is whether the athlete is attempting to use aerobic training to also lose some weight. It is important to remember, as discussed later in this chapter, that total caloric expenditure is closely related to the total duration of exercise.

How often should aerobic training occur per week? Research has shown that the best frequency for most sports is three or four sessions per week (*Coaching theory level 3*, 1981). More than four sessions per week brings into play a sort of law of diminishing returns. That is, more than four training sessions per week appears to lead to additional gains in aerobic fitness at a much lower rate over and above that derived from four sessions per week.

Reprinted by permission: Tribune Media Services.

In some endurance sports, such as track and swimming, some coaches have advocated two and even three workouts per day. There is no scientific evidence, however, to indicate that multiple daily workouts lead to greater fitness and performance gains (Fox and Mathews, 1981). One study even suggested that daily workouts produced better results than multiple daily workouts (Mostardi et al., 1975). Full recovery of the aerobic system after exhausting endurance exercise requires a high dietary intake of carbohydrates over a 2-day (46 hours) recovery period (Fox and Mathews). Approximately 60% recovery can occur after 9 or 10 hours, provided it is accompanied by high carbohydrate intake.

After an athlete has achieved a particular level of aerobic fitness, a number of beneficial training effects can be maintained for several months with two sessions per week. Less than two sessions per week will mean loss of fitness. As we mentioned above, aerobic sports such as distance running and swimming require more frequent workouts.

Planning a Conditioning and Nutrition Program

How long should the aerobic training program continue? The number of weeks that a coach might want to devote to aerobic training will vary considerably from sport to sport and also with the entry level of the athlete. With unconditioned athletes, considerable improvement can be demonstrated in aerobic fitness after approximately 2 months of training. However, if aerobic training continues beyond 2 months, further improvements in aerobic fitness are much more gradual.

There is some evidence that aerobic fitness is lost at approximately the same rate that it is gained, if the previous training guidelines are followed. That is, the gains made in 2 months of aerobic exercising three to four times per week would be lost in approximately 2 months of no aerobic exercising (*Coaching theory level 3*, 1981). Thus, once a certain level of aerobic fitness is attained, a maintenance program should be put into effect.

2. Match the anaerobic training to the demands of your sport. After the aerobic training phase during the pre-season, then what? Most coaches have favorite drills and training routines to get their team in shape for competition. But are those drills matched to the muscular activity and energy requirements of the sport?

Consider the information in Table 8-2. This table illustrates which of the three energy systems provides fuel for muscle activity in terms of

T A B L E   8 - 2

Approximate Percent Contributions of Energy Systems to
Varying Durations of Maximal Effort in Sports

Work Time Maximal Effort	Anaerobic Alactic	Anaerobic Lactic	Aerobic
5 Seconds	85	10	5
10 Seconds	50	35	15
30 Seconds	15	65	20
1 Minute	8	62	30
2 Minutes	4	46	50
4 Minutes	2	28	70
10 Minutes	1	9	90
30 Minutes	Negligible	5	95
1 Hour	Negligible	2	98
2 Hours	Negligible	1	99

From the National Coaching Certification Manual.

the duration of maximal effort of a sport activity. Now consider your sport. For example, in football, how long does the average play last? How long is the average shift in hockey if the players give all-out effort? If your analysis indicates that the average play or shift lasts less than 2 minutes, then anaerobic training is extremely important. Although the anaerobic alactic energy system provides the majority of fuel for all-out muscular activities of up to approximately 10 seconds, that energy system can be trained so that all-out effort can be maintained for 15 to 20 seconds. Similarly, while the anaerobic lactic system yields the majority of the energy for power to peak at approximately 40 to 50 seconds, training can improve this energy system so that high levels of exercise can be maintained for up to $1\frac{1}{2}$ to 2 minutes.

A widely accepted approach for training these energy systems is *interval training*. This means that the part of the practice devoted to developing this energy system is divided into a series of intensive work intervals, with each work interval separated from the next by a rest interval. To improve the anaerobic alactic energy system, you might design your interval training according to the following guidelines:

1. Work time: up to 10 seconds, depending on your sport.
2. Rest time: a 1:3 or 1:4 workrest ratio is recommended, to allow time for ATP to build up during rest times. Full recovery time for the anaerobic alactic system is approximately 3 to 5 minutes. 50% to 70% recovery occurs in 20 to 30 seconds. Thus, if the exercise requires 10 seconds, the athlete should rest (actually jog lightly and move around) for 30 to 40 seconds. This workrest ratio should be sufficient to allow time for considerable ATP to build up again.
3. Repetitions (of work) per set: This is sometimes called the volume of the set, and the total number of repetitions should add up to a total volume of approximately 60 seconds. Thus, a set could consist of six repetitions of a 10-second running burst, with a 40-second rest (light jogging) in between. Alternatively, a set could be 13 repetitions of a 5-second running burst, with 20 seconds active rest in between.
4. Rest between sets: If more than one set is scheduled for a practice, there should be at least 5 minutes rest between sets. Rest time can be devoted to other instructional aspects of practices. As the athletes progress, they may get to the point where as many as five or six sets are completed per practice.

Anaerobic lactic training is also done with interval training similar to that described above. Differences occur in the duration of rest periods and work periods. Once again, the work periods chosen for sets should match the game requirements of the particular sport. Here the work periods might last anywhere from 10 seconds to 2 minutes, depending on the time of the season and the percent of maximum speed that the athletes attempt to perform. Early in the season, the work periods are shorter and the athletes might be performing at as low as 80% of their maximum. As training progresses, work periods can be lengthened and percent of maximum speed can be increased to as high as 95%. Rest periods should be approximately three or four times as long as work periods for shorter work intervals (10 to 30 seconds). At longer work intervals (1 to 2 minutes), the workrest ratio can be decreased to approximately 1:2. As far as the duration of the set is concerned, the total number of work intervals (volume) should add up to approximately 10 minutes. If more than one set is completed, then there should be 10 to 15 minutes or more rest between sets to allow for removal of some of the lactic acid build-up. Total work volume of all the sets could be increased to an upper limit of approximately 20 minutes. Approximately 40% recovery of the anaerobic lactic system can occur within 1 to 2 hours. Complete recovery requires approximately 24 hours (Fox and Mathews, 1981).

How often should anaerobic training occur per week? Sport physiologists differ somewhat in their answers to this question. Some (e.g., *Coaching theory level 3,* 1981) recommend a frequency of three or four times per week for anaerobic lactic training. Martens et al. (1981), on the other hand, suggest that a coach should never schedule more than two high-intensity workouts per week for young athletes. With these guides in mind, the coach should schedule workouts that seem apppropriate for the age and conditioning level of the athletes, while constantly monitoring them for muscular soreness and fatigue.

How long should the anaerobic training program continue? Major gains can be achieved after 6 to 8 weeks of anaerobic training. As with aerobic training, the law of diminishing returns appears to operate with continued anaerobic training beyond approximately 8 weeks. What happens to anaerobic fitness if training is discontinued? Here again, sport physiologists differ somewhat in their answers to this question. Fox and Mathews (1981) report that most of the beneficial effects of training return to pretraining levels within 4 to 8 weeks of lack of training. *Coaching theory level 3* (1981), on the other hand, suggests that if training is discontinued after a 6-week anaerobic training program, 80% to 90% of the anaerobic alactic gains will be maintained over the next 6 weeks, whereas approximately 50% of the anaerobic lactic gains will remain after approximately 6 weeks.

3. **Reemphasis on matching training to game requirements.** An area where many coaches can more effectively improve their training programs is development of training exercises and routines that duplicate the energy requirements of the game itself. Obviously, practices are also designed to improve skills, to enhance play execution, to develop team spirit, and a number of other things. What we want to emphasize here is that the coach should never lose sight of the energy requirements for performing in the game itself. Consider the following examples.

In football, from the time the ball is snapped until the time the play is whistled dead typically takes from 5 to 10 seconds. Barring penalties and time-outs, there is usually 30 to 40 seconds between plays. Thus, the energy demands are drawing heavily on the anaerobic alactic and anaerobic lactic systems. To maximize effects of interval training, these require a workrest ratio of 1:3 or 4. The coach should keep this in mind during various drills such as sled blocking. When sled blocking is done in pairs, each pair should be required to block for approximately 5 seconds, and four more pairs should be lined up and ready to participate, to yield a workrest ratio of 1:4. After a total of 12 repeats on the sled, those 10 players should move on to a different practice drill and the next five pairs should take over. Similarly, scrimmages often can be modified to more closely match the energy demands of games. If a coach allows scrimmages in basketball or hockey, for example, to continue for long intervals without the frequency of whistle stops characteristic of games, then the workrest units are not matching the tempo of the game as closely as they might. Similarly in football scrimmages, if there are usually long pauses while the coaches explain plays, then the tempo does not accurately match that of the game. When planning their training programs, coaches should ask several questions about game requirements. How long does each work interval typically last, and at what intensity of work expenditure? What is the typical workrest ratio of the game? With this information in hand, what are the energy requirements of the sport and how can those be developed in training programs? A more detailed discussion of specific training methods for specific sports can be found in Fox and Mathews (1981).

STRENGTH TRAINING

When most people think of strength, they think of big muscles, weight lifting, arm wrestling, Superman, Conan the Barbarian, or other similar images. That is, we typically think of applying considerable strength for a brief period of time, such as in lifting a heavy weight. In this section, however, we also want to talk about endurance and power. Endurance refers to performing with considerably less than maximum strength over a long period of time, such as a swimmer repeatedly pulling herself through the water while swimming a 200-meter freestyle. Power refers to force (i.e., strength) multiplied by speed.

Should your athletes be encouraged to participate in a weight training program? That depends on the strength demands of the sport, the strength of the athlete entering the sport, and the age of the athlete. Concerning the sport, often the answer is obvious. Football players and weight lifters usually benefit from weight lifting training. A basketball player doesn't need bulging muscles to shoot accurately. On the other hand, a basketball player might need increased weight and improved strength for handling the heavy traffic under the basket. But basketball players also have to jump. If carrying excess weight will seriously affect jumping ability, the basketball player must be very careful about adding irrelevant muscle mass.

Over the past 40 or 50 years, the most popular weight training programs have used free weights such as barbells and dumbbells. Barbell or dumbbell training has been referred to as dynamic, or *isotonic*, muscular contraction. When a person lifts a dumbbell, such as in performing a bicep curl, the force applied to the bicep is variable, depending on the joint angle of the arm. Thus, someone curling a 30 lb dumbbell will feel more pressure on the biceps when the upper and lower parts of the arm are held at a 90 degree angle than when they are at 30- or 150-degree angles. Thus, lifting a constant weight causes varying tensions on the muscles while the muscle shortens. Recognizing this problem, manufacturers of weight training equipment have developed variable-resistance machines that provide for near-constant tension over the entire range of motion while performing an exercise (e.g., Nautilus, Universal Gym). This type of muscular contraction is referred to as *isokinetic*, and the tension developed by the muscle while shortening at a constant speed can be maximal over the full range of motion. A third type of training, called *isometric* training, is characterised by muscle contraction that does not involve movement of joints or extremities. For example, a person might apply maximum pressure to a fixed bar. While tension develops, there is no noticeable change in the length of the muscle.

Which of these three approaches to weight training is superior? Although results of research are not totally consistent, it is generally accepted that progressive weight training programs using either free weights or variable-resistance weights are superior to isometric training programs for increasing both strength and endurance (Fox and Matthews, 1981). Is isotonic or isokinetic training better? Is it better to use barbells and dumbbells, for example, or to work out on Nautilus equipment? In theory, it should be possible to obtain better results with variable-resistance weights (Fox and Matthews, 1981). In practice, however, comparisons between weight training with free weights versus variable-resistance machines has yielded mixed evidence (Pipes, 1978; Sanders, 1980; Stiggins, 1978). Such findings led Rasch (1983), a recognized authority on weight training, to conclude that variable-resistance machines do not produce results significantly better than those obtained by the use of constant-resistance equipment. Because barbells and dumbbells are more likely to be available to the average coach and athlete than the more expensive Nautilus equipment, the following guidelines are based on research of methods of strength-building using free weights. They should also be reasonable guidelines for variable-resistance equipment.

1. Strength training should be carried out approximately 3 times per week, or at most, every other day.
2. During the first few days of weight training, use lighter weights so that each exercise can be performed with a minimum of 10 repetitions.

3. After the first few days, use that amount of weight for a lift that will enable the athlete to do a maximum of five to eight repetitions. Increase the amount of weight when the athlete can do nine or more repetitions.
4. Do two to three sets for each muscle group.
5. A weight training program of approximately 8 weeks can produce considerable gains, with more gradual gains after that.
6. Once a particular level of strength is achieved, that level can be maintained with two workouts per week (Willet, 1976). In general, strength gains are maintained over a longer period of time than are gains from training the various energy systems. After a certain level of strength has been achieved (such as after a 12-week training program), there is very little loss of strength with just one training session per week, provided that weights that require maximal contractions are used (Fox and Mathews, 1981).
7. Considering items 5 and 6, it would be wise to recommend a strength training program during the off-season or pre-season. Also, a minimum of one strength workout per week, using maximal contractions, during most of the competitive season will maintain most pre-season gains (*Coaching theory level 3*, 1981).
8. During workouts, the sequence of exercises should be planned to alternate muscle groups used.
9. As with energy training, strength training should be designed to match the requirements of competing in the sport. Thus swimmers are encouraged to do strength training with equipment that allows them to simulate the arm and hand movements in swimming. Shot putters are encouraged to emphasize development of arm and leg muscles used in putting the shot. In general, the more the athlete can imitate the movements as they are used in competition, the greater will be the benefits of strength training for performing in that particular sport.
10. Finally, heavy weight training is not recommended before puberty (Fox and Mathews, 1981). Not only does it do little good, it can cause various types of bone, muscle, and connective tissue injury to youngsters who are still developing.

What about weight lifting for endurance? Should a swimmer, for example, use weights for lifts that are so heavy that they can only do five to eight repetitions, as suggested above? Some texts (e.g., Martens et al., 1981) recommend that athletes (such as swimmers) who require considerable endurance should do a large number of repetitions (anywhere from 10 to 30) with a lighter weight in their weight lifting program. Other experts (e.g., Fox and Mathews, 1981) question this recommendation. For example, one text states, when discussing the strength versus endurance type of training, "There is little specific evidence for this distinction; and, in fact, the endurance type may have poor carry-over for strength development, while the strength training program involves both strength and muscular endurance" (*Coaching Theory Level 3*, 1981).

What about weight lifting for power? Here again, there are differences of opinion. You will recall that power has been defined as the rate of doing work. In other words, power is applying force with considerable speed. For hockey players who require power, for example, it has been recommended that they do power weight training. This involves practicing a movement as fast as possible using a resistance equal to 30% to 60% of their maximum strength (Martens et al.). It has been further recommended that variable-resistance weight machines that allow control of resistance and speed are better for this type of training than are barbells. On the other hand, another text states, "Only isotonic strength training (i.e., barbells or free weights) has been systematically studied to determine the best methods or programs" (*Coaching Theory Level 3*, 1981).

Where do these controversies leave the coach in selecting an endurance or power program? If you know a sports physiologist who is up-to-date on the latest research, we recommend that you seek his or her advice. In the absence of this luxury, we believe the 10 guidelines listed above for strength training are still the best set of recommendations available.

WARM-UPS, COOL-DOWNS, AND FLEXIBILITY TRAINING

Muscles. Ligaments. Tendons. Cartilage. All athletes have heard of these. Many athletes have damaged or torn them. Surprisingly, few athletes clearly understand how they work or how they are interrelated. An important responsibility of a coach is to spend some time during the pre-season clearly explaining to the athletes how all four of these body parts work together.

We've mentioned that muscle activity requires fuel, and we've explained, in outline form, the three energy systems. But what is a muscle? It's a collection of long fibers grouped in bundles, with each bundle separately wrapped in a sheath that holds it together and protects it. One type of muscle, called striated muscle, is organized in pairs and controls the movements of our bones and joints. When one member of the pair contracts, the other relaxes, causing bones to be moved. It is this type of muscle that we're mainly concerned with when we explain how the three energy systems work to fuel muscles for athletic activity. At the joints themselves (i.e., the places where bones are connected without rubbing against each other), we find the other three components: ligaments, tendons, and cartilage. Cartilage is a type of padding separating two bones at a joint. Tendons connect muscles to bones, and ligaments connect bones to bones.

Concerning warm-up and flexibility, muscles, ligaments, and tendons function kind of like a cheap plastic golf bag. On a frosty fall morning, teeing off on the first hole, the bag is stiff and difficult to unzip. By the ninth hole, when the sun is high overhead and everything has warmed up, the bag is flexible and easy to move. Muscles, tendons, and ligaments are also more flexible when warm.

At the beginning of training sessions, athletes should go through a series of slow stretching exercises. For each exercise, such as bending down and pulling on the ankles with legs straight, the athletes should be encouraged to apply increasing pressure for 10 to 15 seconds. Younger athletes have a tendency to "bounce." Bouncing should be strongly discouraged in all athletes. Stretching should progress through the larger and lower muscle groups, especially the lower back, hamstrings, and groin. Stretching should also emphasize those body parts and joints that are likely to be stressed in the particular sport. For example, swimmers should perform a number of exercises to stretch muscles, ligaments, and tendons at the shoulder joints and the knees. After stretching, athletes should be encouraged to perform vigorous activities, such as running in place, sit-ups, leg raises, and other calisthenics, to increase body temperature and circulation.

In addition to warming up at the beginning of training sessions, athletes should perform light cool-down exercises immediately after competition and training sessions. Fox and Mathews (1981) outlined two important physiological reasons for this practice: (1) lactic acid built up during intense muscular activity will decrease more rapidly during mild exercise than during total rest. Thus, a mild exercise cool-down period will promote faster recovery from fatigue. (2) mild activity during cool-down keeps the blood circulating and prevents it from cooling in the extremities, which reduces the possibility of muscular stiffness and decreases the tendency for fainting or dizziness. Fox and Mathews recommended that the cool-down activities be similar to the warm-up activities, but performed in reverse order. For example, a baseball pitcher after pitching a hard game might throw easy for a few minutes, then do some light calisthenics, and finish with some stretching exercises.

In sports where flexibility is required, such as gymnastics and figure skating, athletes should be encouraged to participate in regular flexibility training beyond the warm-up. Specific flexibility training can increase the range of motion of a particular joint. It is important to remember that training is specific to each joint, and all of the joints that are critical to performance in a particular sport should receive a certain amount of flexibility training. The general rules listed below for any type of training apply to flexibility training as well.

GENERAL PRINCIPLES OF TRAINING

Whether training for fitness, strength, flexibility, or endurance, a number of general principles should be kept in mind:

1. *Start easy.* Warm-up exercises, lifting a few light weights, and some general stretching should be performed at the start of a session in any training program.
2. *Apply overload.* If training is to help an athlete improve, the exercises must place some stress or demand on the body's systems in order to produce a physical change.
3. *Athletes are individuals.* Each athlete must use overload relative to his or her own pretraining fitness level. Requiring the same training of everyone will mean that some will receive too much overload or stress, and others not a sufficient amount to cause a training effect.
4. *As fitness improves, overload must progress.* As athletes become more fit, training demands must be increased for continued progress to occur.
5. *What you train is what you get.* Specific training will bring specific results. Your training should emphasize the energy systems, muscle groups, and range of motions of joints required for effectively performing your particular sport.
6. *Only diamonds are forever.* As indicated in the previous sections, when training stops, gains are lost. Coaches must develop maintenance programs for maintaining preseason gains during the season itself. They should also provide athletes with off-season maintenance programs.
7. *Training is behavior, and behavior requires support.* No matter how keen the athlete, a training program should be complemented with a combination of careful monitoring, goal setting, and feedback.
8. *Everything in moderation.* It is possible to overtrain, especially young athletes. Coaches should be sure to schedule sufficient rest, both between exercises within sessions and between training sessions. Follow the guidelines outlined for frequency of

training sessions. Loss of weight, speed, or interest; poor
school, sport, or work performance; and irritability and fatigue
all may be signs of overtraining. If the coach can rule out other
possible causes of these symptoms, so that overtraining appears to be the culprit, then the workload should be lightened
immediately, and the athlete should be given a few days off
training.

NUTRITION FOR ATHLETES

Why is nutrition for athletes important? Because all energy for
muscle contraction comes from ingested food. Unfortunately, most
young people (athletes included) have experienced deficient nutritional
education programs and have considerable misinformation about nutrition. Athletes need to know about the three main food groups:
carbohydrates, fats, and proteins. They also require some understanding of the vitamins and minerals necessary to help regulate the chem-
istry of the body. They should appreciate the importance of drinking
lots of water. They should know about the pregame meal, and about
nutrition during competition. Finally, they should understand how
eating habits established in childhood are likely to persist and affect
susceptibility to heart attack, general health, and longevity.

Reprinted with special permission of King Features Syndicate, Inc.

Carbohydrates, Fats, and Proteins

Carbohydrates are an extremely important part of an athlete's
diet. Although the average North American diet contains an estimated
45% carbohydrate, it is recommended that the diet for athletes should
contain at least 65% carbohydrate (Martens et al., 1981). Carbohydrates include starches and sugars. Many athletes misunderstand,
however, the role of sugar. Natural carbohydrates include foods that
are normally considered starchy, such as potatoes, whole-grain

products, beans, rice, and corn. These products should be Number 1 on the list for athletes. They are referred to as unrefined carbohydrates, as contrasted with table sugar, which is a concentrated or refined carbohydrate.

Carbohydrate is the major fuel used to regenerate ATP during intense exercise. Carbohydrate is stored in the body as a sugar (glucose) in the blood, and as glycogen (which contains glucose units) in muscle and the liver. Although carbohydrate is the major fuel used during intense exercise, the body stores will last for only a limited period of time (approximately 2 to 3 hours at a moderately intense rate of exercise, and substantially less at all-out speeds of exercise). When carbohydrate stores are used up during exercise, two things tend to happen. First, blood glucose levels can become dangerously low, causing physical reactions such as light-headedness or blacking out. Second, the rate of activity must slow down so that the body can use either stored fat or protein as fuel. The potential for use of carbohydrate stores during exercise, and the resulting low blood glucose levels, has led some individuals to recommend that athletes eat chocolate and other sweets during competitions. However, this practice should be avoided (Lemon, 1984). Ingestion of sugar can cause the body to produce a large amount of insulin very quickly, which can result in an even lower blood glucose level and a greater need to rely on muscle carbohydrate as an exercise fuel. Such a situation can hasten exhaustion, rather than postponing it. Moreover, refined sugars tend to draw fluid from other parts of the body into the stomach. This can contribute to dehydration and be problematic in sports in which sweating is excessive.

Fats are needed for healthy functioning, but in much smaller amounts than most North Americans consume. The average North American diet consists of approximately 40% fat; it is recommended that this be cut to 20% or less for a high performance athletic diet (Martens et al., 1981). Fat is a source of fuel during low to moderately intense exercise, or after intense exercise has consumed all of the carbohydrate stores. As a source of fuel during exercise, fat requires oxygen to be metabolized.

When most athletes think of fat in foods, they probably think of the layer of fat on a big T-bone steak. However, a great deal of our fat intake comes from butter, margarine, cheese, oils, and other sources of saturated fats. Unfortunately, a diet heavy on eggs, cheese, whole milk, red meat, ice cream, and butter—believed healthy for growing children—is also high on cholesterol and saturated fat. These are the substances that progressively clog arteries and contribute to heart attack later in life. But more about that later.

Proteins provide what are referred to as the building blocks of the body. These building blocks, called amino acids, are essential for growth and development, and tissue repair. A number of the amino acids can be manufactured by the body, but some of them must come from the diet. Although there is some evidence that protein may also provide some of the fuel for exercise, it seems clear that carbohydrates, and to a lesser extent fats, are the major sources of fuel. Common sources of the amino acids that must come from foods include dairy products, meat, fish, eggs, and poultry. Minimum protein intake for adolescents or children is approximately 2 gm/kg, and 1.8 gm/kg for adults (Lemon, 1984). Athletes striving for large muscle mass (such as football players or weight lifters) might require extra protein to ensure optimal growth. It is equally important, however, to ensure that the extra protein is not taken at the expense of a high carbohydrate diet.

Vitamins and Minerals

The body needs a number of vitamins and minerals daily to perform at maximum efficiency. Vitamins, for example, help cause chemical reactions that make it possible for carbohydrates to provide fuel for muscle activity. Vitamin deficiency, therefore, could contribute to decreased athletic performance. In spite of claims to the contrary, however, there is no evidence that megadoses of various vitamins and minerals will improve performance. On the contrary, excessive intake can be hazardous.

Concerning vitamins, it is important for the athlete to understand that there are both water-soluble and fat-soluble vitamins. Water-soluble vitamins are washed away in the urine. Thus, although excessive intake of water soluble vitamins may not necessarily enhance performance, they are also not likely to cause a decrease in performance. Fat-soluble vitamins are a different story. Vitamins A, D, E, and K, and a number of minerals (iron, zinc, and selinium) are poisonous when taken in excess.

Reprinted by permission: Tribune Media Services.

Guidelines for Healthy Diet

The objectives of good nutrition are to eat a wide variety of foods; limit cholesterol, sweets, fats, salt, and greasy foods; and maximize intake of carbohydrates (e.g., bread, pizza, cereals, pancakes, pasta). If you supplement your diet with vitamins and minerals, take a multiple vitamin, and iron. Be careful of consuming excessive fat-soluble vitamins (A, D, E, K) and minerals (zinc, selenium).

Four Main Food Groups	Junk Food
Breads and cereals (3 to 5 servings daily)	1 serving of sweets, fats, or greasy foods
EXAMPLE OF A SERVING	EXAMPLE
2 Pieces toast	1 Chocolate bar
1 Bowl cereal	1 Soft drink (with sugar)
Meat and meat alternatives (2 servings daily)	1 Slurpee
	1 Bag of salted chips
EXAMPLE OF A SERVING	1 Order of french fries
1 Piece fish	1 Pizza pop
1 Serving chicken	1 Pack of sweetened gum
1 Hamburger (also classified as junk food, if fried)	1 Small bag candies
	1 Piece cake
Dairy products (3 to 4 servings daily)	2 Cookies
	1 Piece pie
EXAMPLE OF A SERVING	1 Fried hamburger
8-ounce glass of skim milk	
$\frac{1}{2}$ cup of yogurt	
$\frac{1}{2}$ cup of low-fat cheese	
Fruits and vegetables (4 to 5 servings daily)	
EXAMPLE OF A SERVING	
1 Large carrot	
Salad	
1 Apple	
1 Orange	

FIGURE 8-2

So what does this mean with respect to recommendations for vitamin and mineral supplements? Most young people adequately supply their daily vitamin and mineral needs by eating several servings each day from each of the four main food groups, listed in Fig. 8-2. If athletes get into the habit of assuming that they are meeting their daily vitamin and mineral requirements through supplements, it could result in their eating a nutritionally poor diet. Having said that, they might be encouraged to take modest supplements "just to be on the safe side." In particular, young athletes who consume excessive junk foods or those on food-restricted diets, might be encouraged to take a multiple-vitamin supplement.

Water

Water is absolutely essential to body functioning. An individual can survive as much as four times as long without food than without water. Although approximately 50% of the body's protein and more than 90% of the reserve carbohydrate and fat stores can be lost without danger, a loss of 10% of water in the body can be serious. Thus coaches must be continually sensitive to loss of body water through vigorous activity. During practices and games, coaches should ensure that water is continuously available. Athletes should be encouraged to (1) drink one or two cups of water about 15 minutes before exercising or competition, (2) drink small volumes (about a half cup) of cool water at regular intervals (approximately 15 minutes) during heavy exercise, and (3) drink one or two cups of water after an exercise session or competition. In addition, in hot climates coaches should schedule heavy practice sessions during the cooler parts of the day, gradually increase the duration of practice sessions over the first 1 to 2 weeks of the season to allow for acclimatization, and allow the athletes to wear light-colored, porous uniforms to minimize heat gain and maximize heat loss.

Pre-Game Meal

During my playing days with the Varsity hockey team at Colorado College, the pregame meal consisted of a steak, baked potato, tea with honey, and little or no bread. Today, as a coach of the Manitoba Marlin Swim Club, I encourage the swimmers to consume a pre-swimming-meet meal consisting of pancakes and cereals or pizza (with minimal topping), bread (with little butter), and lots of water or unsweetened orange juice. Which meal is likely to enhance competition? The latter—by far! We can now say a number of things with considerable certainty about the pregame meal:

1. The meal itself cannot produce a super performance, but it can help to some degree.
2. The pregame meal could impair performance.
3. It is better to eat too little than too much during the pregame meal.
4. The meal should consist mainly of unrefined carbohydrates.
5. The meal should be eaten 2 to 3 hours before competition.
6. The nearer to the competition, the less should be eaten. Some nutritionists recommend consuming liquid meals as proximity to game time increases, because of the faster rate of digestion.
7. Undigested food at game time not only provides no fuel, it reduces aerobic energy by decreasing oxygen available for muscle activity, because oxygen in the blood is diverted to the gastrointestinal tract.

In general, foods to definitely stay away from in the pregame meal and throughout the day of competition include highly spiced and gas-forming foods such as onions and baked beans, and fatty or greasy foods that slow digestion and leave the athlete feeling "stuffed." Also, proteins should be kept to a minimum, because they only minimally contribute to energy production, and also stimulate acid secretion in the stomach. You can see now why the pregame steak, with its high fat and high protein content, is simply not recommended for a pregame meal.

As it became increasingly clear that carbohydrates provided the fuel for muscle activity during intense exercise, athletes began to experiment with increasing carbohydrate intake before important competitions. During the past dozen or so years, a procedure known as *carbohydrate loading* has become popular. However, the different strategies for carbohydrate loading are not recommended for use by young athletes still in developmental stages. Some nutritionists recommend that carbohydrate loading not be practiced by adult athletes as well (e.g., see Pritikin, 1983). A detailed discussion of different strategies for carbohydrate loading in adult athletes can be found in Lemon (1984).

Misunderstandings About Nutrition

The first misunderstanding about nutrition that must be stressed concerns the previous advice that young athletes should eat a balanced diet consisting of the four main food groups. This is true. But we would be remiss if we did not caution readers about the long-term dangers of eating diets high in cholesterol and saturated fats. The United States has one of the highest heart attack rates in the world.

Why? One of the factors identified is the high blood cholesterol levels attributed to high dietary intake of eggs, fatty red meats, milk, and cheese. For example, a study comparing a group of schoolchildren in Wisconsin with a group of schoolchildren living in a rural mountain village in Mexico revealed average blood cholesterol levels of 187 versus 100, respectively. The difference in blood cholesterol levels between the two groups of children was attributed largely to the higher intake of dietary cholesterol and saturated fat by the Wisconsin children (Farquhar, 1978). Thus, when advised to eat lots of dairy products (as one of the four main food groups), athletes should also be advised that they can obtain needed calcium from skim milk as well as from whole milk without, at the same time, consuming excessive cholesterol. They should be cautioned that most of the protein in an egg is in the white and that all of the cholesterol is in the yolk (which could be thrown away from a nutritional point of view). Young athletes should understand that a piece of red meat that appears lean is still loaded with animal fat. They should understand that fish, poultry, beans, and peas offer alternative ways to obtain needed protein while keeping saturated fat intake at desirable levels. While we're on the topic of protein, a caution is necessary for young football players or weight lifters who may be taking considerable protein supplements. As stated in *Coaching theory level 3* (1981), "There is no evidence to suggest that the training effect can be improved by protein supplements over and above the protein available through a balanced diet." Not only that, it is important for young athletes to understand that large amounts of water are required to screen by-products of excessive protein, which may thereby overload the kidneys.

Additional cautions are needed concerning sugar and salt. The problem with refined sugars is that they stimulate increased insulin, which causes the blood sugar level to become dangerously low (a condition called hypoglycemia). The complex carbohydrates (starches), on the other hand, enter the bloodstream more slowly and at a steadier rate. We recognize that it is common practice for athletes to eat chocolate and other refined sugars just before and during competitions. The evidence suggests, however, that the practice not only does not help, it is likely to be harmful (Lemon, 1984). Concerning salt, some athletes take salt tablets during hot weather and when sweating profusely. However, recent evidence suggests that not only does sweating not cause a deficiency of salt or other electrolytes, but that salt ingestion reduces the rate of fluid absorption from the gastrointestinal tract (Lemon, 1984).

In summary, the best nutritional advice for athletes is:

1. Eat three to five servings each day from the four main food groups.
2. Control cholesterol by emphasizing skim milk products.
3. Eat lots of unrefined carbohydrates and drink lots of water.
4. Keep junk foods (sweets, fats, greasy foods, and excessively salty foods) to a minimum. A reasonable goal would be three or fewer junk foods per day.

Some Tips for Losing Weight

What about the young athlete who is a little on the chubby side and wants to lose weight? What about the young athlete who is considerably overweight? Weight loss is a serious business, and it is important for coaches to be cautious about making off-hand comments or recommendations to young athletes. If coaches recommend that their athletes lose weight, they should consider the following:

1. Preliminary steps. Any serious weight control program should include: a medical check-up to determine the physical status of the athlete; a consultation with a nutritionist to set up a reasonable, gradual weight loss program; and a support system of coach, friends, and family to encourage the athlete to adhere to his/her program.

2. Careful monitoring of calories in, calories out, and weight. It is important to impress on youngsters that to lose weight they must use more calories than they take in. Most overweight adults, let alone overweight teenagers, grossly underestimate the calories they consume in foods, while at the same time grossly overestimating the calories that they burn off in certain exercises. Athletes need to be educated about weight loss. They need to know, for example, that walking an extra 4 miles daily burns about 200 calories. Table 8-3 provides an estimate of the total calories expended per minute in various sports or activities. Athletes who need to lose weight should study that table. As another example, they also need to know that one sugared donut has approximately 450 calories. Athletes who need to lose weight should have a list of foods and their calorie content as well as a calorie counter. They need to learn that excess calories at the end of the day means excess weight on the scales.

3. Consideration of energy sources for different types of exercise. Educate your athletes about the sources of energy used for different types of exercise. As indicated earlier in this chapter, body fat is the major contributor to energy supply during low to moderately intense exercise and during prolonged exercise (60 minutes or longer). Thus,

T A B L E 8 - 3

Total Calories Expended per Minute in Various Sports or Activities _____

Sport or Exercise	Total Calories Expended per Minute of Activity
Climbing	10.7-13.2
Cycling 5.5 mph	4.5
9.4 mph	7.0
13.1 mph	11.1
Dancing	3.3-7.7
Football	8.9
Golf	5.0
Gymnastics	
Balancing	2.5
Abdominal exercises	3.0
Trunk bending	3.5
Arms swinging, hopping	6.5
Rowing 51 strokes/min	4.1
87 strokes/min	7.0
97 strokes/min	11.2
Running	
Short distance	13.3-16.6
Cross-country	10.6
Tennis	7.1
Skating (fast)	11.5
Skiing	
Moderate speed	10.8-15.9
Uphill, maximum speed	18.6
Squash	10.2
Swimming	
Breaststroke	11.0
Backstroke	11.5
Crawl (55 yd/min)	14.0
Wrestling	14.2

From Nutrition for the Athlete.

jogging or walking is highly recommended for individuals trying to lose excess fat stores in the body. Some individuals who begin running programs to lose weight make the mistake of pushing themselves at excessive speeds that draw primarily on carbohydrate stores. But it is their fat stores that they need to lose. Whereas it is necessary to maintain a fairly intense level of exercise for aerobic fitness, this is not the case for losing weight. Rather, to lose weight an individual is better off maintaining a lower level of exercise for a longer period of time on each exercise occasion.

4. Consideration of referral for behavior therapy. For young athletes who have a serious weight problem, we recommend referral to a behavior modification expert. One of the most successful approaches to childhood obesity is behavior therapy. A comprehensive review of this treatment can be found in LeBow (1984). Because obesity is an independent risk factor for both heart disease and cancer, and because childhood obesity is strongly related to adult obesity, the plight of excessively overweight young athletes should not be taken lightly.

SUMMARY

Muscle activity is fueled by three different energy systems. The anaerobic alactic system provides most of the energy for high-intensity, short-duration exercises requiring a burst of speed or high resistance movement lasting up to 10 seconds. This system uses stored energy, does not require oxygen, and does not produce lactic acid (a waste product). For intense muscular activity lasting from 20 to 30 seconds to approximately 2 minutes, the majority of energy is supplied by the anaerobic lactic system. This system uses carbohydrate fuels stored in the body, does not require oxygen, and produces lactic acid, which causes fatigue. Beyond approximately 2 minutes of muscular exercise, the majority of energy for the muscles is provided by the aerobic system. This system uses carbohydrate fuel (and to a lesser extent, fats or proteins) stored in the body, and oxygen, and does not build up lactic acid (provided that the pace is not too great). Some activities draw primarily on anaerobic energy systems, some draw primarily on aerobic energy, and some draw on both anaerobic and aerobic metabolism.

It is recommended that all conditioning programs begin with aerobic training. Even though some sports require primarily anaerobic energy, athletes are likely to recover faster between plays if they have a higher level of aerobic fitness. Moreover, aerobically fit athletes are less susceptible to injury, and aerobic fitness later in life minimizes the possibility of heart attack. Guidelines are presented for the frequency, intensity, and duration of aerobic conditioning programs.

An effective strategy for anaerobic training is the interval training system. Interval training involves alternating bouts of hard work with periods of lighter work or rest. Coaches can effectively match their training program to the energy requirements of their sport by manipulating, within the interval training system, the rate and distance of the work interval, the number of repetitions, and the time and type of rest interval. Guidelines are presented in this chapter for appropriate weight training for strength and endurance, both during the off-season as well as the competition season. All training activity should be preceded by warm-up and stretching activities to increase the flexibility of muscles, tendons, and ligaments. After a training session, athletes should also perform cool-down exercises to promote faster recovery from fatigue and to reduce muscle stiffness and any tendency for fainting and dizziness after strenuous activity. General principles of training include individualization for each athlete, warm-up and cool-down exercises for each session, muscular overload to stress the body's systems, progressive increases in training demands (as fitness improves), specific training for specific results, and an appropriate system of goal setting, monitoring, and feedback to help keep the athlete keen.

Concerning nutrition, athletes should eat a minimum of three to five servings each day from the four main food groups; control cholesterol by emphasizing skim milk products; eat lots of unrefined carbohydrates and drink lots of water; and keep sweets, fats, cholesterol, greasy foods, and salt to a minimum. The pregame meal should consist mainly of unrefined carbohydrates, and be eaten 2 to 3 hours before competition. Strategies for athletes to lose weight include (1) preliminary medical and nutritional consultations, and a social support system; (2) consideration of minimal calorie requirements for growth (of young athletes); (3) careful monitoring of calories in, calories out, and weight; and (4) if the problem is serious, possible referral to a behavior therapist who specializes in weight control.

Coach's Checklist

The steps for planning and implementing a conditioning and nutrition program for athletes in the sport that you coach, or hope to coach, are outlined in Fig. 8-3. We recommend that you use the checklist to ensure appropriate planning before the season and to monitor your implementation of the program during the season.

COACH'S CHECKLIST

Planning Conditioning and Nutrition Program

	Date Completed					
Assess energy demands of your sport during games or competitions						
1. Identify average duration of each play or activity (work interval) during games.						
2. Identify intensity of work expenditure during average play at games.						
3. Identify typical work/rest ratio of game.						
4. On basis of previous questions, identify energy requirements of your sport.						
5. Identify strength requirements of your sport.						
6. Identify flexibility requirements of your sport.						
Design aerobic portion of your training program						
1. Write out aerobic training workouts for your athletes so that:						
a. Aerobic training is emphasized during first 8 weeks of season.						
b. Aerobic training will occur three to four sessions per week during first 8 weeks.						
c. Aerobic maintenance program will continue during season at frequency of two sessions per week.						
d. Initial aerobic training sessions meet rules of thumb for intensity (see page 169).						
e. Subsequent aerobic training sessions during 8-week training program include progressive overload.						
2. Explain to your athletes rationale for and benefits of being aerobically fit.						
Design anaerobic portion of your training program to match demands of your sport						
1. Considering the information that you collected in part A, write out training activities for practices so that they:						
a. Match anaerobic alactic and/or anaerobic lactic demands of your sport.						

FIGURE 8-3

	Date Completed

b. Include interval training with appropriate work/rest ratio and work/volume per set.

c. Include frequency of anaerobic training of three to four times per week and duration of approximately 8 weeks prior to major competitions.

d. Give due consideration to need for overload progression.

2. Explain to your athletes differences between anaerobic and aerobic energy systems, and need for your athletes to be anaerobically fit as well as aerobically fit.

Design strength training and flexibility training program for your athletes (if appropriate)

1. Write out details of 2-month strength training program for your athletes (follow guidelines on pages 176-177).

2. Write out flexibility training program for your athletes (follow guidelines on pages 178-179).

3. Explain to your athletes importance of strength training and flexibility training (if appropriate).

4. Explain to your athletes importance of warm-ups and cool-downs.

Plan nutrition information package for your athletes

1. Prepare handouts that include information on the four main food groups and junk food (Fig. 8-2), vitamin supplements, pregame meal, and some misunderstandings about nutrition.

2. Schedule meeting to discuss importance of nutrition with your athletes.

3. For overweight athletes, schedule separate meeting and discuss guidelines for weight control program (see pages 188-190).

Review Questions

1. What is ATP?
2. What is lactic acid, where does it come from, and what is its effect?
3. In what sense do muscles work like engines?
4. Outline in table form the anaerobic alactic, anaerobic lactic, and aerobic energy systems in terms of
   a. Type of fuel used.
   b. Whether oxygen is required.
   c. Whether lactic acid is produced.
   d. Which duration of all-out activity receives the majority of energy from which of the three systems.
5. Which energy system provides the majority of energy for the following activities:
   a. Bench-pressing 400 lb once
   b. Blocking a play in football
   c. Making a serve in tennis
   d. Swimming a 50 M sprint swim
   e. Skating all-out on a breakaway in hockey
   f. Executing a fast break in basketball
   g. Wrestling for 3 minutes
   h. Swimming a 1500 M race
   i. Running a 400 M race
6. How does the aerobic energy system differ from the anaerobic energy system?
7. List four reasons why athletes should be encouraged to develop their aerobic fitness levels as a foundation for further training.
8. Outline the minimum requirements of an aerobic training program in terms of the intensity of each session, the duration of each session, the number of sessions per week, and the duration of the entire aerobic training program.
9. What is an interval training program?
10. Consider the following situation for 10 football players. They are lined up in pairs to do sled blocking. Each pair blocks for approximately 5 seconds, and then goes to the back of the line. After each pair has blocked a total of 10 times, they jog around the track for about 5 minutes. Then they repeat the whole routine four more times.
    a. Within a set, what is the workrest ratio?
    b. What is the work volume within a set?
    c. What is the work volume across all of the sets?
    d. Which energy system is being used?

11. For interval training for the anaerobic alactic and the anaerobic lactic energy systems, outline the important points to remember for each of the two systems concerning:
    a. Work time per set.
    b. Workrest ratio per set.
    c. Work volume per set.
    d. Recommended rest between sets.
    e. Recommended total work volume.
12. What are some considerations in deciding whether athletes in the sport that you coach should participate in a weight training program?
13. What would you consider to be the minimal frequency per week and the minimal number of weeks of a pre-season weight training program for athletes in many sports?
14. Let's suppose that an athlete has been training for approximately 8 weeks, and then stops training. At what rate will gains be lost if the training program was primarily aerobic? If the training program was primarily anaerobic?
15. With respect to ligaments, tendons, cartilage, muscles, and bones, what connects what to what?
16. What is the overload principle of training?
17. What is the progression principle of training?
18. What is the specificity principle of training?
19. List various symptoms that a coach should watch for that might be signs of overtraining.
20. Why are carbohydrates an extremely important part of an athlete's diet?
21. Why should athletes not eat chocolate and other sweets just before and during competition?
22. Is fat a source of fuel for muscular activity? Explain your answer.
23. Why should athletes be cautious of taking megadoses of vitamins and minerals?
24. Outline several guidelines that coaches should follow to ensure that their athletes consume a sufficient amount of water.
25. Outline the content of an ideal pregame meal. Why should fats and proteins be avoided during the pregame meal? Should young athletes consume large doses of protein supplements? Why? Should athletes who sweat a lot take salt tablets? Why?
26. In a sentence or two each, list four guidelines that coaches should follow when advising overweight athletes in weight control programs.

Mini-Lab Exercises

1. Choose a sport that you played or hope to coach. Consider typical competition requirements for that sport. How long does each work interval typically last, and at what intensity of work expenditure? What is the typical workrest ratio during competition? With this information in mind, what energy systems should you emphasize during training? If you are not sure of the answers concerning workrest ratios and durations, watch the sport on TV or go to a live performance, use a stop watch, and take some data.
2. Using the information that you obtained in question 1, outline an appropriate 8-week interval training program in terms of (a) training activity and (b) interval training components per practice session.

Day of Week/ Week	Work Time (Sec)	Rest Time (Sec)	No. of Repeats per Set	Rests Between Sets	Number of Sets	Work Volume

3. To help you become aware of calories consumed and burned during the day (which in turn will help you to advise athletes), monitor your total calorie intake and your total calorie expenditure over 24 hours. To help you, take a sheet of paper and divide it into five columns. In the left column, indicate at 1-hour intervals the hours from 1 to 24. In column 2, list all of the foods you consume. In column 3, record the number of calories consumed. In column 4, indicate activities that occupied the majority of each hour. In column 5, indicate the calories expended per hour. In addition to the information in Table 8-3, you can count 60 calories/hour for each hour of sleep, and 75 calories/hour for each hour of restful activity such as reading or watching TV. A good strategy so that you remember to record everything is to carry the paper with you and record calories consumed every time you eat something. At the end of each hour, figure out approximate calories burned during that hour and record on the sheet. Just after waking in the morning, record the total calories expended while sleeping. At the end of 24 hours, compare your totals. You might be interested to know that you need to burn off approximately 3500 calories in excess of calories consumed in order to lose approximately 1 pound of body fat.

References

Coaching theory level 2 (1979). National Coaching Certification Program, Ottawa, Canada.

Coaching theory level 3 (1981). National Coaching Certification Program, Ottawa, Canada.

Cooper, K. (1982). The aerobics program for total well-being: Exercise, diet, emotional balance. New York: Bantam Books.

Farquhar, K.W. (1978). The American way of life need not be hazardous to your health. New York: W.W. Norton.

Fox, E.L., and Mathews, D.K. (1981). The physiological basis of physical education and athletics, 3rd ed. New York: Saunders.

LeBow, M.D. (1984). Child obesity: A new frontier of behavior therapy. New York: Springer.

Lemon, T.W.R. (1984). You are what you eat: Energy metabolism and nutrition for the coach and athlete. Coach. Sci. Update 5:35-40.

Martens, R., Christina, R.W., Harvey, A.S. Jr., and Sharkey, B.J. (1981). Coaching young athletes. Champaign, Ill.: Human Kinetics Publishers.

Mostardi, R., Sandee, R., and Campbell, T. (1975). Multiple daily training and improvement in aerobic power. Med. Sci. Sports 7:82.

Pipes, T.V. (1978). Variable resistance versus constant resistance strength training in adult males. Eur. J. Appl. Physiol. 39:27-35.

Pritikin, N. (1983). The Pritikin promise: Twenty-eight days to a longer, healthier lifestyle. New York: Pocketbooks, Division of Simon & Shuster.

Rasch, P.J. (1983). *Weight training*. Debuque, Iowa: William C. Brown Publishers.

Sanders, N.T. (1980). A comparison of two methods of training of the development of muscular strength and endurance. J. Ortho. Sports Phys. Ther. 1:210-213.

Stiggins, C.F. (1978). Nautilus and free weight training program: A comparison of strength development at four angles in the range of motion. Unpublished Masters thesis, Brigham Young University.

Willet, J.E. (1976). The effects of an in-season weight training program on the muscular strength of intercollegiate football players. Unpublished Masters thesis, South Dakota State University.

Selected Readings

Bomba, T.O. (1983). Theory and methodology of training: The key to athletic performance. Dubuque, Ia.: Kendall/Hart Publishing Co.

Haas, R. (1983). Eat to win: The sports nutrition bible. New York: Signet, New American Library.

Jensen, C., and Jensen, C.R. (1978). Update on strength training. Scholastic Coach 48:90-100.

Sharkey, B.J. (1984). Physiology of fitness, 2nd ed. Champaign, Ill.: Human Kinetics Publishers.

Wells, C.L. (1985). Women, sport and performance: A physiological perspective. Champaign, Ill.: Human Kinetics Publishers.

Wolf, M.D. (1984). The complete book of Nautilus training. Chicago: Contemporary Books.

Psychological Preparation for Competition in Sports: Sports Psyching

Experts acknowledge that top athletes must be prepared in four main areas: physical, technical, tactical, and psychological. Obviously, top athletes have to be in excellent physical condition. Second, their technical skills must be highly practiced, correct, and second nature so that they occur without even thinking about them. Third, tactical strategies are important. The fourth area, psychological preparation, is an area that has received increased attention during the past few years (Rushall, 1979; Silva and Weinberg, 1984). At the level of international competition, there is often very little difference between athletes in terms of their physical conditioning or technical skills. Often the difference between individuals in competition boils down to psychological preparation. On the day of a competition at the international level, there is little that athletes can do to enhance performance. They can't get in better condition on that particular day. They can't learn any new techniques in such a short period of time. However, there are many distractors and other factors that can detract from performance.

The athletes that have mastered a variety of psychological coping skills are much less likely to be influenced by those distractors and therefore are much more likely to perform to their full potential. You might be thinking, "So what does this have to do with coaching beginning athletes?" The answer is that there are a number of psychological coping techniques that can be taught to young persons or beginning athletes. Not only can these enhance performance of beginning athletes, but they can also prove extremely useful in meeting life's daily trials and tribulations. This chapter will provide guidelines for teaching some useful psychological coping skills to beginning athletes. First, however, we will briefly review major areas of applied sports psychology, and discuss some of the myths about sports psychology.

SOME MAJOR AREAS OF APPLIED SPORT PSYCHOLOGY

It is interesting that physical educators—not psychologists—have been largely responsible for the growth of sports psychology in America (Wiggins, 1984). Hundreds of research papers have been published by physical educators in the area of sports psychology, with many examining aspects of motor learning. Since the early 1970s, there has also been a growing desire on the part of practicing coaches for more applied sports science experimentation, particularly in the area of sports psychology (Gowan et al., 1979). The 1970s saw the development of both national and international organizations devoted to sports psychology, including the International Society for Sport Psychology, the North American Society for the Psychology of Sport and Physical Activity, and a European sports psychology association.

Applied sport psychology has been defined as the use of psychological knowledge to enhance the development of performance and satisfaction of athletes and others associated with sports (Blimkie et al., 1984). Individuals currently providing services in applied sports psychology come from diverse backgrounds, including coaching, education, motor learning, psychology, medicine, and physiology. It is important to understand, however, that the term "psychologist" is legally restricted to individuals who have formal training in psychology and who are subsequently licensed by the state or province in which they work. Although individuals other than licensed psychologists may provide a quality service in an area that fits the definition of "applied sports psychology," they must offer their services under another title, such as sports consultant or motor behavior specialist. Whether they are licensed psychologists or not, practitioners in the general area of applied sports psychology have made a number of contributions.

Techniques for Effectively Improving Skills of Athletes

What is the most effective way of helping an individual learn new skills? Eliminate or unlearn, or decondition bad habits? Combine simple skills into complex behaviors or patterns of execution? Considerable research has examined techniques for effectively improving skills of athletes (Martin, in press; Martin, and Hyrcaiko, 1983). Practical strategies for applying these techniques are outlined in earlier chapters.

Strategies for Motivating Practice and Endurance Training

How can a coach effectively improve attendance at practices? Motivate athletes to get the most out of practice time? Organize practices so that there is very little down time in which athletes are inactive? As with the previous section, many of the techniques for solving these types of problems are summarized in earlier chapters in a way that they can be easily applied by coaches. Goal-setting techniques, effective use of reward strategies, self-recording and self-monitoring by individual athletes, team-building sessions—all are potentially effective motivational techniques that can be readily learned by coaches.

Dealing with Personal Problems of Athletes

When most people hear the word "psychologist," they envision someone sitting in an office conducting therapy to help clients solve various personal problems of daily living. Obviously, athletes can also experience such problems, and might seek help from a clinical psychologist to solve those problems. Because personal problems can detract from performance, some countries send psychologists with teams to international competitions so that help is readily available to deal with emotional or other problems that some athletes might experience. In this sense, a trained and licensed clinical psychologist is providing a service for athletes in the same way he or she would with any other individual.

Helping Coaches to Become Better Coaches

Researchers have identified a number of inadequacies seen in many coaches, suggesting that many coaches rely on homespun psychologies for their coaching procedures, do not know how to motivate athletes so that they will consistently perform at high levels, use skill development procedures that are inefficient and are seldom better than trial and error, and have a tendency to implement stop-gap programs (Rushall, 1976; Ziegler, 1980). While recognizing the possible validity of some of these criticisms with regard to some coaches, we must also recognize that coaches have a very difficult job and in the past have not been provided with sufficient opportunities for adequate training. Many coaches spend hours of their free time coaching, often with very little by way of tangible benefits to show for it. Also, with increasing research into sports psychology, physiology, medicine, sociology, and sports equipment, there is a large and growing literature for coaches to attempt to master. Sports psychologists, along with other professionals, are contributing to this body of knowledge.

An underlying theme of this book is that a coach must effectively and efficiently help athletes to modify their behavior to improve and maintain skilled athletic performance. From a behavior modification perspective, a coach must effectively instruct, set goals, praise, reprimand, and perform other activities that, collectively, determine his or her effectiveness as a behavior modifier. To develop behavior modification skills in coaches, we must be able to assess their presence or absence and their effect on the specific athletic performance of the athletes. Numerous research studies have also been conducted in this area (Hrycaiko and Martin, 1983; Martin, in press).

"Sports Psyching" to Prepare for Competition

The final area that we would like to comment on, and to which the rest of this chapter is devoted, is "sports psyching." In commonsense terms, sports psyching is concerned with the "mental" part of the game. We've all heard expressions like, "The reason so-and-so lost was because he was psyched out," or "If you want to do your best, you have to get psyched up," or "So-and-so just gets too high for important matches and has to learn how to psych down." While we all may have some general idea as to what these kinds of phrases mean, knowing generally what they mean and learning how to teach psychological coping skills to athletes (especially young athletes) are two different things. The material in later sections in this chapter provides specific guidelines for teaching psychological coping skills to young athletes.

Brent Rushall, an internationally known sport psychologist who has worked with many of Canada's Olympic athletes, has divided psychological preparation for serious competition into pre-competition and competition strategies (Rushall, 1979). A pre-competition strategy is a specific plan to follow on the day of a competition up to the time just before the event itself. It includes things that the athlete should do, say, think about, concentrate on, and attend to from the time he or she gets up in the morning until just before the event is about to start. The competition strategy refers to what the athlete should do, say, concentrate on, or attend to from a few minutes before the competition, and throughout the entire competition, to maximize performance. Both pre-competition and competition strategies require that potential distractions be identified and that the athlete has practiced well-rehearsed, specific coping responses for dealing with them.

SOME REASONS FOR PRACTICING SPORTS PSYCHING

Rushall (1979), Tutko and Tosi (1976), Nideffer (1981), and others have outlined numerous reasons why athletes should learn and practice sports psyching strategies. Some of those reasons are as follows:

1. During the day of competition there is little that can be done to enhance performance (e.g., in terms of level of physical fitness, additional practice). However, there is every opportunity for numerous events to distract an athlete and detract from performance. A sports psyching program can minimize the effects of these distractions.

2. There is considerable evidence to support the view that, in many situations, what you say to yourself and how you think is how you perform. It therefore makes no sense to spend hours each day for many months preparing for an important competition, and then leave thought patterns to chance.

3. If athletes have a detailed plan of action to follow during the day of competition, then they are determining the things that can influence them. If athletes don't have a detailed plan, then the things that can influence them are left to chance or in the hands of others.

4. As described below, opponents in sports may knowingly or unknowingly do things to psych out or deliberately disrupt an athlete's performance. A sports psyching program may help minimize the effects of psych-out attempts by the opposition.

5. If an individual is excessively nervous or anxious just before an important competition, then chances are that individual will not perform to full potential. A sports psyching program can teach the athlete how to reduce excess nervousness and anxiety.

6. Highly successful athletes perform many of the activities that are taught in sports psyching programs.

7. Finally, the psychological skills necessary for developing and executing successful competition plans can be useful in many areas of daily living.

It is important to emphasize that psychological preparation cannot substitute for the other three areas of athletic preparation (physical, technical, and tactical). However, psychological preparation can help athletes perform near the best they are capable of, given their preparation in other areas. As expressed by Tutko and Tosi (1976), sports psyching can help you play your best game all the time.

SOME MYTHS ABOUT SPORT PSYCHOLOGY

Occasionally, quotes in newspapers by famous coaches and athletes make psychologists cringe. Perhaps the coaches and athletes are misquoted. Or perhaps some of the coaches and athletes quoted are misinformed about sports psychology. And perhaps some sports psychologists themselves have been misleading the sports community about the benefits of sports psychology. Whatever the reasons, some statements that you might hear about sports psychology are clearly myths or misunderstandings. Some of the more common misunderstandings are presented on the following pages.

"To do well in competition you have to get yourself really psyched up." Usually such a statement implies that athletes have to learn to increase their physiological arousal and show the sorts of behaviors that are likely to be described as "pumped up." That may be true about certain individuals or certain sports, but it certainly does not apply across the board. Some weight lifters, for example, might benefit from increasing their physiological arousal just before attempting to make a particular lift. Skeet shooters, however, must be extremely relaxed. A swimmer about to swim a 50-meter sprint race should be physiologically aroused. A swimmer about to swim a 1500-meter race, however, should be very relaxed. Physiological arousal for the 1500-meter swim will simply take away from the energy needed to swim the long race. Just as there are differences across sports, there are also differences among individuals. Psychological assessments might demonstrate that some people are simply too "laid back" in sporting situations, and their performance might be improved by increasing their physiological arousal. Other individuals, however, might show an improvement by learning how to relax before important events.

"Before important events, a coach should give an athlete some new, last-minute advice in order to give the athlete an advantage." As mentioned in the introduction to this chapter, an athlete cannot improve his or her physical condition or techniques on the day of an important competition. On that particular day they are capable of performing at a particular level as a function of their preparation. However, there are many things that can detract from performance. If an athlete is well rehearsed and knows what to do to perform at or near the level of which he or she is capable, then any last minute advice from a coach could simply be one more distractor. One of the contributions

of sports psychology has been to emphasize the need in many sports for moving from coach control to athlete or self-control. On the day of competition, if the coach has done the best job possible, then last-minute advice might not be an advantage but a distraction and a disadvantage instead.

There are, of course, some situations where last-minute advice from a coach can be very helpful. For example, a volleyball coach watching the opposition warm up, or noting the rotation of players during the first game of a match, might identify some important factors that can profitably be communicated to the team in order to make a tactical adjustment. It is a definite mistake, however, for coaches to assume that they must always give athletes some new last-minute advice in the hope that that will benefit performance. In many cases, it will have the opposite effect.

"Coaches of team sports have to be really good at motivating the athlete, through locker room pep talks just before the big game." Again, this is a myth. First, there is very little evidence that locker room pep talks significantly enhance team performance. More important, however, a locker room pep talk to the entire team ignores the fact that some athletes might benefit from being psyched up, whereas others might benefit from being psyched down. In a football game, for example, linemen may need to increase their physiological arousal in order to constantly bash away at each other at an intense level, play after play after play. The quarterback and the receivers, however, should be extremely relaxed and loose. You can imagine how difficult it would be for a highly aroused, tense, uptight receiver to try to get finger-tip control of a pass from the quarterback. Rather than learning how to give locker room pep talks just before the big game, coaches have to learn how to conduct individual assessments of athletes and how to deal with the athletes as individuals in order to maximize their respective performances.

Reprinted with special permission of King Features Syndicate, Inc.

"If athletes aren't nervous before a big event, that's a sign that they don't care." Once again, this is outmoded thinking. It's another example of the error of trying to offer across-the-board generalizations. Skeet shooters, gymnasts, figure skaters, and athletes in many other sports have to learn to go into the big event totally relaxed and confident, not nervous.

"By using hypnosis or some other psychological procedure, psychologists can quickly get you to control your mind and become a super athlete." You've probably read of many instances where professional athletes have undergone hypnosis to improve performance. A hockey player is concerned about a scoring slump. A batter is concerned about not hitting home runs. A pitcher all of a sudden loses control and can't find home plate. A basketball player makes only 30% of his free throw attempts. A golfer can't make a putt. In all of these situations, psychological procedures might help the athlete to improve

performance. It's a mistake, however, to think that such procedures are quick and simple. It's also a mistake to assume that such procedures can make one into a super athlete if that person has not already experienced considerable success. There is nothing especially complex about the psychological coping skills that can help improve the above types of problems, and which are described later in this chapter. However, like other skills, they must be practiced. The activities involved in what's referred to as psychological preparation are skills that can be practiced and learned, like any other skill. They are not mystical, not magical, and they cannot enable one to perform miracles. What they can do is to help an individual perform consistently at or near potential.

A TEACHABLE PROGRAM OF SPORTS PSYCHING

On the following pages we describe a plan to use to teach subtopics of sports psyching to the athletes that you coach. The techniques described can be used to help athletes in a number of close-ended individual sports, including speed swimming, synchronized swimming, diving, figure skating, gymnastics, track and field, weight lifting, golfing, downhill ski racing, cross country ski racing, archery, ski jumping, target shooting, cross-country running, and speed skating. The program could also be used, as is, to improve performance of close-ended activities in open-ended sports, such as shooting free throws in basketball or kicking field goals in football. Many of the components might also be adapted to enhance performance of individuals participating in open-ended, individual or team sports.

Sports Psyching Strategy No. 1: Controlling Problem Thoughts Before Competitions

PROBLEM: *Thinking distracting problem thoughts just before competitions*

Persistent and recurring thoughts can distract athletes from thinking about desirable technique thoughts, goals for the event, and other planned preparation activities. Such things as worrying about other competitors, about losing, about the poor quality of the playing facilities, about personal, family, or school problems, can all detract from top-level performance in competition. After young athletes have experienced a number of competitions, the form in Fig. 9-1 can be used as a questionnaire to help an athlete and coach pinpoint particular problem thoughts that may detract from performance. Give the athlete about 15 to 20 minutes to complete the questionnaire. Then ask the athlete various questions to clarify the kinds of examples de-

Problem Thoughts That Can Detract from Performance

Have you ever experienced the following thoughts during the last half hour before important competitions?

1. Self put-downs in comparing yourself with other competitors (you frequently feel inferior to other competitors and think about how much better they are). Describe examples: _____

   _____

   _____

   Frequency with which these occurred at past competitions:

   Almost never   1   2   3   4   5   Very often

2. Fear of failure (you do not necessarily feel inferior, but think that if you fail others might think badly of you). Describe examples: _____

   _____

   Frequency with which these occurred at past competitions:

   Almost never   1   2   3   4   5   Very often

3. Pain or fatigue (you think of getting hurt or feeling the pain from excessive fatigue and therefore do not put out full effort). Describe examples: _____

   _____

   Frequency with which these occurred at past competitions:

   Almost never   1   2   3   4   5   Very often

4. Climate or facility (e.g., you are overly concerned that it is too sunny, the pool is slow). Describe examples: _____

   _____

   _____

   Frequency with which these occurred at past competitions:

   Almost never   1   2   3   4   5   Very often

5. Other preoccupations (e.g., school problems, family problems, financial problems, or other problems that reduce your concentration). Describe examples: _____

   _____

   _____

   Frequency with which these occurred at past competitions:

   Almost never   1   2   3   4   5   Very often

FIGURE 9-1

scribed and the accuracy of the estimate of frequency with which those problems thoughts occurred.

If specific problem thoughts are rated as occurring with a frequency of often (four times) or very often (five times) during competitions, and if comparison of practice and competitive performance suggests to the coach that the individual frequently performs below potential in competitions, then the following program might be used to teach the athlete to cope with the problem thoughts.

TREATMENT: *Centering and coping self-statements*

When people experience problem thoughts and worry about things, such as other competitors, they are likely to become increasingly nervous. The muscles in the neck and shoulders might tighten up, and they are likely to breathe high in the chest. When they inhale, their chest expands and their shoulders rise. This combination of activities is likely where the expression "uptight" came from. People literally breathe in the upper part of their chest and are tense or tight in their upper musculature. The centering procedure* can help to produce the opposite effect.

Centering is a procedure that emphasizes thought control, a particular way of breathing, and muscle relaxation. When centering, the athlete should be encouraged to consciously relax and droop the neck and the shoulder muscles, letting the arms hang down at the side as low as possible. This can be done while standing or sitting. When breathing, the athlete should breathe from very low down in the abdomen. An easy way to teach this is as follows. Have the athlete place his hands on his abdomen and inhale, and then while exhaling, consciously push the abdomen in, to force all of the air out of the lungs. Have him watch his hands move forward each time he inhales, as the abdomen bulges out while the lungs fill with air. Some athletes give an imitation of being pregnant when they effectively inhale while centering; rather than the chest and shoulders rising and falling, the abdomen extends (when inhaling) and collapses (when exhaling). While they are exhaling, encourage athletes to think "relax." Breathing slowly in this manner for a half a dozen or so breaths helps the individual to quickly relax. Centering also effectively stops problem thoughts, and prepares the athlete to go on to the second part of the treatment.

In addition to centering, the athlete should be taught specific coping self-statements to counteract problem thoughts. As indicated pre-

---

*For a more detailed discussion of centering, see Nideffer, 1981.

viously, there is considerable evidence to support the view that "how you think is how you perform." Encourage your athletes to actually write out things that they can say to themselves and think about to counteract problem thoughts. For example, if an athlete frequently worries about other competitors, that athlete can practice saying such things as:

"What they do is their problem. I'm just concerned about my performance."

"I can't control what they do, but I can control what I do."

"I have my own reachable realistic goals. That's what I'm going for."

"To heck with them. I'm going for my own goals in my own race in my own way."

If an athlete frequently thinks and worries about losing just before an important competition, he or she can be encouraged to practice rehearsing such statements as the following:

"This is a competition, not an evaluation of me as a person. I know I'm a worthwhile person."

"What happens if I lose this competition? Will my house burn down? Will it cause a nuclear war? Of course not."

"Every thinking, feeling, living human being experiences losing at some time. But I can keep it in perspective because I have coping techniques to deal with it. Besides, meeting my own realistic, reachable goals is not losing."

Athletes should be shown a number of such examples of coping self-statements for the particular worrisome thoughts that occur with high frequency. They should then be encouraged to describe four or five specific examples (such as those above, or their own comparable examples) on 3″ × 5″ cards. They should be encouraged to practice rehearsing those statements in a variety of situations, and to have their 3″ × 5″ cards with them at important competitions.

Thus, to deal with various types of problem thoughts, the athlete should center, rehearse specific coping self-statements, and then return to his or her own precompetition and competition planning program.

Sports Psyching Strategy No. 2: Coping with Excessive Nervousness and Anxiety

PROBLEM: *Excessive nervousness and anxiety*

In many sports, a high level of nervousness and anxiety may detract from performance. A high level of anxiety is correlated with several behavioral effects for athletes in competition. First, those things that have been practiced while an athlete is relatively calm are less likely to occur in competition if an athlete is highly anxious. We know from stimulus generalization research that a response that has been well learned in one situation is more likely to occur in another situation if that situation is highly similar to the one in which the response was learned. We also know that one's body contributes cues to the general practice situation in which an athlete learns to perform. If the bodily sensations (e.g., from anxiety vs. relaxation) are quite different in competition than in practice, then performance may be different. In many cases, performance may be poorer. Second, athletes are likely to be less responsive to cues in their environment if they are highly anxious. High anxiety is correlated with a narrowing of attention. Cues that would normally control behavior in a relaxed state do not necessarily exert control when one is anxious. In a general sense, we are not nearly as responsive to our environment and are therefore likely to miss critical cues and make lots of mistakes and perform poorly when we are highly anxious. A third effect of a highly aroused and anxious state is that it takes energy. Although increasing the flow of adrenalin is desirable when a burst of energy is needed for a short time, such as when lifting a heavy weight in weight lifting or doing a 50-meter sprint in swimming, it is undesirable when sustained output is needed over a long time. High anxiety in the latter situation, such as distance swimming, takes energy that is needed for effective performance.

How does a coach measure level of anxiety in athletes? Although it would be nice to be able to assess the various physiological indicators directly, the coach usually has to rely on general observation of behavior patterns of the athletes. The form provided in Fig. 9-2 can be useful to help systematize the coaches' observations.

TREATMENT A: *Centering and coping self-statements*

Athletes can be taught a variety of strategies for decreasing anxiety and nervousness. One strategy that can often be effective is the centering procedure described in the previous section. Centering is especially helpful if the level of anxiety is not too great. Centering can be enhanced as a relaxation strategy if it is combined with the use of appropriate coping self-statements. For example, when faced with a stressful situation, an individual is likely to feel even more anxious if he or she says things like, "Oh no! I feel really nervous! What if I screw up? This is going to be terrible!" Alternatively, individuals can make other kinds of coping self-statements to confront and handle the stressful situation. For example:

Anxiety Behavior in a Stressful Situation _____

Individuals react quite differently to highly stressful situations. There-fore, no one set of symptoms will indicate potential loss of control or high anxiety for everyone. The key is to know the individual under normal circumstances and to be sensitive to changes in the way he or she is behaving. If you are concerned about a particular individual, you might complete the following checklist.

SCORING KEY: 1 = *Much less than average*
                    2 = *Less than average*
                    3 = *Average*
                    4 = *More than average*
                    5 = *Much more than average*

Behavior patterns	STEP 1 Observe the individual in a number of non-stressful situations and rate symptomatic behavior	Step 2 In a potentially stressful situation, look for changes in *either* behavior pattern A or behavior pattern B or behavior pattern C, and score below. A "More than normal" rating indicates anxiety.		
		Normal	More than normal	Much more than normal
Behavior Pattern A				
1. Drowsiness	1 2 3 4 5			
2. Drinking, yawning, stretching	1 2 3 4 5			
3. Preoccupied, unresponsive to questions, unresponsive to events around him/her	1 2 3 4 5			

FIGURE 9-2

Behavior patterns	STEP 1 Observe the individual in a number of non-stressful situations and rate symptomatic behavior					Step 2 In a potentially stressful situation, look for changes in *either* behavior pattern A *or* behavior pattern B *or* behavior pattern C, and score below. A "More than normal" rating indicates anxiety.		
						Normal	More than normal	Much more than normal
Behavior Pattern B								
4. Overactivity (can't sit still)	1	2	3	4	5			
5. Highly distracted by things, unable to stick to a topic, constantly shifting focus of attention	1	2	3	4	5			
Behavior Pattern C								
6. Tension								
In neck	1	2	3	4	5			
In shoulders	1	2	3	4	5			
In back	1	2	3	4	5			
7. Rapidity and shallowness of breathing (up in chest)	1	2	3	4	5			
8. Complaints of lightheadedness, dizziness, nausea, headaches	1	2	3	4	5			
9. "Set" jaw, grinding teeth, chewing on something unusual	1	2	3	4	5			

"There is no sense in worrying; worrying never helps anything."

"One step at a time. I know I can handle this one step at a time."

"I won't think about the problem; I'll concentrate on what I can do about it. That's better than getting nervous."

"Everybody gets a little nervous once in a while. But I have ways to manage it."

"I'll center, relax, and slow things down."

"If I get really nervous, I'll just do muscle relaxation, and calm right down."

As with the previous coping statements, athletes should be encouraged to write four or five examples on a $3'' \times 5''$ card. Whenever they feel a little nervous, they should do the centering procedure, and immediately follow centering with a review of coping self-statements. To increase the chance that the athletes will in fact do this in a stressful situation, the coach should practice what cognitive behavior therapists refer to as "stress innoculation" (Meichenbaum, 1977). The coach can arrange several sessions in which a highly stressful situation is described in detail. The athletes should be encouraged to imagine feeling nervous and anxious in that situation. When they indicate that they feel some anxiety, they should then go through the centering procedure and their coping self-statements. Afterward, the coach should provide supportive statements to the athletes, and impress on them that they are fully capable of coping with nervousness or anxiety in real, competitive situations.

TREATMENT B: *Progressive relaxation*

An additional tactic to decrease anxiety is to teach athletes to practice progressive relaxation. With this strategy, athletes are taught how to alternately tense and relax their muscles. They learn to think about the relaxed state of their muscles in contrast to the tension. The coach should prepare a tape that athletes can listen to over a number of sessions. It would be maximally effective to have someone with a low, even, soothing voice record the relaxation instructions. A set of instructions that we have used in our relaxation program is provided in Fig. 9-3.

An athlete should practice using the tape on at least five successive nights while in the comfort and quiet of his or her own room just before bedtime. Then, over the next three or four nights, the athlete should practice the relaxation exercises just before going to bed, but without the tape. Finally, the athlete should practice the muscle tensing and relaxation exercises in a sports environment. A program of approximately five practices with the tape and three without the tape, in his or her room, and five in a sports environment should enable an athlete to be able to relax totally in a few minutes in almost any situation. Those athletes who have difficulty relaxing without the tape should be encouraged to take it along with a tape player to important competitions.

Sports Psyching Strategy No. 3: Minimizing Effects of "Psych-Out Attempts" from Opposition
PROBLEM: *"They're trying to psych me out!"*

We frequently hear reports that a player or team has intimidated the opposition. For example, in the NFL play-off in January 1984, after the Los Angeles Raiders defeated the Seattle Sea Hawks, Raiders defensive end Lyle Alzado was quoted as saying, "I was doing a lot of talking to Curt Warner [of the Sea Hawks]. Just stupid things, trying to rattle him. I told him if he came my way again I would tear his head off. Stuff like that" (*Winnipeg Free Press*, Jan. 9, 1984). Such tactics fall under the general category of "psyching out the opposition." In some cases, attempts at psyching out the opposition are deliberate, such as in the above quote. In other situations, such as among friends playing a weekend game of golf, players may do things that disrupt opponents even though the disruptive tactics are not deliberate or even done consciously by the individuals involved.

"... AND IS IT TRUE, COACH, THAT NO VISITING TEAM HAS MADE A LAY-UP THIS YEAR?"

Relaxation Instructions

The instructions on this tape will help you learn to relax. Included is a series of exercises in which you first tense various muscles, then relax them, while at the same time noticing the difference between how they feel when they're tense and how they feel when they're relaxed. Before you start listening to the instructions, find a comfortable place where you can sit or lie down and where you won't be disturbed for 10 minutes or so. Listen closely to the instructions.

Each time I pause, continue doing what you were doing just before the pause. Now close your eyes and take three deep breaths. (p) (p)* Now squeeze both fists really tight and raise your fists up to your shoulders to make the muscles in your biceps tight. *Squeeze them tight. Note how they feel.*† Now relax. Just relax and think of the tension disappearing from your fingers. (p) (p) Once again, squeeze both fists at once and bend both arms to make them feel totally tense throughout. *Hold it. Keep them tight. Think about the tension you feel.* And now relax. Feel the total warmth and relaxation flowing through your muscles, (p) all the way down from your biceps, down to your forearms, and out of your fingertips. (p) (p)

Now wrinkle your forehead and squint your eyes very tight and hard. *Squeeze them tight and hard. Feel the tension across your forehead and through your eyes.* Now relax. Note how it feels in your eyes. They feel warm and relaxed. (p)

Now squeeze your jaws down tight together. Bite down hard and raise your chin. Stick your chin out to make your neck muscles hard. *Hold it. Bite down hard. Tense your neck. Squeeze your lips really tight together.* And once again, just relax. Just breathe deeply and relax. (p) (p)

Now squeeze both your shoulders forward as hard as you can, so that you feel your muscles pull tight across your back, especially between your shoulder blades. *Squeeze them. Hold it.* And relax. (p) Just breathe deeply. (p) One more time, squeeze your shoulders forward again, but this time at the same time suck in your stomach as far as you can, and make your stomach muscles hard. *Feel the tension in your stomach? Hold it.* And relax. (p) (p)

Paraphrased from Martin, G.L., and Pear, J.J.
*Each (p) represents a pause of 5 seconds.
†Each italicized phrase should be stated a little more loudly and quickly than the other statements.

FIGURE 9-3

Taped relaxation instructions.

Now your legs. Bend your knees so that you can push down hard on your heels. *Push down hard. Raise your toes, make your calf muscles and thigh muscles tight. Hold it.* And relax. (p) (p) Just feel the warmth flowing down your legs, down to your ankles, down to your toes. (p) One more time with your legs. Bend your legs so you can push down hard on your heels, and squeeze your toes up toward your shins. *Make the muscles in your legs tight. Hold it.* And relax. (p)

Take three deep breaths. (p) (p) Now, when I call out the names of the muscles and the body parts, tense them just as you've been practicing. Ready? *Both fists—squeeze them tight. Bring your fists up to your shoulders; make your arms tight. Wrinkle your forehead; squint hard. Bite down hard with your jaw; squeeze your lips together. Round your shoulders forward; suck in your stomach. Push down hard on your heels; squeeze your toes up. Hold it. Hold it.* And relax. (p) (p) Just breathe deeply, and notice how relaxed all your muscles feel. (p) (p)

Take three deep breaths. (p) (p)

One more time, as I call out the names of the muscles and the body parts, squeeze them the way you've practiced. Ready? *Both fists—put your fists up to your shoulders; make your arms tight. Bite down hard. Wrinkle your forehead; squint hard. Round your shoulders forward; suck in your stomach, and push against your stomach. Squeeze down with your heels; curl your toes up. Hold it. Everything tense. Hold it.* And relax. (p) (p) Just enjoy the feeling of complete relaxation. (p) (p) Breathe slowly and deeply. (p) (p) Now turn the tape off.

The different types of behaviors that have the effect of psyching out the opposition might be divided into two main categories. First, some psych-out behaviors affect the motivation of the opposition. In some cases, because of the psych-out attempts, the opposition tries extra hard, and his or her technique is disrupted as a consequence. For example, when discussing various examples of psych-outs, Tutko and Tosi (1976) described an example where a golfer might tease an opponent by saying, "OK, go ahead and drive," when the preceding group is only 150 yards in front of the tee. The effect of this comment might be to cause the golfer at the tee to deliberately wait until the preceding group is about 300 yards in front, and then swing especially hard at the ball. The result is likely to be a poor drive that dribbles off the tee or that slices or hooks to the right or left. Some strategies influence the opposition so that motivation is affected in the opposite direction. These strategies are designed so that the opposition won't try very hard and therefore not perform up to full potential. For example, a basketball team may show considerable razzle-dazzle and lots of slam dunks during warm-up. Lyle Alzado was quoted as telling Curt Warner that he was going to "tear his head off." The message in these types of strategies seems to be, "There's no sense in your trying, because I'm much better than you are," or "If you try, you are going to get hurt." Another strategy that weakens motivation is to play on the sympathy of the opposition. For example, the weekend golfer might say to his friends, "My bum knee is really bothering me today," or "I only get to play once or twice a year." The psych-out effect here is to influence the opposition to play at something less than full potential.

The second major category of psych-out attempts consists of strategies to distract the opposition so that the cues controlling effective performance are disrupted. Sometimes the psych-out attempts consists of subtle comments about the condition of the facilities, such as a figure skater loudly complaining about the cracks in the ice so that the other skaters hear the comments (and perhaps think about them while they're performing). Sometimes the psych-out attempt consists of a comment about the opponent's technique, such as one golfer asking another, "How can you twist your hips so far back on your backswing?" You can bet that the next time that person is about to hit the ball, he is going to be thinking about how far his hips twist on the backswing, which is also likely something quite different than what that golfer usually thinks about on the backswing. A third strategy that falls into this category consists of temper tantrums or other antics to distract an opponent. John McEnroe's tantrums in tennis are well-known. All of these tactics serve as distractions to the opposition. They are likely to have the effect of disrupting the usual thought patterns that occur when the opposition is playing well.

TREATMENT: *Centering, coping self-statements, and rehearsal of form*

In our opinion, athletes should not be encouraged to deliberately psych out the opposition. If athletes have their own precompetition and competition strategies so well rehearsed that they can play close to their top potential in most situations, then that may be the most effective psych-out strategy of all. If others attempt to disrupt an athlete and are consistently unsuccessful, two things are likely to occur: future attempts at psyching out by that particular person are likely to decrease; and the failure to be able to affect a particular athlete may be highly disruptive to the person who is attempting the psych-out in the first place.

Because psych-out attempts are common in sports environments, the coach should discuss them with the athletes. The athletes should be encouraged to identify various types of psych-out attempts that the opposition has shown in the past. They should then be taught that a psych-out attempt by the opposition should be a cue to perform a particular routine. Specifically, the psych-out attempt by the opposition should be a cue for the athlete to center, rehearse specific coping self-statements about the opposition, and then to immediately rehearse or role-play the specific components of the technique that are "well grooved" (and likely to be resistant to disruption). For example, let's assume that golfer A has been commenting on golfer B's technique, on various hazards on particular holes, and complaining about a sore shoulder. Should any of these occur, golfer B should center (while walking or standing or sitting), then recite specific coping self-statements about the opposition. If the psych-out attempts have occurred just before golfter B is about to make a shot, golfer B should center, recite coping self-statements, and then perform practice swings until feeling comfortable that the "perfect swing" has occurred. Golfer B should then proceed with the usual routine for selecting a club, setting up, and making the shot. Once again, coaches should not expect athletes to be able to respond in this way to psych-out attempts from the opposition just on the basis of verbal instruction. Deliberate sessions of modeling and role playing, and deliberate practice sessions under real playing circumstances should be repeated on several occasions.

Sports Psyching Strategy No. 4: Reliving Your "Best" Performance
PROBLEM: *Sometimes athlete has "one of those days"*

On some days of competition, everything seems to go right, and an athlete performs exceptionally well. On other days, in spite of being in good physical condition and having spent hours and hours practicing, the athlete somehow doesn't perform up to potential. Often the athlete is not quite sure what went wrong. In these kinds of situations, we are likely to hear such cliches as, "I guess I lost my concentration" or "I just couldn't seem to get into it" or "I wasn't mentally prepared."

TREATMENT: *Relive "best" performances*

One strategy for maximizing the frequency of "best performances" is for an athlete to repeat things that were done on the day of a competition at which that athlete performed at his or her best. On the day of a previous best performance, what did the athlete do, say, think about, concentrate on, and attend to? Was there a particular wake-up routine in the morning? What kinds of meals were eaten, and where were they eaten? What activities filled the day before the competition? Who was around? What about getting the equipment ready? What happened at the field setting or the arena? What about the details of the warm-up routine? The stretching? Detailed planning for all such eventualities minimizes the possibility of various distractors influencing or detracting from performance. Also, detailed planning increases the chances that the athlete will be able to repeat the various activities that occurred during the day of a previous best performance.

Encouraging athletes to analyze their best performances is also a useful strategy for helping them to come out of a slump. Roger Neilson, former NHL coach of the Toronto Maple Leafs and the Vancouver Canucks, is well known for his creative use of videotaped replays to help hockey players relive best performances. When asked about how he helped his star players come out of a slump, "Captain Video" Neilson replied, "Here's a guy who's gone five or six games, and we can't figure out what's the matter. We'll go through all our old [taped] scoring chances and pick out all the best things he's done over the first 30 games, put them on a tape, and call him in. It might take a whole day to put the tape together, but we've done it for Lanny McDonald, Tony McKegny, Thomas Gradin, Glen Hanlon, goalies especially. We'll find they'll come back and watch that tape 10 times in a year, just seeing themselves playing well" (Newman, 1982). Another example of helping athletes relive best performances was reported for the University of

Cincinatti golf team. Kirschenbaum and Bale (1978) designed a multi-component sports psyching program that they referred to as "brain power golf." One of the components was positive self-monitoring. After each hole, a golfer recorded the shots that he made effectively. As he did so, he recalled everything he could about the shot—positioning, feel of the swing, target selection, club selection, and so on. In addition, the golfers were instructed to "file away the poor shots in your memories and recall them after the game." In other words, the golfers relived their good shots and learned not to dwell on their bad shots.

Sports Psyching Strategy No. 5: Realistic, Short-Term Goal Setting
PROBLEM: *Unrealistic, short-term goal setting*

Anxiety, disappointment, and other problems for athletes can derive from unrealistic, short-term goal setting. This is frequently a problem with young and beginning athletes. If beginning athletes go into a competition expecting to win a gold medal, beat the superstar, improve their time or performance greatly, then they are frequently doomed to be disappointed. To minimize disappointment and maximize rewards for competing, athletes should be encouraged to set realistic self-improvement goals for each competition.

TREATMENT: *Realistic, short-term goal setting*

We should point out that we're not talking here of long-term goal setting. Strategies for setting a variety of performance goals for practices and competitions for the season, and perhaps for several years, are described in Chapter 10 (*see also* Botterill, 1983; Rushall, 1979). The emphasis here is on realistic goal setting for a particular competition.

First, in conjunction with the athlete, design a goal-setting sheet on which the athlete can summarize his or her level of preparation and identify numerous goals for each competition. A sample of such a sheet for competitive speed swimmers is shown in Fig. 9-4. For each competition, the athlete should be encouraged to realistically appraise his or her degree of preparation. Second, the athlete should be encouraged to set several realistic goals with respect to the competition. Multiple goals increase the likelihood of the athlete achieving some of them in each and every competition. The goals should be realistic, but they should also include a reasonable amount of "stretch" or challenge. It is also recommended that the multiple goals be prioritized in order of importance.

Goal-Setting Sheet for Swimmers Before Meet _____

Name _____ Date of meet _____

This sheet is set up for a 1-day meet. If the meet lasts more than 1 day, use one sheet for each day.

APPRAISAL OF MY PREPARATION

Number of weeks since I last swam this event? _____

Average number of practices per week that I have attended during past _____ months? _____

Average distance swum per week during past _____ months? _____

How would I rate my overall effort at the practices that I have attended during the past _____ months?

Usually very lazy   1   2   3   4   5   6   7   Consistently worked very hard

Did I taper before this meet? _____

Have I had lots of rest during the past few days before the meet? _____

Have I been stress and illness free during the last few days before the meet? _____

MY GOALS

My events in order	My previous best times	Will I be going all out for best times?	Realistic target times that I will shoot for	Splits that I need to hit my goals	Actual race times
_____	_____	_____	_____	Target / Actual	_____
_____	_____	_____	_____	Target / Actual	_____
_____	_____	_____	_____	Target / Actual	_____
_____	_____	_____	_____	Target / Actual	_____
_____	_____	_____	_____	Target / Actual	_____
_____	_____	_____	_____	Target / Actual	_____

Total number of target times achieved _____

Percent of target times achieved _____

Total number of best times achieved _____

Percent of best times achieved _____

Do I have any specific technique goals for any of the strokes?	Did I achieve those goals?
Back	
Breast	
Fly	
Free	

Do I have any "sports psyching" goals?	Did I achieve those goals?

FIGURE 9-4

Sports Psyching Strategy No. 6: "Psyching Up," If Needed
PROBLEM: *Athlete is not "up" for competition*

Sometimes, athletes do not seem to be ready to perform. They might be described as too laid back, too relaxed, disinterested, too complacent, or not "hungry." If we were to measure it, they would probably show a very low level of physiological arousal. Although such a relaxed state might precede optimal performance in some sports, many athletes in many sports have performed at their best when their behavior just prior to performance was characterized as pumped up, charged up, psyched up, confident and aggressive, or ready to go. The athlete who appears far too laid back before a competition should know of various strategies for "psyching up."

TREATMENT: *Psyching up strategies*

Different athletes have used different strategies for increasing their arousal prior to competition. It is recommended that you discuss each of the following strategies with your athletes, and encourage them to choose those that they feel most comfortable with or identify some new ones. Common strategies have included the following:

1. *Physical pumping,* or burst of physical activity, such as a few fast push-ups, running in place for a few seconds, shadow boxing for a few seconds, or finding a partner so that they can grab each other's shoulders and push each other back and forth, as in Greco-Roman–style wrestling.
2. *Rehearsal statements* that the athlete can say to himself, such as, "I know I can do it," "I'm going to go for it," "It's now or never," "I've trained hard, and there's no sense in holding back," "I'm going to give it all I've got," "No matter what happens, I want to be able to say I did my best when it's finished."
3. *Listening to music,* for example, wild rock music or fast marches.
4. *Use of imagery,* for example, thinking of sitting on a keg of dynamite about to explode, imagining a space ship taking off from Cape Canaveral, or dancing to a fast beat.
5. *Explosive words,* such as "pow," "bam," "blast," "charge."

These techniques will help an athlete only if they are practiced. After a session in which they choose their favorite arousal strategies, encourage your athletes to say or describe them out loud or listen to the music in sessions where they are imagining themselves at the competition site, approximately 3 to 5 minutes before having to perform. Over several competitions, encourage them to practice the spe-

cific strategies and take notes to determine whether they have a higher
, frequency of top performances when they practice the strategies or
when they don't.

**Sports Psyching Strategy No. 7: Controlling Thought Content
During Competition**
PROBLEM: *Certain thought patterns during competition can detract
from performance*

What do athletes think about during competitions? The answer
varies considerably from athlete to athlete and from sport to sport. In
some sports, such as tennis, hockey, and basketball, the athletes must
react so quickly that there's little time to think of anything. In fact, if a
defenseman takes time to think in the process of checking Wayne
Gretzky, Wayne Gretzky will likely be long gone. In other sports, such
as swimming, private thoughts just before and throughout the competition can play an important role. Even in sports where reaction time
in the heat of the battle is so fast that there is little time to think, there
is usually an opportunity for thoughts to play a role between instances
of action. What does a tennis player think about when walking back to
the serve line? What does a hockey player think about on the ice while
waiting for the other team to change players? The answers vary considerably from athlete to athlete, and surveys of top athletes in various
sports have revealed some interesting findings. For example, many
athletes, when they require a burst of energy or speed, think explosive
thoughts such as "blast," "charge," "explode." On the other hand, if
agility is required, such as in fencing, an athlete might think such
thoughts as "dance," "flow," "whip." Both types of thoughts are called
"mood" thoughts or words. A different type of thought is "technique"
thoughts, in which athletes rehearse various aspects of their form. For
example, a swimmer might think about specific aspects of hand entry,
pull, recovery, breathing, and kick, while swimming. On the basis of
his work with some of Canada's Olympic athletes, Rushall (1979) has
provided detailed guidelines for helping athletes to plan the content of
competition thinking. His work has mainly been with national or
international performers, and we strongly encourage coaches to seriously study Rushall's publications.

In our work with young age-group athletes, we have attempted to
follow Rushall's guidelines. Although more research is needed, subjective reports from the young athletes involved suggests that planning of
content of competition thinking for young athletes can also be beneficial.

TREATMENT: *Prepare detailed plan of thoughts and self-statements to be used during competition*

The first step is to help your athletes record the specific thought content that they might use during a competition. Your recording form should identify those situations during the competition when there is an opportunity for thoughts to play a role. In hockey, what should the players be thinking about between shifts while they are resting on the bench? In tennis, what should a player be thinking about while walking back to the line to get ready for the next serve after just hitting an ace? In swimming, what should the swimmer be thinking about throughout a 100-meter race? Some examples of self-statements for ice hockey players are shown in Fig. 9-5.

Working with the athletes on a one-to-one basis, help them to write out thought content for the specific competition for which they are preparing. Obviously, there will be some real differences here from sport to sport. Recommended guidelines for planning thought content include the following:

1. In sports like middle and distance swimming, cross-country skiing, and rowing, which involve repetitive movements, at least two thirds of the thought patterns and statements should involve self-statements about technique (Rushall, 1979).

2. If the event requires a short burst of energy, such as a 50-meter freestyle sprint, or a particular lift in weight lifting, there should be a major emphasis on mood words that imply explosive power.

3. In sports like golf or target shooting, where each shot is under the control of the athlete, use mood words that connote smooth, relaxed control just before going through the preshot ritual.

4. In general, performances should be segmented, and athletes should be encouraged to use natural cues to prompt particular thoughts. For example, coming up for a turn in a swimming race prompts one type of thought. Breaking to the surface and beginning to stroke after the turn prompts a different type of thought.

5. As an athlete begins to experience fatigue, use more anti-fatigue thoughts. In sports such as swimming, cross-country skiing, or rowing, the onset of fatigue should prompt an increase in the technique thoughts used. Similarly, hockey players in between shifts, or offensive football players when the defense is on the field might also use technique thoughts to

Coping Self-Statements for
Ice Hockey Players

Situation	Coping Self-Statements
An "aggravator" type pushes you after the whistle:	• "Can't help the team from the penalty box." • "Get to the face-off circle and play your game." • "Don't play down to him (play your own game)."
You get caught deep in offensive zone:	• "Get back on defense!" • "Turn this into an offensive advantage!"
You've been sitting on the bench for a period:	• "Keep in the game." • "You have to be able to play 100% when you get the chance." • "Lots of chatter, keep the team up."
Teammate takes a dumb penalty:	• "Let's kill this penalty. We can do it!" • "I make mistakes, too." • "Worry about your own game."
Coach loses self-control during game:	• "So what? Play the game." • "Salvage what's left of the game." • "Bear down and concentrate on your assignment."
Center facing off against someone you haven't won a face off against all night:	• "Try something new." • "Relax, and concentrate on the puck." • "I'll get him this time"

Prepared by Paul Milton.

FIGURE 9-5

counteract fatigue. An offensive tackle, for example, might say to himself, "Pass blocking—butt down, straight back, hands out in front, foot movement and lead steps, contact on chest." Individuals can also have specific coping self-statements to deal with fatigue: "As soon as I begin to feel tired, I'm going to concentrate harder than ever on my technique," "Sure it hurts, but I can manage it if I concentrate. It'll be worth it."

As with all the other techniques, the athletes will use them only if they are well rehearsed. The athletes can be encouraged to memorize them and imagine that they are performing and report the thoughts out loud to the coach (or into a tape-recorder for later play-back by the coach). After each competition, the coach should check with the athlete to determine if the thoughts were used, if they were helpful, and how they might be modified for subsequent competitions.

Sports Psyching Strategy No. 8: Imagery
PROBLEM: *How to improve performance*

Imagery (or mental rehearsal*) as a sports psyching strategy is somewhat different than any of those listed above. With each of the previous strategies, a particular problem was identified. The problem was something that detracted from maximum performance. A strategy was designed to minimize the effects of that particular problem. With imagery, the concern is not so much to deal with a particular problem as to simply teach athletes one additional tactic that might improve overall performance.

Have you ever watched Jack Nicklaus play golf on TV? It seems like he takes forever standing over the ball before each shot. Have you ever thought about what he might be doing? Nicklaus himself claims that he goes through mental rehearsal of every shot throughout an entire round (Nicklaus, 1974). First he pictures the target spot where he wants the ball to land. Then he visualizes the arc of the ball flying through the air to land on that target spot. Next he imagines himself executing the swing needed in order to produce a shot that will give the ball that particular flight pattern. When imagining himself performing the swing, he imagines how it feels to him when he is addressing the ball, on his backswing, on his follow through, weight transfer, and so forth. In other words, he does not mentally picture how someone else watches him hit the ball from the outside. He imagines how he feels

---

*While some authors distinguish between imagery and mental rehearsal (e.g., Harris and Harris, 1984), we use the terms interchangeably.

from the inside while executing the shot. Nicklaus has suggested that success on any one shot in golf depends 10% on technique, 40% on set up (e.g., club selection for the particular shot), and 50% on mental rehearsal of the correct form for the shot. Of course, we don't know that these percentages are correct. What we do know is that many highly successful athletes have learned to image specific aspects of performance in considerable detail. At the very least, as suggested by Simek and O'Brien (1981), rehearsing imagery just before a competition is likely to have the effect of minimizing distractors. The athlete who is mentally rehearsing a particular performance is less likely to be thinking about any problem thoughts that can cause excessive nervousness and that clearly detract from performance. Also, if practiced just before participation in an event, mental rehearsal can serve to maintain the athlete's attention on task-relevant factors. Finally, it may serve to put the athlete "in the mood" to perform at his or her best, and in that sense it may also serve a psyching up function to help prepare the body for competition. Detailed reviews on research on mental preparation, including imagery, are provided by Weinberg (1982; 1984).

TREATMENT: *Imagery*

We cannot emphasize too often the need to practice the various sports psyching techniques if they are to be used effectively by athletes. The first step in learning imagery, therefore, is to have several sessions with the athletes in a noncompetitive environment. The athlete should then practice on his or her own. The coach should review the athlete's practice attempts. Finally, the athlete should attempt imagery at competitions. The steps through which this might proceed are as follow:

Step 1. Coach leads athletes through imagery. The coach should arrange for a session to be held in a quiet relaxed atmosphere. Depending on the sport and the activity to be rehearsed, the session could be done as a group or with individuals. For example, mentally rehearsing freestyle figure skating routines would have to be done individually, because each skater individualizes his or her routines. A synchronized swimming team, however, can mentally rehearse their routine as a group. The coach should first have the swimmers go through the progressive relaxation tape (described previously) in order to totally relax them and put them in a receptive frame of mind. Next, the coach should provide specific prompts—auditory, visual, and tactual cues that normally exist in the competitive environment. For example, for the synchronized swimming team, the coach might say, "Imagine that you are in the water at the pool, waiting near the edge for your event to be announced. You can see out of the corner of your eye where the judges have just raised the scores for the previous swimmers. Feel the water lapping gently against your arm," and so on. If music is a part of the routine, such as in figure skating, then the music can be playing in the background. After setting the mood, the coach should then ask the athletes to visualize and feel as though they were performing. The coach should describe the specific routine or series of actions that would normally be performed.

Step 2. Athlete records private recitation of rehearsed imagery on tape. Once the athletes have the idea of what imagery is all about, have them go through a personalized mental rehearsal experience and record it on tape. You can then listen to the tape with the athlete and provide suggestions for improving the content. For example, they may want to add certain mood words, words about specific parts of the environment (such as feeling the water lapping against them, hearing the crunch of the snow while skiing), and time the thought content to suit the event. *Coaching Theory, Level III* (1981) of the Canadian National Coaching Certification Program recommends the following as critical features for successful imagery:

1. The skill or event should be performed in its entirety.
2. Athletes should concentrate on imagining the feel of the action.
3. The imagined skill or event should approximate the rate or speed of actual performance.
4. The athletes should imagine themselves being successful in the rehearsal.
5. If possible, the mental rehearsal should take place in the performance environment, and meet a realistic performance goal.
6. At least one mental rehearsal should precede each performance at the competition site.

Step 3. Athlete practices with tape night before competitions and at competition itself. As with other techniques, the athletes must be encouraged to practice imagery and to keep notes on both their rehearsals and their performances over several competitions. All of the sport psyching strategies are skills that can be improved with practice.

Sports Psyching Strategy No. 9: Goal Setting and Assessment of Psychological Factors During Games with a Team

It's not uncommon for coaches to suggest that, for optimal performance during games, players must maintain a certain level of intensity, communicate effectively on the field, concentrate on techniques and tactics throughout the entire game, and maintain a posi-

Assessment of Psychological Factors During Game _____

Before each game, set a goal for each factor by placing an X on the number that you would like to score during the game.

After the game, circle the appropriate number for each factor as it applied to you during the game. Then circle the appropriate number for each factor as it applied to the team.

SCORING KEY: +3 = *Frequently throughout game, on most opportunities*
0 = *So-so, neutral, some of the time*
−3 = *Frequently throughout game, on many opportunities*

Opponent _____ Date _____

Positive	+3 +2 +1 0 1 2 3	Negative
Was relaxed, loose, rhythmic	*S: 3 2 1 0 1 2 3 T: 3 2 1 0 1 2 3	Was nervous, tense, uptight, forced, anxious
Was physically energized, ready to play, showed lots of hustle, wanted to be in the action	S: 3 2 1 0 1 2 3 T: 3 2 1 0 1 2 3	Was lethargic, dragging, or wanted to sit out or get the game finished
Was mentally alert, attentive, maintained concentration	S: 3 2 1 0 1 2 3 T: 3 2 1 0 1 2 3	Was dopey, tuned out, made many mental errors, lost concentration
Was proudly and responsibly assertive	S: 3 2 1 0 1 2 3 T: 3 2 1 0 1 2 3	Was intimidated, submissive
Used positive self-talk ("We can out-hustle them." "Let's play our best right to the final whistle.")	S: 3 2 1 0 1 2 3 T: 3 2 1 0 1 2 3	Used negative, defeatist self-talk ("We'll never beat them." "What's the use?" "Let's get this over with.")
Showed quick reaction to losing the ball or puck or getting beat; got right back into play	S: 3 2 1 0 1 2 3 T: 3 2 1 0 1 2 3	Got mad or down on myself when I got beat or made a bad play, and showed temporary mental lapse

*S = self, T = team.

FIGURE 9-6

Positive	+3 +2 +1 0 −1 −2 −3		Negative
Accepted "bad" calls by the referee and was immediately ready to play	S: 3 2 1 0 1 2 3	T: 3 2 1 0 1 2 3	Got mad at "bad" calls, showed a temporary mental lapse
Was generally encouraging to teammates in words ("Let's go!" "Keep hustling!") and body language (encouraging slap on back)	S: 3 2 1 0 1 2 3	T: 3 2 1 0 1 2 3	Was generally quiet or discouraging to teammates in words ("What's the use?") and body language (throwing up hands in disgust)
Communicated tactically with teammates ("I've got her/him. You take the other forward.")	S: 3 2 1 0 1 2 3	T: 3 2 1 0 1 2 3	Did not communicate with teammates
Specifically praised good performance of teammates in words ("Great shot!" "Way to go!") and body language (showing clenched fist victory sign)	S: 3 2 1 0 1 2 3	T: 3 2 1 0 1 2 3	Specifically and harshly criticized poor performance of teammates ("What kind of dumb play was that?")
Gave verbal emotional support to teammates if they made a mistake ("That's ok, let's get it back.")	S: 3 2 1 0 1 2 3	T: 3 2 1 0 1 2 3	Did not give emotional support to teammates following their mistakes, or made unpleasant comments
Enjoyed competition and felt good about my/our performance and sportsmanship	S: 3 2 1 0 1 2 3	T: 3 2 1 0 1 2 3	Did not enjoy competition, felt bad about my/our performance, showed poor sportsmanship

Total individual score out of 36 _____

Total team score out of 36   _____

tive attitude. The team that shows behaviors representative of these more general characteristics is more likely to play up to its potential than the team that doesn't show such behaviors. The checklist shown in Fig. 9-6 can be used for self-evaluation as well as for overall team evaluation. It can also be used for goal-setting. Players can be encouraged to review the checklist before games and to set individual goals that they hope to meet on each of the factors. Players can then use the checklist for evaluation after games. Consistent goal setting and evaluation of these factors will help individuals and the team play to their full potential.

STRATEGY FOR FOLLOW-UP ON SPORTS PSYCHING TACTICS

We have emphasized throughout this chapter that sports psyching involves skills that can be taught by coaches and learned by athletes. As with any other skill, they require some support to be maintained. A useful strategy for influencing the athletes to maintain sports psyching and for helping the coach keep track of who's doing what is to prepare a self-monitoring checklist. This checklist should list the specific behaviors to be performed by the athletes, and should provide them an opportunity to indicate their presence or absence in relation to competition. A sample checklist is shown in Fig. 9-7.

SUMMARY

Applied sport psychology is the use of psychological knowledge to enhance the development, performance, and satisfaction of athletes and others associated with sport. Subareas of applied sport psychology described in this book include techniques for effectively improving skills, strategies for motivating practice and endurance training, dealing with personal problems, helping coaches to become better coaches, and "sport psyching" to prepare for competition. This chapter emphasized sports psyching.

Several myths or misunderstandings about sport psychology were discussed. Many of the myths relate to overgeneralizations about sports psyching. However, the procedures are not mystical, not magical, and they cannot enable an athlete to perform miracles. Sport psyching procedures must be individualized. They also must be practiced. They involve skills that an athlete can learn and that can help an athlete consistently perform at or near potential.

Sports psyching strategies discussed include (1) centering and coping self-statements to minimize distracting problem thoughts just before competitions; (2) centering, coping self-statements, and progressive relaxation to decrease excessive nervousness and anxiety; (3) centering, coping self-statements, and rehearsal of form to minimize psych-out attempts by the opposition; (4) reliving "best" performances to decrease the frequency of "off" days or to help an athlete come out of a slump; (5) realistic short-term goal setting to minimize disappointment from unrealistic goals; (6) psyching up strategies before competitions; (7) planning thought content during competition to enhance performance and minimize distractions; and (8) imagery rehearsal to improve performance. Finally, a checklist was provided to help the coach monitor the sport psyching techniques used by an athlete during a competition.

Coach's Checklist

We believe that, after studying this chapter, you will be able to implement these strategies with your athletes. We have summarized the components in a checklist for teaching sports psyching (Fig. 9-8). We recommend that you consider scheduling 1 hour each week to be devoted to sports psyching. As can be seen in the checklist, implementation of the entire program will require a total of 12 sessions. Individual athletes would be expected to do additional practice on their own, and will also require a few minutes of guidance and feedback before and after each competition to ensure that they are obtaining maximum benefit from the techniques. If it is not possible for you to devote the necessary time to implement the entire program, then select those components that you think will be most valuable, and implement them. If you decide that you do not have time to implement any of the strategies in this chapter, then we encourage you to consider the following:

> Attributions given by coaches and athletes for not performing up to expectations generally involve those related to the mental aspects of performance! "They weren't hungry enough," "We lost our momentum," "I got psyched out," "I just didn't want it enough," or "I wasn't psyched up enough" are comments frequently used to describe competitive disappointments. Rarely do you find the coach who says that the team had not been taught the proper psychological skills and strategies. An athlete seldom concludes a loss was related to poor or inadequate preparation of psychological strategies. However, after the game, the greatest percentage of excuses are generally attributed to the mental and emotional aspects of the game. Yet, almost no time has been spent in incorporating these into the training routine (Harris and Harris, 1984, p. 16).

Record of Sports Psyching Techniques Attempted ___

Name ___

Competition ___ Date of competition ___

	Yes	To Some Extent	No
Month Before Competition			
1. Did you keep careful records of your practice performance?			
Week Before Competition			
2. Did you complete a realistic goal-setting sheet before the competition?			
3. If you completed a goal-setting sheet, did you *carefully* and *realistically* consider your preparation (e.g., in swimming, distance swum during previous months, presence or absence of taper, presence or absence of illness or stress) in order to set *realistic* goals?			
4. Did you *plan* and *write out* thought content for your events so that it included "mood" words?			
5. Did you *plan* and *write out* thought content for your events so that it included technique thoughts?			
6. Did you check to see if your thought content for your events followed the guidelines previously given to you?			
7. Did you practice the thought content during at least one practice?			
8. Did you practice imagery before the competition?			
9. Did you practice *progressive muscle relaxation* at least once?			
10. Did you write out specific coping statements to counteract a variety of possible problem thoughts (about other competitors, about losing, about the facilities)?			
11. Did you practice *centering and coping self-statements* at least once to prepare to deal with nervousness or problem thoughts that might be experienced at the competition site?			

FIGURE 9-7

	Yes	To Some Extent	No
12. Did you plan specific "psyching up" strategies that could be used if needed at the competition (e.g., physical activity, roughhousing, fast music, sexual fantasies)?			
At Competition			
13. Did you review your goal-setting sheet just before competing?			
14. Approximately 15 minutes before competing, did you self-assess or talk to your coach to judge your level of arousal to see whether you needed to relax or psych up?			
15. Following your self-assessment as indicated in question 14, did you use an appropriate relaxation or psyching up strategy to achieve optimal arousal?			
16. Did you use centering and specific coping statements to counteract various distracting problem thoughts during the last 15 minutes before competing?			
17. Did you practice at least one complete imagery rehearsal just before competing?			
18. *During competition,* did you use "mood" thoughts and technique thoughts to maximize performance?			
19. Did you record your results on your goal-setting sheet after competing?			
After Competition			
20. Did you review your results and sports psyching strategies and discuss possible improvements with your coach or sport psychologist?			
TOTAL YES'S			

Percent of total sports psyching program used:

$$\frac{\text{Total yes's}}{20} \times 100 = \frac{}{20} \times 100 = \underline{}\%$$

Teaching Sports Psyching

	Date Completed
1. Provide an introductory lecture/discussion on characteristics. misconceptions, and potential advantages of sports psyching (one session)	
2. Complete Checklist of Problem Thoughts (Fig. 9-1) and Checklist of Anxiety Behavior (Fig. 9-2) (one session)	
3. Teach athletes about centering and coping self-statements to deal with problem thoughts (one session. plus self-practice by athletes)	
4. Teach athletes about centering. progressive relaxation. and coping self-statements to deal with excessive nervousness and anxiety (one session, plus self-practice by athletes)	
5. Teach athletes about centering and coping self-statements and rehearsal of form to minimize "psych outs" by opposition (one session, plus self-practice by athletes)	
6. Teach athletes how to relive "best" performances to enhance consistency (one session, plus after successful competitions and before future competitions)	
7. Teach athletes about realistic goal setting for competitions to minimize disappointment and anxiety from unrealistic goal setting (one session, and before every competition)	
8. Teach athletes how to "psych up" if needed to enhance physiological arousal (one session, plus self-practice by athletes)	
9. Teach athletes how to plan and control thought content during competitions (one session, and during each competition)	
10. Teach athletes how to use imagery to improve performance (two sessions, and before competitions)	
11. Teach athletes to use self-monitoring checklists to maintain application of sports psyching techniques across competitions (one session, and after every competition)	

FIGURE 9-8

Review Questions

1. Name and briefly describe the four main areas for athletic preparation.
2. Briefly describe five major areas of sports psychology.
3. List at least five reasons for practicing sports psyching.
4. List five misconceptions about sports psychology. Briefly explain why they are misconceptions.
5. Give examples of three different types of problem thoughts that can detract from an athlete's performance if they occur prior to competition.
6. Briefly describe a plausible treatment program for minimizing problem thoughts before competition.
7. Assume that you become extremely nervous and anxious before competing in athletic events. Briefly outline a plausible treatment strategy that you might use to learn to control your excessive anxiety.
8. What is meant by "reliving your best performance"? Why do you suppose that learning to relive best performances might enhance consistency? Explain in behavioral terms (e.g., in terms of stimuli, behaviors, rewards).
9. Describe at least three important characteristics of realistic short-term goal setting.
10. Describe at least three different ways for influencing athletes to psych up for a competition.
11. Should all athletes be taught to psych up? Why?
12. Describe two different types of thoughts that athletes might deliberately program to occur during competition.
13. What is meant by imagery or mental rehearsal? According to Simek and O'Brien, why might mental rehearsal seem to help performance?

Mini-Lab Exercises

1. Consider a sport that you played or would like to coach. Describe three different examples of psych-out attempts that athletes who play that sport often show to try to psych out the opposition.
2. Considering your answer to question 1, describe a plausible treatment strategy that you might teach an athlete to help that athlete minimize the effects of psych-out attempts by the opposition.
3. Consider the guidelines for controlling thought content during competition (Sports Psyching Strategy No. 7). Now consider a sport that you have played or would like to coach. In two or three pages, describe a set of self-statements and planned thought content that an athlete could practice while playing that particular sport.

References

Blimkie. J.. Gowan. G.. Patterson. P.. and Wood. N. (1984). Sport and psychology: What ethics suggest about practice. Sports Science Periodical on Research and Technology in Sport. Ottawa, Ontario, Canada: Coaching Association of Canada.

Botterill. C.B. (1983). Goal-setting for athletes. with examples from hockey. In G.L. Martin and D. Hrycaiko. eds. Behavior modification and coaching: Principles, procedures and research. Springfield. Ill.: Charles C Thomas, pp 67-85.

Coaching theory level 3 (1981). National Coaching Certification Program. Ottawa, Ontario, Canada: Coaching Association of Canada.

Gowan. G.R.. Botterill. C.B.. and Blimkie. C.J. (1979). Bridging the gap between sport science and sport practice. In P. Klavora and J. Daniel. eds. Coach. athlete and the sport psychologist. Toronto. Ontario. Canada: School of Physical and Health Education. University of Toronto.

Harris. D.V.. and Harris. D.L. (1984). Athletes' guide to sports psychology: Mental skills for physical people. New York: Leisure Press.

Hrycaiko. D.. and Martin. G.L. (1983). Effective behavioral coaching: Current status and suggestions for future research. In G.L. Martin and D. Hrycaiko. eds. Behavior modification and coaching: Principles, procedures and research. Springfield. Ill.: Charles C Thomas.

Kirschenbaum. D.S.. and Bale. R.M. (1980). Cognitive behavioral skills in golf: Brain power golf. In R.M. Suinn. ed. Psychology and sports: Methods and applications. Minneapolis: Burgess.

Martin. G.L. (in press). Applied behavior analysis in sport and physical education: Past. present. and future. In L. Hamerlynck and R.P. West. eds. Designs for excellence in education: Legacy of B.F. Skinner. Hillsdale. N.J.: Lawrence Erlbaum Associates.

Martin. G.L.. and Hrycaiko. D.. eds. (1983). Behavior modification and coaching: Principles. procedures and research. Springfield. Ill.: Charles C Thomas.

Martin. G.L.. and Pear. J.J. (1983). Behavior modification: What it is and how to do it. 2nd ed. Englewood Cliffs. N.J.: Prentice-Hall.

Meichenbaum. D.H. (1977). Cognitive behavior modification: An integrative approach. New York: Plenum.

Newman. S. (1982). Roger Neilson. Coach. Rev. 5:6-12.

Nicklaus. J. (1974). Golf my way. New York: Simon & Shuster.

Nideffer. R. (1981). The ethics and practice of applied sport psychology. Ithaca. N.Y.: Mouvement Publications.

Rushall. B.S. (1976). A direction for contemporary sports psychology. Can. J. Appl. Sport Sci. 1:13-21.

Rushall. B.S. (1979). Psyching in sports. London: Pelham.

Simek. T.C.. and O'Brien. R.M. (1981). Total golf: A behavioral approach to lowering your score and getting more out of your game. Huntington, N.Y.: B-Mod Associates.

Silva. J.M. III. and Weinberg. R.S.. eds. (1984). Psychological foundations of sport. Champaign. Ill.: Human Kinetics Publishers.

Tutko. T.. and Tosi. U. (1976). Sports psyching: Playing your best game all of the time. Los Angeles: J.P. Tarcher.

Weinberg. R.S. (1982). The relationship between mental preparation strategies and motor performance: A review and critique. Quest 33(2):196--213.

Weinberg. R.S. (1984). Mental preparation strategies. In J.M. Silva III and R.S. Weinberg. eds. Psychological foundations of sport. Champaign. Ill.: Human Kinetics Publishers.

Wiggins, D.K. (1984). The history of sports psychology in North America. In J.M. Silva III and R.S. Weinberg, eds. Psychological foundations of sport. Champaign, Ill.: Human Kinetics Publishers.

Ziegler, S. (1980). Applied behavior analysis: From assessment to behavioral programming. In P. Klavora and K.A. Whipper, eds. Psychological and sociological factors in sport. Toronto, Ontario, Canada: Publications Division, University of Toronto.

Selected Readings

Bird, A.M., and Cripe, B. (1986). Psychology and sport behavior. St. Louis: Times Mirror/Mosby College Publishing.

Nideffer, R.M. (1985). Athletes' guide to mental training. Champaign, Ill.: Human Kinetics Publishers.

Orlick, T. (1980). In pursuit of excellence. Ottawa, Ontario, Canada: Coaching Association of Canada.

Orlick, T., Partington, J.T., and Salmela, J.H., eds. (1983). Mental training for coaches and athletes. Ottawa, Ontario, Canada: Coaching Association of Canada.

Pre-Season Planning and Post-Season Evaluation

"You can't see the forest for the trees." You've no doubt heard that expression. And there is some truth to it. In Chapter 2 we outlined some general characteristics of effective behavioral coaching. In some respects, that was kind of like a map of the forest. Since then, however, we've been giving you lots of trees—lots of specific procedures and strategies for effectively influencing athletic behavior in desirable directions. Things like behavioral assessment; the specifics of conditioning and nutrition; checklists for teaching new skills, decreasing errors, motivating athletes, and decreasing problem behaviors; and even a detailed program of sports psyching. But what about some overall goals for the team? No, we don't mean winning the league championship. We're talking about an overview of the four main areas of athletic preparation: physical, technical, tactical, and psychological.

Top executives spend a lot of time planning. The higher up in the organization they are, the more time they are likely to spend on planning. In many respects, coaches are like top executives. They have assistants. They control budgets. They are responsible for directing the organization (i.e., team). And like executives, they must do a considerable amount of planning. Some aspects of pre-season planning are discussed in the following chapters. In Chapter 11 we talk about preparing some sample practice plans. In Chapter 12 we offer some guidelines for selecting and managing assistant coaches, team managers, and team captains. And then there's the money problem. Chapter 13 presents guidelines for preparing and administering a budget, purchasing and caring for equipment, and developing and caring for the home facility. Chapter 14 presents a system for putting all this planning to good use. It will introduce a planning calendar to regularly prompt you to take the steps necessary to accomplish all of your goals in order to maximize your pay-offs during the coming year. In this chapter, we restrict the discussion to pre-season planning to maximally prepare your athletes.

There are so many subcomponents to athletic preparation that it's easy to get lost in specifics. During the off-season, it's very helpful for a coach to consider the subcomponents of athletic preparation within an overall perspective. That's what this chapter is all about.

To plan for the season, identify a realistic set of subgoals within each of the four major areas of physical, technical, tactical, and psychological preparation. We will illustrate the steps that a coach might take with reference to pre-season planning in these four areas for a high school boys basketball team. The procedures, however, could be applied to coaching any sport. Now let's consider the process in more detail.

SETTING GOALS FOR PHYSICAL PREPARATION OF ATHLETES

What are the important physical factors in your sport? In which of the various subcategories of physical conditioning should you plan for improvements during the coming season? No, we're not thinking about recruiting a couple of 7-footers for the basketball team. Rather, considering the athletes from last year that will be returning to the team, the rookies that will probably be trying out, the relative strengths of some of the opposition that you will be playing against— where should you put emphasis in the conditioning and nutrition programs? The first step is to make a list of the physical factors necessary for the development of the athletes, such as shown in Fig. 10-1 for high school basketball players.

Next, consider the "importance for improvement" scale in Fig. 10-1. You are not asking which of these factors are important for the sport. Obviously, they're all important. Rather, you want to identify which of the factors require special attention during the coming season. For example, the basketball coach may have been unhappy with the speed of the fast break last year. Or perhaps the team played poorly during the second half in many games, and must build more endurance. Maybe some of the team members loaded up on junk foods at tournaments, and require information and guidance about nutrition and the importance of the pregame meal.

The next step is to consider when during the season the important factors should be emphasized (Fig. 10-1).

SETTING GOALS FOR TECHNICAL PREPARATION OF ATHLETES

How do your athletes perform on the fundamentals? In addition to an appropriate level of physical fitness, skilled performance in any sport requires mastery of some basic skills. The next step in pre-season planning is to consider the fundamental skills and their important variations for the sport that you coach. For example, in the technical area for high school basketball, fundamentals include footwork, dribbling, passing, receiving, shooting, and rebounding. Each of these can

Physical Factors for Development of
High School Basketball Players _____

	Relative Importance as Goal for Improvement			When Will Factor Receive Attention?				Priority
	Low	Medium	High	Off-Season	Pre-Season	Mid-Season	Peak Season	
Speed (anaerobic lactic system)	1 2 3 4 5							
Quickness (anaerobic alactic system)	1 2 3 4 5							
Endurance (aerobic conditioning)	1 2 3 4 5							
Recovery (aerobic conditioning)	1 2 3 4 5							
Strength for rebounding	1 2 3 4 5							
Strength for jumping	1 2 3 4 5							
General nutrition for practice energy	1 2 3 4 5							
Specific nutrition for games and tournaments	1 2 3 4 5							

FIGURE 10-1

be further divided into a number of important subskills. For example, passing could include chest, two-hand overhead, bounce, baseball, hook, and hand off. For most sports, detailed lists of fundamental skills are available in books and are available in most book stores.

Once you have prepared a detailed list of the technical factors, use the scale indicated in Fig. 10-2 to assess their relative importance as goals for improvement. Again, remember that assigning a skill a value of 1 (low importance) does not mean that that skill is unimportant for your players. It simply means that, for various reasons, you are not identifying it as an area of high priority for emphasis during the coming season. After you have assessed the relative importance of the various factors for emphasis during the coming season, indicate when during the season the particular factors will receive attention.

SETTING GOALS FOR TACTICAL PREPARATION
OF ATHLETES

Tactical factors are a bit more difficult to plan ahead of time than are physical and technical factors, at least in certain sports. To some extent, offensive and defensive strategies will depend on the opposition. They also depend, in some sports, on the personnel available on a particular team. For example, in basketball, a coach with a smaller, faster team is likely to emphasize a fast break offense and frequent full court press. A taller but slower team might want to slow the game down and emphasize ball control. In spite of that, there will no doubt remain a variety of maneuvers and team tactics that can be targeted as goals for improvement.

As with technical preparation, the first step is to make a detailed list of the various maneuvers and team tactics that characterize the sport. If you coach an individual sport, then the tactical strategies must be highly individualized to capitalize on the strengths of the individual athletes.

After you have prepared a list of tactical factors for yo'ır sport (such as those in Fig. 10-3 for basketball), rate their relative importance as goals for improvement, and target when during the season they will be emphasized.

SETTING GOALS FOR PSYCHOLOGICAL PREPARATION
OF ATHLETES

In Chapter 9 we described eight strategies for "sports psyching." We argued that athletes who have mastered a variety of psychological coping skills are much less likely to be influenced by various distractors during competition, and therefore are much more likely to perform up to their full potential. Which of those sports psyching strategies might be helpful for your athletes in the sport that you coach? We encourage you to examine each of the strategies in Chapter 9 and think about how they might be adapted to your sport. With respect to high school and college basketball, for example, a combination of relaxation and mental rehearsal procedures have been demonstrated to improve free throw performance (Hall and Erffmeyer, 1983; Lane, 1980; Silva, 1982). What about coping self-statements? Scott Martin, a point guard for the University of Manitoba Varsity Men's Basketball team, identified five different game situations that sometimes disrupted his performance. To help him minimize the effects of those, he identified and practiced the following coping self-statements:

Text continued on p. 250.

Technical Factors for Development of High School Bask

	Relative Importance as Goal for Improvement					When Will Factor Receive Attention?				Priority
	Low		Medium		High	Off-Season	Pre-Season	Mid-Season	Peak Season	
Footwork										
Forward/backward running	1	2	3	4	5					
Stopping/starting	1	2	3	4	5					
Change of direction	1	2	3	4	5					
Shuffling/sliding	1	2	3	4	5					
Pivoting										
Lead-up	1	2	3	4	5					
Front	1	2	3	4	5					
Reverse	1	2	3	4	5					
Offensive ready position	1	2	3	4	5					
Defensive stance	1	2	3	4	5					
Combination moves	1	2	3	4	5					
Dribbling										
Ball familiarization	1	2	3	4	5					
Right/left hand	1	2	3	4	5					
Stop/start	1	2	3	4	5					
Alternate hands	1	2	3	4	5					
Front crossover	1	2	3	4	5					
Change of direction	1	2	3	4	5					
Reverse (spin)	1	2	3	4	5					
Crab	1	2	3	4	5					
Change of pace	1	2	3	4	5					
Between legs	1	2	3	4	5					
Behind back	1	2	3	4	5					
Passing										
Chest	1	2	3	4	5					
Two-hand overhead	1	2	3	4	5					
Bounce	1	2	3	4	5					
Baseball	1	2	3	4	5					
Hook	1	2	3	4	5					
Handoff	1	2	3	4	5					

From Basketball Development Model.

FIGURE 10-2

	Relative Importance as Goal for Improvement					When Will Factor Receive Attention?				Priority
	Low		Medium		High	Off-Season	Pre-Season	Mid-Season	Peak Season	

Receiving

Funnel	1	2	3	4	5					
Block-and-trap	1	2	3	4	5					

Shooting

One-hand set shot	1	2	3	4	5					
Lay-up	1	2	3	4	5					
Jump shot	1	2	3	4	5					
Reverse lay-up	1	2	3	4	5					
Crossover lay-up	1	2	3	4	5					
Power lay-up	1	2	3	4	5					
Hook	1	2	3	4	5					
Jump hook	1	2	3	4	5					
Tipping	1	2	3	4	5					
Dunking	1	2	3	4	5					

Rebounding

Offensive positioning	1	2	3	4	5					
Defensive										
Footwork										
Front turn	1	2	3	4	5					
Reverse	1	2	3	4	5					
Securing ball	1	2	3	4	5					
Outlet pass	1	2	3	4	5					
Ball side	1	2	3	4	5					
Off side	1	2	3	4	5					
Vs. shooter	1	2	3	4	5					
Vs. post player	1	2	3	4	5					
From overplay position	1	2	3	4	5					

Tactical Factors for Development of High School Basket

	Relative Importance as Goal for Improvement					When Will Factor Receive Attention?				Priority
	Low		Medium		High	Off-Season	Pre-Season	Mid-Season	Peak Season	
Team Offense										
1. *Player maneuvers*										
Square-up	1	2	3	4	5					
Quick step	1	2	3	4	5					
Jab step	1	2	3	4	5					
Leveling	1	2	3	4	5					
Post play	1	2	3	4	5					
Cutting	1	2	3	4	5					
2. *Player maneuvers*										
Give and go	1	2	3	4	5					
Screen on ball	1	2	3	4	5					
Back door	1	2	3	4	5					
Pass and follow	1	2	3	4	5					
3. *Player maneuvers*										
Screen away from ball	1	2	3	4	5					
Floor balance (rotation)	1	2	3	4	5					
Ball movement (reversal)	1	2	3	4	5					
Downscreens	1	2	3	4	5					
Horizontal screens	1	2	3	4	5					
5. *Player maneuvers*										
Player positioning	1	2	3	4	5					
Floor balance	1	2	3	4	5					
Transition	1	2	3	4	5					
Advantage situations	1	2	3	4	5					
Special situations										
• Jump ball	1	2	3	4	5					
• Throw-in	1	2	3	4	5					
• Free throw	1	2	3	4	5					
Fast break										
• By number	1	2	3	4	5					
• By rules	1	2	3	4	5					
• By concepts	1	2	3	4	5					
Principles of man-to-man	1	2	3	4	5					
Principles of zone	1	2	3	4	5					
Vs. man-to-man presses	1	2	3	4	5					
Maneuvers complementing post play	1	2	3	4	5					
Vs. special defenses	1	2	3	4	5					
Vs. zone presses	1	2	3	4	5					
Early offense	1	2	3	4	5					
Delay offense	1	2	3	4	5					

From Basketball Development Model.

FIGURE 10-3

	Relative Importance as Goal for Improvement			When Will Factor Receive Attention?				Priority
	Low	Medium	High	Off-Season	Pre-Season	Mid-Season	Peak Season	

Team Defense

1. *Player maneuvers*
   Vs. player with ball

• Passer	1 2 3 4 5							
• Dribbler	1 2 3 4 5							
• Shooter	1 2 3 4 5							
Vs. player without ball	1 2 3 4 5							
Vs. post	1 2 3 4 5							

2. *Player maneuvers*

Vs. give and go	1 2 3 4 5							
Vs. screen on ball	1 2 3 4 5							
Vs. back door	1 2 3 4 5							
Vs. ball cuts	1 2 3 4 5							
Help and recover	1 2 3 4 5							
Deny defense	1 2 3 4 5							

5. *Player maneuvers*

Help concept/position	1 2 3 4 5							
Ball side vs. help side	1 2 3 4 5							
Vs. special situations								
• Jump ball	1 2 3 4 5							
• Throw-in	1 2 3 4 5							
• Free throw	1 2 3 4 5							
Vs. outnumbering situation	1 2 3 4 5							
Principles of man-to-man	1 2 3 4 5							
Principles of zone	1 2 3 4 5							
Forcing/influencing	1 2 3 4 5							
Overplay	1 2 3 4 5							
Double teaming	1 2 3 4 5							
Principles of pressing								
• Man-to-man	1 2 3 4 5							
• Zone	1 2 3 4 5							
Vs. delay game	1 2 3 4 5							
Trapping zones	1 2 3 4 5							
Match-up zones	1 2 3 4 5							
Combination defenses								
• Box and 1	1 2 3 4 5							
• Diamond and 1	1 2 3 4 5							
• Triangle and 2	1 2 3 4 5							
Denying	1 2 3 4 5							
Transitions	1 2 3 4 5							

Situation	Coping Self-Statements
Referee doesn't call a foul when you think he should.	"So what, play the game." "I got away with one earlier." "Last time he didn't even foul me, and the referee called it."
Teammate doesn't pass you the ball when you're wide open, or you should be getting the ball (e.g., open for an easy shot, or don't get the ball to lead the break)	"There are four other people on the floor." "You make mistakes, too." "Quit whining, and play." "Keep working to get open" (i.e., play your own game).
You make a mistake (e.g., a poor turn-over or a foul).	"Concentrate and play." "Why worry about it? It doesn't help." "Get back on defense."
You shoot an air ball or a bad shot.	"Big deal. I'll still hit my percentage." "Get back on defense." "Square-up and form." "I'm still great."
A teammate makes a mistake.	"Get back on defense." "I make mistakes, too." "Worry about your own game."

What about the problem of motivation for practices? Do you re-member Jim Dawson, the coach of the junior high school basketball team in Columbus, in Chapter 1? Jim and Dr. Daryl Siedentop devel-oped a highly effective motivational system for improving performance in lay-up drills, jump shooting drills, free throw drills, and being a "team player" at daily practices. What about motivation to improve consistency of key behaviors in games? Continuing with our example of basketball, Dale Bradshaw, a highly respected high school coach in Canada, assigned point values to a variety of basketball behaviors as follows (Bradshaw, 1984):

Field goals made	+2
Field goals attempted	−0.8
Free throws made	+1
Free throws missed	−1
Assists	+1
Defensive rebounds	+0.75
Offensive rebounds	+1
Deflections	+0.5
Recoveries of loose balls	+1
Steals	+2
Charges drawn	+3
Blocked shots	+1
Jump balls won	+1
Tie-ups for held balls	+0.5
Turnovers	−2

Coach Bradshaw states, "Coaches who use this system believe it helps motivate their players by (1) assigning a final numerical grade to their game, (2) emphasizing the importance of role playing to the final grade, (3) providing objective data for discussion, and (4) establishing baselines for goal setting. These coaches also believe it helps motivate their feeder programs, because young players realize coaches are looking for complete players, not just scorers" (Bradshaw, 1984, pp. 52-53).

The psychological factors that might be especially appropriate for high school basketball coaches to emphasize are listed in Fig. 10-4.

As with other factors, identify those that are priority goals for improvement. Then determine when during the season those goals will receive emphasis.

Psychological Factors for Development of High School Basketball Players

	Relative Importance as Goal for Improvement			When Will Factor Receive Attention?				Priority
	Low	Medium	High	Off-Season	Pre-Season	Mid-Season	Peak Season	
Centering for foul shooting	1	2 3	4 5					
Mental rehearsal for foul shooting	1	2 3	4 5					
Centering and coping self-statements so as not to dwell on mistakes	1	2 3	4 5					
Relaxation training to control nervousness	1	2 3	4 5					
Realistic goal setting to maintain intensity	1	2 3	4 5					
Team building sessions	1	2 3	4 5					
Team player awards for practices and games	1	2 3	4 5					
Basketball behavior statistics for motivation during games and practices	1	2 3	4 5					
Psyching strategies for games	1	2 3	4 5					

FIGURE 10-4

ADDITIONAL STEPS IN PRE-SEASON PLANNING

You now have a detailed list of subcomponents in the areas of physical, technical, tactical, and psychological preparation of your team that require emphasis during the coming season. These objectives are somewhat general at this point, and are attainable over a period of time varying from a few practices to a year. The next step is to prioritize the objectives across the four major areas of athletic preparation. Consider all of the items that you have given a value of either 4 or 5 in terms of their relative importance as goals for improvement. Chances are, you won't be able to accomplish everything. It is therefore important to arrange them in order of importance. If you have set up your lists similar to those in Figs. 10-1 through 10-4, use the column on the right-hand side to indicate the relative priority of the items assigned a 4 or 5 value. Put a number 1 beside the top priority item in the right-hand column; put a number 2 beside the second priority item; and so on.

Once you have identified and prioritized goals for the season, you are ready for some additional input. How do your assistants feel about

FIGURE 10-5
Involvement of assistant coaches is important to successful pre-season planning.

your list of priorities? Involvement of assistant coaches is important to pre-season planning (Fig. 10-5).

What about the athletes themselves? Because your pre-season planning is likely to be done during the off-season, it may not be possible to have input from all of the athletes that you will be coaching. However, it is likely that you can arrange for a meeting with some of the returning athletes. As stated by Botterill, "In addition to analyzing your own goals, priorities, and expectations, the good coach wants to discover the goals, priorities, and expectations of his/her athletes" (Botterill, 1983, p. 68).

Once you have a concensus about specific goals, subsequent steps include task analyzing the goals, setting performance standards, and identifying strategies for accomplishing those goals. These three steps are discussed in Chapters 4 through 7, and 11. If you follow the guidelines presented, they will enhance the chances that you will accomplish the goals that you have identified in this chapter.

POST-SEASON EVALUATION

Did you have a winning season? There's no doubt that's the yardstick by which many people will evaluate the success of your season. The win-loss record is not unimportant, but it should by no means be the only statistic to evaluate the success of a season. An effective behavioral coach evaluates a season by collecting detailed information from a number of sources.

Athletes

We encourage you to ask your athletes to evaluate the season in two respects. First, to help them focus on specific skills that were goals in the first place, we recommend that you prepare questionnaires based on the components listed in Figs. 10-1 through 10-4. For example, the questionnaire with respect to physical factors for the high school basketball team might be constructed as shown in Fig. 10-6.

In addition to examining how the athletes feel about the extent to which specific goals were accomplished, and their suggestions for future directions, it is often valuable for a coach to evaluate how the athletes feel about a number of general characteristics about you as a coach. An assessment tool that is very useful for that purpose is the Coach Evaluation Questionnaire developed by Rushall and Wiznuk (1985; Fig. 10-7). Their questionnaire has been shown to be a valid, reliable, and standardized instrument capable of providing useful information to the coach as well as a total score that can be interpreted by a coach as a measure of how much of the "ideal" coach exists in himself or herself.

If you coach younger athletes, you will not want to overwhelm them with a detailed questionnaire that they have difficulty relating to. A questionnaire developed by the National Coaching Certification Program that can be used to assess how young athletes feel about their season with you as a coach is presented in Fig. 10-8.

After you have had a chance to examine the evaluations by your athletes, we encourage you to schedule a post-season rap session with them. This should be done within a couple of weeks after the final

Post-Season Questionnaire on Physical Factors for Development of High School Basketball Players

Consider the following factors concerning conditioning and nutrition. Consider how well we performed during the past season. In the middle column, circle the number that indicates how well you think we did with respect to each of the factors listed. In the right-hand column, circle the number that indicates whether that factor needs to be improved for next year.

	How Well Did We Do During Past Season?			Which Factors Do We Need to Improve for Next Year?		
	Very Poorly	So-So	Very Well	Definitely Not	To Some Extent	Definitely Yes
Speed (anaerobic lactic system)	1	2 3	4 5	1	2 3	4 5
Quickness (anaerobic alactic system)	1	2 3	4 5	1	2 3	4 5
Endurance (aerobic conditioning)	1	2 3	4 5	1	2 3	4 5
Recovery (aerobic conditioning)	1	2 3	4 5	1	2 3	4 5
Strength for rebounding	1	2 3	4 5	1	2 3	4 5
Strength for jumping	1	2 3	4 5	1	2 3	4 5
General nutrition for practice energy	1	2 3	4 5	1	2 3	4 5
Specific nutrition for games and tournaments	1	2 3	4 5	1	2 3	4 5

FIGURE 10-6

Questions Contained in
Coach Evaluation Questionnaire

1. The coach is dedicated to the sport.
2. The coach is patient.
3. The coach communicates with the athletes.
4. The coach uses abusive and foul language.
5. The coach dresses appropriately. setting a good example for athletes to follow.
6. The coach is a source of motivation.
7. The coach's judgment is based on reasoning and/or is well thought out.
8. The coach is strict.
9. The coach gives attention to each athlete.
10. The coach encourages athletes even after a loss or defeat in competition.
11. The coach's physical appearance sets a good example for the athletes.
12. The coach has a sense of humour.
13. I feel that I can trust the coach.
14. I like the coach.
15. I respect the coach.
16. The coach is interested in me as a person.
17. The coach finds ways to make all the athletes feel good about themselves.
18. At meetings of athletes. the coach gives everyone a chance to make their opinions known.
19. The coach sets a positive example during competitions.
20. The coach's conduct toward athletes at competitions is sportsmanlike.
21. The coach's conduct toward officials at competitions is sportsmanlike.
22. The coach encourages social activities for the athletes.
23. The coach is interested in the athlete's schoolwork or occupation.
24. The coach provides training sessions that are organized.
25. The coach is in command during practice.
26. The coach is concerned about the health and safety of the athletes during practice.
27. The coach makes the best use of the time available for practice.
28. The coach interacts with each athlete at training.
29. The coach encourages athletes to keep logbooks so that they can measure their own improvement.
30. The coach makes sure the athletes are physically prepared for each competition.
31. The coach's instructions are easily understood.
32. The goals that the coach sets for the athletes are possible to achieve.
33. After a performance. the coach indicates the good part of the performance but also points out the areas that could be improved upon.
34. The coach knows how to teach difficult skills.
35. The coach attends clinics and workshops to stay abreast of new coaching methods.
36. The coach knows when to use discipline and when not to.

From Rushall. B.S., and Wiznuk. K.

FIGURE 10-7

Post-Season Questionnaire for
Young Athletes

1. Think back to what you expected at the beginning of the season. Were your expectations met? Not met? Surpassed?

2. Think back to what you thought you would have to put into the season. Did you do about what you expected? More? Less?

3. Did you improve your skills in any way over the season?

4. What did you like best about this season?

5. What did you like least?

6. Do you have any suggestions for improving anything (practice. games. coach. other players)?

7. On a scale from 1 to 10 (10 being the best). rate how satisfied you were:

	Not very satisfied	1 2 3 4 5 6 7 8 9 10	Extremely satisfied
Team		1 2 3 4 5 6 7 8 9 10	
Coach		1 2 3 4 5 6 7 8 9 10	
What you learned		1 2 3 4 5 6 7 8 9 10	
How much fun you had		1 2 3 4 5 6 7 8 9 10	

Comments: _____

_____

_____

8. Are you going to play (compete) again next year?

From the National Coaching Certification Manual.

FIGURE 10-8

competition of the season. If you let it go much longer than that, the athletes will be dispersing or involved in other activities. At your rap session, point out all the good things and improvements that you witnessed over the season. Emphasizing mistakes or problems at this point can have absolutely no benefit for the past season. It's already finished. Leave on a positive note so that athletes look forward to the next season.

By permission of Johnny Hart and News America Syndicate.

You can also use the rap session to distribute off-season goals and training programs to various individuals. This is an ideal time to emphasize to the athletes that all of the fitness and strength gains they have made can be maintained with a certain amount of exercise during the off-season. Some athletes will want to improve. Depending on the age and commitment of your athletes, you may want to identify specific days by which they return progress notes to you during the off-season so that you can monitor their progress.

Parents

As a general rule, the younger the athletes the more time you should spend developing a good working relationship with their parents. In Chapter 16 we strongly advise that you hold a parent clinic or orientation session at the beginning of the season to coincide with athletics registration. We also advise that you formally ask parents for feedback at the end of the season. A useful evaluation form for that purpose can be found in Martens et al. (1981).

SOME FINAL THOUGHTS ON PRE-SEASON PLANNING

It is widely recognized that pre-season goal setting can have a number of potential benefits. Botterill (1978:55) suggests that effective pre-season goal setting can contribute to the following:

Clarified goals and priorities—everyone has a better idea as to what the season or activity is all about and why it is important.

Increased commitment and motivation toward group goals.

Fairly immediate success because many specific achievable goals (other than just winning games) have been identified.

Improvement in the athletes' self-confidence and in group morale.

The development of psychological maturity in athletes, which is reflected in self-discipline and skills in self-control and self-management.

Increased poise and improved abilities to adapt, cope, "keep things in perspective," and concentrate on the right things.

The elimination and prevention of problem behaviors.

Leadership usually becomes less autocratic and much more enjoyable and effective.

Increased appreciation of the importance of planning and goal setting in any activity.

Increased empathy and respect for the rights and feelings of others.

Improved communication and understanding among all parties concerned and control over "unintentional" problem behavior.

Happier athletes, better performance, and much more fun.

In addition to guidelines for pre-season goal setting in sport environments, as proposed by Botterill and others, it is useful to examine the research that has been done on goal setting as a promising strategy for improving performance in organizational settings. After all, an athletic team is an organization, and a coach is often in the position of organizational behavior manager. A recent review of research on goal setting in organizational behavior management (Fellner and Sulzer-Azaroff, 1984) makes it possible for us to identify several guidelines that coaches should keep in mind when they attempt to pursue the pre-season goals that they have set according to the guidelines in this chapter. First, goals are more likely to be met if they are specific rather than a "do your best" reminder. Second, goal setting in combination with feedback on degree of goal attainment is likely to be more effective than either goal setting alone or feedback alone. Third, self-selected goals are likely to be at least as effective for improving performance— and sometimes more effective—than are externally imposed goals. Further research needs to be done on all of these variables in athletic settings; however, the best current advice for coaches is to *involve athletes* in setting *specific goals,* and provide *frequent feedback* for approximations of goal attainment.

SUMMARY

Successful coaches, like top executives, must spend a considerable amount of time on planning. To plan for the season, the coach should identify a realistic set of subgoals within each of the four major areas of physical, technical, tactical, and psychological preparation. Each subgoal should be assessed for relative importance as a goal for improvement during the coming season. The coach should further target when during the season that the high-priority subgoals will be emphasized. A further step is to obtain a consensus about the importance of the subgoals from the assistant coaches and from the athletes. Athlete input is critical for goal-attainment.

An important companion of pre-season goal setting is post-season evaluation. At the end of the season, coaches are encouraged to use formal questionnaires to obtain the athletes' views of their progress over the season and their assessment of a number of general characteristics of the coach. The coach should conclude with a post-season rap session with the athletes, to point out good things and improvements that occurred during the season and to distribute off-season goals and training programs. Finally, coaches working with young athletes are encouraged to obtain post-season feedback from the parents as well.

Coach's Checklist

A list of the steps that you might follow in effective pre-season planning and post-season evaluation is presented in Fig. 10-9. We suggest that you use the list as a continued reminder sheet to ensure that you practice all of the steps.

Review Questions

1. Suppose that you have prepared a detailed list of the subcomponents in the areas of physical, technical, tactical, and psychological preparation for your athletes as illustrated in this chapter for high school basketball. Outline some additional steps that you might take in pre-season planning.
2. In two or three sentences each, describe the different types of questionnaires that you might administer to your athletes to aid you in post-season evaluation.
3. Describe the kinds of things that you might do in a post-season rap session with your athletes.
4. What recommendations can we draw from research on goal setting in organizational behavior management that might help in further refining pre-season planning?

COACH'S CHECKLIST

Pre-Season Planning and Post-Season Evaluation ___

	Date Completed
Pre-Season Planning	
1. Physical preparation for your athletes	
a. Prepare checklist of physical factors important for your athletes (see Fig. 10-1).	
b. Assess their relative importance as goals for improvement.	
c. Identify when during season various factors will receive attention.	
2. Technical factors	
a. Prepare list of fundamental skills and techniques important for athletes that you coach (see Fig. 10-2).	
b. Assess their relative importance as goals for improvement.	
c. Identify when during season various factors will receive attention.	
3. Tactical factors	
a. Prepare list of offensive and defensive strategies appropriate for competition for athletes that you coach (see Fig. 10-3).	
b. Assess their relative importance as goals for improvement.	
c. Identify when during season various factors will receive attention.	
4. Psychological factors	
a. Prepare list of sports psyching and motivational techniques that you might use to help athletes that you coach (see Fig. 10-4).	
b. Assess their relative importance as goals for improvement.	
c. Identify when during season various factors will receive attention.	
5. Reconsider all factors above that were rated as either 4 or 5 in terms of their relative importance. Compare all of those factors against each and prioritize them in terms of their relative importance as goals for improvement.	

FIGURE 10-9

	Date Completed
6. Schedule meeting with some of the seniors or returning athletes and ask for their opinions as to your list of priorities.	
7. Schedule meeting with your assistant coaches and ask for their opinions with respect to your list of priorities.	
8. Reassess your priorities for improvement on basis of combined rankings from yourself. your athletes. and your assistants.	
9. Review guidelines in Chapters 11 through 14 and plan to take steps to accomplish your goals.	

Post-Season Evaluation

1. Prepare checklists (see Figs. 10-6 through 10-8) to be used by you. your assistants. and your athletes to evaluate your success in meeting the goals that you set in your pre-season planning.
2. Complete assessments yourself.
3. Ask your assistants to complete assessments.
4. Ask your athletes to complete assessments.
5. Within approximately 2 weeks after end of season. hold post-season rap session with your athletes.
   a. Summarize good things and improvements that occurred during season.
   b. Distribute information about off-season programming.
6. If you coach young athletes. ask parents to complete post-season questionnaire to give you feedback.
7. Use post-season evaluations to make preliminary list of areas and subcategories in which you would like to improve in following season.

Mini-Lab Exercises

1. Consider a sport that you have played or would like to coach. What are the important physical factors for that sport? Organize those factors in a table similar to the example illustrated for basketball in Fig. 10-1.
2. For the sport that you chose in question 1, what are the important technical factors (fundamental skills) for the age group of the athletes that you would like to coach? Arrange them in a table similar to the illustration for the technical factors of high school basketball players listed in Fig. 10-2.
3. For the sport and the age group of athletes that you choose in question 2, what are important offensive and defensive tactics that those athletes should be able to execute in competitions? Arrange them in a table similar to the illustration of tactical factors for high-school basketball shown in Fig. 10-3.
4. Consider the motivational system described by Dale Bradshaw in which a variety of basketball behaviors were assigned point values. Develop a similar system for competitions for the sport that you chose above; that is, prepare a list of key behaviors for competitions and assign to them what you consider to be plausible point values representing their relative importance.
5. For the sport that you chose, prepare a list of important sports psychology strategies that might be helpful for the athletes. Arrange them in a table similar to the illustration of psychological factors for high school basketball players listed in Fig. 10-4.

References

Botterill, C. (1978). Psychology of coaching. Coaching Review 1:46-65.

Botterill, C. (1983). Goal setting for athletes, with examples from hockey. In G.L. Martin and D. Hrycaiko, eds. Behavior modification and coaching: Principles, procedures and research. Springfield, Ill.: Charles C Thomas.

Bradshaw, B. (1984). Motivation through basketball statistics. Coaching Review 7:52-54.

Coaching theory level 2 (1979). National Coaching Certification Program. Ottawa, Ontario, Canada: Coaching Association of Canada.

Fellner, D.J., and Sulzer-Azaroff, B. (1984). A behavioral analysis of goal-setting. Journal of Organizational Behavior Management 6:33-52.

Hall, E.G., and Erffmeyer, E.S. (1983). The effect of visuo-motor behavior rehearsal with video taped modeling on free throw accuracy of inter-collegiate female basketball players. Journal of Sport Psychology 5:343-346.

Lane, J.F. (1980). Improving athlete performance through visual motor behavior rehearsal. In R. M. Suinn, ed. Psychology in sports: Methods and applications. Minneapolis: Burgess Publishing.

Martens, R., Christina, R.W., Harvey, J.S. Jr., and Sharkey, B.J. (1981). Coaching young athletes. Champaign, Ill.: Human Kinetics Publishers.

Rushall, B.S., and Wiznak, K. (1985). Athletes' assessment of the coach: the coach evaluation questionnaire. Canadian Journal of Applied Sport Sciences **10**:157-161.

Silva. J.M. III. (1982). Competitive sport environments: Performance enhancement through cognitive intervention. Behavior Modification **4**:443-463.

Selected Readings

Albrecht. K. (1978). Successful management by objectives: An action manual. Englewood Cliffs. N.J.: Prentice-Hall.

Creel, J. (1980). Objectives for winning. Athletic Journal **60**:42, 64.

Hogue. M. (1980). Awards and rewards. Coaching: Women's Athletics **6**:18-19.

Locke. E.A.. and Latham. G.P. (1985). The application of goal setting to sports. Journal of Sport Psychology **7**:205-222.

O'Block. F.R.. and Evans. F.H. (1984). Goal-setting as a motivational technique. In J.M. Silva III and R.S. Weinberg. eds. Psychological foundations of sport. Champaign. Ill.: Human Kinetics Publishers.

11

Planning and Managing Practices

Carefully planned and well-managed practices have a number of benefits, including more efficient use of practice time by both coaches and athletes; increased commitment and motivation by the athletes to achieve practice objectives; increased respect for the coaches by the athletes; more fun for the athletes; prevention of problem behaviors; better alternation and sequencing of conditioning, technical, and tactical drills across practices; and an increased likelihood of meeting the season's goals. All too often, unfortunately, many coaches appear to just "wing it" at practices. However, as George Allen, the former Washington Redskins' coach, said, "Practice doesn't make perfect. Perfect practice makes perfect." In this chapter, we discuss planning and writing out the overall content of practices, and managing them efficiently and effectively.

CROCK by Rechin & Wilder © by and permission of News America Syndicate.

When scheduling practices, the following need to be considered: the commitments and availability of yourself and your athletes, availability of practice facilities, conditioning level of your athletes, limitations on practice frequency and scheduling that may be imposed by your league or conference, and the schedule of games or competitions for the particular season.

Books have been published for virtually every sport imaginable, and describe detailed practice plans, diagrams of plays, and a wide variety of conditioning and skill development exercises. In our experience, however, the sample practice plans for specific sports provided in these books often represent personal experience of the authors. While such experience may be extensive, it does not mean that the sample practice plans provided have been prepared with careful attention to all of the important components that characterize well-organized practices. We therefore strongly encourage you to draw on the sample of practice plans in such books for the sport that you coach, but to consider such examples in terms of the goals of your own program, the developmental and conditioning levels of the athletes that you coach, and the considerations and specific components described in this chapter.

GENERAL CONSIDERATIONS FOR DETERMINING PRACTICE CONTENT

Athletes obviously spend far more time at practices than they do at competitions. For that reason alone, coaches must spend a considerable amount of time planning practices in order that they will be utilized effectively and will be challenging and fun for the athletes. A coach should consider each of the following points in planning a particular practice.

1. **Practice environment, number of athletes, and number of coaches.** It is important to consider the simple logistics of who does what, where, when, and who will supervise. The number of players, the area, the available equipment, the total available practice time, where you and your assistants will be to maximize instructions and feedback—all require careful planning if practice time is to be used effectively.

2. **Conditioning level of athletes.** The amount of practice time devoted to conditioning activities will depend on the time of the season in which practice occurs and the particular levels of physical fitness that each athlete brings to the practices. However, every practice should include at least some conditioning drills (*see* Chapter 8).

FIGURE 11-1
Practices should include a review of basic skills.

3. Skill level of athletes. Early in the season, with younger athletes and with individuals who have not yet learned the basics, a great deal of practice time should be devoted to learning basic skills (*see* Chapter 4). Even with skilled athletes, review of the basics can be very valuable (Fig. 11-1).

4. Season goals. Remember the pre-season goal-setting process described in Chapter 10? Particular practices should be devoted to certain activities necessary for meeting the goals for the season.

5. Written objectives for every practice. We strongly recommend that you prepare written behavioral objectives for each practice. The objectives should be kept simple, few in number for any given practice, and should identify measurable outcomes. Avoid general statements such as "Practice take-downs and counter-to-take-downs" in wrestling. A better objective would be "Practice arm-drag take-downs until the wrestlers demonstrate at least three take-downs each on an opponent offering moderate resistance."

A good behavioral objective has five characteristics (Albrecht, 1978; Piper and Elgart, 1979; Thompson, 1977). First, it identifies a specific behavior. In the above example, the wrestlers were not told to "work on some holds." Rather, they were told to practice "arm-drag take-downs," a very specific behavior. Second, it should identify the circumstances surrounding the performance. In the above example, wrestlers were instructed to practice arm-drag take-downs with an opponent offering "moderate resistance." Third, an objective should identify a particular quantity, level, or standard of performance. In the above example, the wrestlers were instructed to demonstrate at least three take-downs. Fourth, a behavioral objective should be realistic. A coach must set practice objectives that are reasonably obtainable in the time available and given the skill level of the athletes. Finally, an objective should be pay-off oriented. The athletes must clearly understand that accomplishing a practice behavioral objective will contribute to improvement of their overall athletic performance.

6. **Mastery criteria for practice drills.** Before beginning actual instruction, you should decide on some criteria for success. At what point are you going to say, "O.K.! That behavior is *learned! Now we move on to step 2!"* Coaches often design their practice sessions to meet "time goals" rather than "learning goals." A basketball coach might decide to spend 10 minutes on a dribbling drill, 10 minutes on foul shooting, and so on. This is better than no organization at all. However, the "time goal" plan can be improved simply by adding a learning goal that should be met within that time period. For example, the basketball coach could decide that foul shooting will be practiced until each player makes three successful foul shots in a row (or until 10 minutes pass); a swimming coach could choose the goal that each beginning swimmer will swim three lengths freestyle with high elbow recovery on every stroke; a golf instructor might decide the beginner will practice 4-foot putts until he or she sinks four putts in a row.

These types of learning goals are called "mastery criteria." They are an important part of behavioral coaching. Whenever you attempt to teach a skill or part of a skill, set a mastery criterion that must be met before you move on. Part of the value of this is that it can tell you if you're asking too much of the athlete. If the criterion cannot be achieved within a reasonable period of time, something is wrong. The steps in your task analysis may be too large. You may not have selected rewards from the athlete's point of view. There may be too many distractions in the learning situation. Each potential difficulty can be checked out.

There is no hard and fast rule about how many correct tries in a row indicate that the athlete has acquired the skill. Examples of practice repetitions for specific task components for various sports are shown in Fig. 11-2. Criteria are set on the basis of a coach's experience with similar athletes, their present skill level, the need to keep everybody active during much of a practice, and several other considerations. The basic assumption is that if the athlete has met the mastery criterion, he or she has learned that part of the skill well enough so that, if asked to do it 30 minutes later, the skill would be performed correctly. Another important assumption is that if the athlete has met the mastery criteria during practice, there is a high probability that the skill will be executed correctly during competition.

7. **Activity.** There is obvious room for improvement in a practice where many of the athletes spend large amounts of time just standing around or waiting for an opportunity to perform. Unfortunately, recent research shows that most practices in many sports are not organized to maintain high levels of activity for the athletes involved. Rushall (1983) gathered observations in practices of swimming, women's volleyball, men's basketball, women's basketball, ice hockey, and physical education classes. Only swimming kept the participants at practices active from 70% to 80% of the time. In the other sports, most commonly 10% to 40% of time was spent in physical activity, with ice hockey and physical education showing the lowest values. Careful planning will enable you to improve on these values.

8. **Practice routines.** A number of specific components should be considered for each practice. However, the order in which these components are practiced and the amount of time devoted to each should be varied in order to make practices as interesting as possible.

9. **Program success for athletes.** The practice routine should be designed to challenge the athletes. However, the athletes should also achieve a considerable amount of success in practices. If the drills or skills required and the attitude of the coach continually give the impression that no one is ever good enough at anything, then many athletes will likely become discouraged.

10. **"Fun" activities as rewards.** Fun activities should be scheduled for every practice, especially in youth sports. It is important, however, that the fun activities be scheduled as rewards to be experienced *after* the athletes demonstrate some performance objectives.

Goals for Subcomponents of Skilled Tasks _____

Tennis	10 backhands in a row down the line 10 volleys in a row, alternating left and right corners 5 first serves in a row in left third of service court, 5 in middle third, 5 in right third 5 returns of serve in a row deep to the add court

Football	Wide receiver:
	    5 over-the-head catches in a row of a 40-yard pass
	    5 one-handed catches in a row of a 15-yard pass
	Defensive back:
	    5 interceptions in a row with receiver using preannounced route
	    2 or fewer completions allowed out of 5 tries with receiver running unknown route
	Kicker:
	    10 field goals in a row from 40-yard line

Baseball	Infielder:
	    10 hard grounders in a row fielded without error, 5 to left and 5 to right
	Outfielder:
	    20 fly balls caught on the run without error (5 to left, 5 to right, 5 in back, 5 in front)
	Hitter:
	    5 curve balls in a row hit out of infield

Wrestling	6 takedowns using at least two different techniques against an inferior but motivated opponent in (?) minutes 6 escapes using at least three different techniques in (?) minutes against same opponent
Basketball	20 foul shots in a row 30 uncontested lay-ups in a row 10 jump shots in a row from 10 feet 5 out of 10 jump shots from 40 feet Dribbling 2 minutes man-on-man against best defensive player without losing ball
Soccer	10 shots into left corner of goal from 30 feet with goalie not moving from center of goal 5 goals out of 10 shots from 20 feet with goalie free to move

From Locke, E.A., and Latham, G.P.

FIGURE 11-2

Hockey	Goalie: Stops 10 of 15 shots from 20 feet Stops 5 of 10 one-on-one situations Forward: Passes successfully 8 of 10 times to open man in front of net with one defender in between
Lacrosse	Similar to soccer and hockey
Golf	6 drives in a row over 200 yards and landing on fairway 15 12-foot putts in a row 10 9-irons in a row onto green from 75 yards

SPECIFIC COMPONENTS OF PRACTICE PLANS

Although there will undoubtedly be considerable variability from one practice to the next, consideration should be given to include each of the following components in all practices:

1. Review of practice objectives with athletes
2. Warm-up
3. Review and rehearsal of some recently acquired skills
4. Teaching and practice of new skills
5. Teaching and practice of tactical strategies and style of play
6. Scrimmages or competitions under gamelike conditions
7. Additional physical conditioning drills
8. Fun activity chosen by the athletes
9. Cool-down
10. Team discussion of strengths and weaknesses of the practice
11. Coach's comments
12. Clean-up

Provided that you have behavioral objectives and specific activities planned for each of the above components, you are more likely to use your practice time efficiently if you also carefully monitor the duration of each of the planned components. Of course, clear instructions to the athletes concerning expectations for each of the components, and sufficient numbers of coaching staff to provide frequent positive feedback for each athlete are essential. Finally, practices are likely to go much smoother for all concerned if the coach prompts appropriate people concerning the "extras," such as cleaning up the facilities, putting away the equipment, doing a quick check of the showers, and checking the locker room after practice. An effective strategy is to get the team captain involved in rotating assignment of such duties to the team members.

RECORDING AND CHARTING OF IMPORTANT PRACTICE BEHAVIORS

Let's review the examples described in previous chapters of practice behaviors of athletes that have been recorded and charted:

Coach monitoring of components of backstroke at swimming practice (Chapter 2)

Coach monitoring of fundamental skills of a hockey player (Chapter 3)

Coach monitoring of components of a drive block in football (Chapter 3)

Coach monitoring of execution of the backfield in Pop Warner football (Chapter 3)

Coach monitoring of components of windmill-style fastball pitcher (Chapter 4)

Coach monitoring of a golfer's performance on a learning progression checklist (Chapter 4)

Coach monitoring of components of a serve in tennis (Chapter 5)

Coach monitoring of components of foul shooting in basketball (Chapter 5)

Athlete monitoring of performance during a swimming practice (Chapter 6)

Athlete monitoring of offensive blocking by a university football player (Chapter 6)

Athlete and coach monitoring of gymnastics performance on a progression chart (Chapter 6)

Student manager monitoring of lay-ups, jump shots, and free throws at a junior high basketball practice (Chapter 6)

Athlete monitoring of various jumps and spins at a figure skating practice (Chapter 7)

Coach monitoring of important behaviors during a basketball scrimmage (Chapter 10)

In addition to the above examples, there is also a checklist at the end of each chapter for monitoring the performance of a coach. Important practice behaviors can be recorded by coaches, athletes, team managers, or other appropriately trained volunteers. As indicated in Chapter 3, there are a number of reasons for recording and charting practice behaviors of athletes and coaches. Although we do not want to repeat those reasons here, nor restate all of the guidelines for recording and charting of important behaviors described in previous chapters, we do want to reemphasize the importance of this aspect of behavioral coaching. If, as a coach, you take concrete steps to ensure that important practice behaviors are recorded (either by coaches, or athletes, or team managers, or some combination of all three), then you are greatly increasing the chances of seeing those behaviors improve.

SUMMARY

Carefully planned and well-managed practices greatly increase the likelihood of meeting the season's goals. When preparing a practice plan, a coach should:

1. Devote some time to conditioning activities
2. Include drills for skill development appropriate for the skill level of the athletes
3. Design some skills specifically to accomplish the goals for the season

4. Set written behavioral objectives for every practice
5. Identify mastery criteria for practice drills
6. Vary the practice routines across practices
7. Ensure that the practice drills and routines program some success for the athletes
8. Plan fun activities as rewards
9. Try to keep everyone active throughout the practice
10. Ensure that the logistics of who does what, where, and when is planned to include an acceptable coach/athlete ratio and full utilization of the playing facilities.

At the start of a practice, the coach should arrive early enough to allow ample time for necessary organizational activities and positive interactions with the athletes. During the practice, in addition to executing the practice plan, the coach should ensure that the athletes receive appropriate positive feedback and that specific practice behaviors are recorded. After the practice, the coach should praise athletes who performed well, encourage athletes to self-evaluate their practice performance, and evaluate the practice for future improvements.

Coach's Checklist

Fig. 11-3 is a summary checklist to remind you of the steps that you should follow before practice, at the start of a practice, during practice, and after practice. We encourage you to review the checklist several times during the season to ensure that you are following effective strategies for managing and planning practices.

Review Questions

1. Briefly list seven benefits of carefully planned and well-managed practices.
2. Briefly describe 10 considerations that a coach should keep in mind when planning a particular practice.
3. Describe five characteristics that a good behavioral objective should have. Illustrate each with an example.
4. What is meant by the term "mastery criteria"? Illustrate with an example.

C O A C H ' S   C H E C K L I S T

Managing and Planning Practices _____

SCORING KEY: $\sqrt{}$ = *Satisfactory (performed by coach at appropriate times)*
X = *Less than satisfactory*

	Date							

Practice plan

1. Included conditioning drills appropriate for athletes
2. Included skill drills appropriate for athletes
3. Contained behavioral objectives and mastery criteria for skill exercises
4. Was designed to keep all athletes active most of the time
5. Included "fun" activities as rewards
6. Was written out

At start of practice, the coach

1. Arrived early enough to organize practice area
2. Arrived early enough to talk to athletes to create positive atmosphere, to encourage them to support each other, to set goals, and so on
3. Led or assigned someone to lead warm-up
4. Reminded athletes of at least some "good news" and "bad news" behaviors and told them how they could earn fun activity
5. Reviewed practice objectives with athletes

During practice, the coach

1. Instructed athletes on new skills (see Fig. 4-5)
2. Gave instructions to athletes at start of routine to help them concentrate on particular aspect of technique
3. Used audiovisual aids (e.g., picture prompts, videotaped feedback, models)

FIGURE 11-3   *Continued.*

COACH'S CHECKLIST

Managing and Planning Practices—cont'd _____

	Date							

During practice, the coach—cont'd

4. Gave each athlete corrective feedback or prescriptive praise at least once per practice on some aspect of technique
5. Praised each athlete at least once per practice for effort
6. Maintained higher frequency of praise as compared with reprimands or yelling at athletes
7. Dealt with problem behaviors (see guidelines in Chapter 7)
8. When disciplining was necessary (e.g., after one or two reprimands were ignored by athlete), disciplined privately
9. Looked for something to praise in athlete later in practice after athlete had been yelled at or reprimanded
10. Avoided using physical activity as punishment

After practice, the coach

1. Praised specific athletes who had excellent practices
2. Asked some athletes to self-evaluate for effort, and gave feedback on their evaluations
3. Asked some athletes to set specific personal goals for future practices
4. Ensured that area was cleaned up and that equipment was put away
5. Reviewed practice data that was recorded, and provided positive feedback where appropriate

FIGURE 11-3, cont'd

Mini-Lab Exercises

1. Consider a sport that you played or would like to coach. Prepare a specific practice plan for that sport following the guidelines in this chapter. To make your plan realistic, write out some preliminary details concerning the age group of the athletes, the number of athletes and coaches involved, some characteristics of the playing facility or field, and the particular time during the season when your practice plan might be followed. After completing your practice plan, try to find a coach and a situation fairly close to your description of preliminary details, and ask that coach to give you some feedback on the strengths and weaknesses of your practice plan.

2. Consider the coach's checklist for managing and planning practices (Fig. 11-3). Now try to find a coach who is willing to let you attend and observe a practice. Use the checklist to evaluate the extent to which that coach performs the various behaviors. In addition to observing the coach before, during, and after the practice, you will also have to ask the coach some questions about the practice plan in order to score all items on the checklist.

References

Albrecht, K. (1978). Successful management by objectives: An action manual. Englewood Cliffs, N.J.: Prentice-Hall.

Piper, T.J., and Elgart, D.B. (1979). Teacher supervision through behavioral objectives: An operationally described system. Baltimore: Paul H. Brookes Publishers.

Rushall, B. (1983). Coaching styles: A preliminary investigation. In G.L. Martin and D. Hrycaiko, eds. Behavior modification and coaching: Principles, procedures and research. Springfield, Ill.: Charles C Thomas.

Thompson, D.G. (1977). Writing long-term and short-term objectives: A painless approach. Champaign, Ill.: Research Press.

Selected Readings

Coaching theory level 1 (1979). National Coaching Certification Program. Ottawa, Ontario, Canada: Coaching Association of Canada.

Hoehn, R.G. (1984). Nagging problems. Coaching Review **7**:39-40.

Martens, R., Christina, R.W., Harvey, J.S. Jr., and Sharkey, B.J. (1981). Coaching young athletes. Champaign, Ill.: Human Kinetics Publishers.

Nesbitt, R. (1984). Periodization: A coach's example. Coaching Review **7**:16-18.

Pate, R.R., McClenaghan, B., and Rotella, R. (1984). Scientific foundations of coaching. New York: Saunders College Publishing.

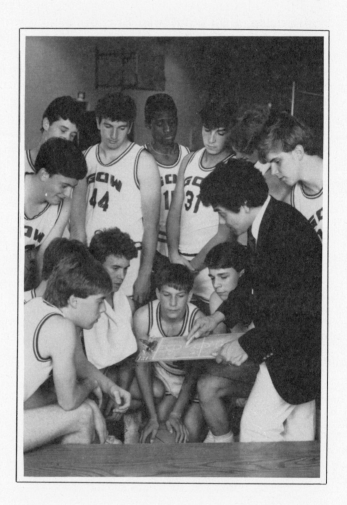

ORGANIZING AND ADMINISTERING ATHLETIC PROGRAMS

12

Assistant Coaches, Team Managers, and Team Captains

Most coaches will tell you that behind every successful coach can be found competent assistants. This is especially true for a coach who hopes to practice effective behavioral coaching. Behavioral coaching is a lot of work. Frequent monitoring of performance of athletes and coaches alike should occur in every practice and every game. Who's going to do all that monitoring? Who's going to provide all that feedback? Who's going to set all those goals, evaluate progress toward the goals, and reward goal attainment? Obviously, the Head Coach can't do it all. In professional sports in recent years, there has been ample evidence of a move toward expanded coaching staffs. Offensive coaches, defensive coaches, backfield coaches, line coaches, coaches for goalies, coaches for pitchers, coaches for forwards, and on and on. As a coach of a high school or junior high team, however, it's not likely that you will have the luxury of a large coaching staff. As a volunteer coach of a community club soccer team, you may be it—Head Coach, Assistant Coach, and Chief Cook and Bottle Washer, all rolled into one. Nevertheless, you can't escape two facts. First, to practice effective behavioral coaching, you will need a lot of help. Second, valuable help is always available provided that you (1) take the necessary steps to obtain it, (2) select your help with care, and (3) manage your assistants with the same attention to detail that we hope you will devote to managing yourself and your athletes. The guidelines that we provide in the next two sections are directed at paid assistant coaches. Many of these guidelines, however, also apply to selecting student managers or parent volunteers to assist you in practicing effective behavioral coaching.

SELECTING ASSISTANT COACHES

Not all coaches at the club or high school level have the luxury of selecting their own assistants. If you do have such luxury, there are some definite pitfalls to be avoided when selecting assistant coaches. First and foremost, we strongly recommend that you not select an assistant who has a totally different coaching philosophy from yours. When interviewing assistants, be up front about your beliefs, expectations, and approach to coaching. Coaching philosophies can differ drastically. Failure to clarify philosophies when selecting assistant coaches can become a source of considerable frustration and discontent later for head coach, assistant coach, and athletes. If you wholeheartedly endorse the philosophy and procedures of effective behavioral coaching as outlined in this book, then it's important that you select assistant coaches who will feel comfortable with behavioral coaching. In other words, choose someone who is willing to adopt this approach.

Second, you should not evaluate an applicant primarily in terms of his or her athletic accomplishments, medals, and awards. Remember what you expect an assistant coach to do. You will want your assistant to be able to instruct, praise, reprimand, and perform other activities that will effectively improve and maintain skilled athletic performance in your athletes. Your assistant is not there to perform as an athlete. People who were outstanding athletes are not necessarily going to be outstanding coaches.

Third, constantly guard against the view that the head coach knows everything and does everything well, and the assistant coach is second best in all categories on which the two might be compared. In any head coach–assistant coach pair, there will always be things that the assistant coach does better than the head coach. Thus, although you want an assistant who adopts a similar coaching philosophy, you should also look for assistants who have certain skills that are not your outstanding suit. This approach can only lead to a better overall coaching staff.

Fourth, avoid any tendency to select an assistant primarily on the basis of his or her performance in an interview. Andrew Carnegie once said, "As I grow older I pay less attention to what people say. I just watch what they do." Some people can sound fantastic in an interview, but perform much less than satisfactorily when it comes to doing the job itself. Therefore, we strongly endorse a competency-based approach for selecting and evaluating assistants. Discuss the possibility of directly observing the prospective assistant in action. If he or she agrees, then you will have an opportunity to directly monitor a number of the coaching competencies that you believe to be critical to effective assistants.

Those are some of the don'ts about selecting assistants. What are some of the do's? Numerous books on coaching have identified desirable characteristics and qualities for assistant coaches, for example, teaching skills, loyalty, enthusiasm, knowledge of the sport, initiative, dependability, philosophy, desire to be a head coach, playing experience, attendance at clinics, rapport with athletes, liaison between players and head coach, willingness to work, and contributing ideas (Sabock, 1985). Whereas such a list is useful as a preliminary list of categories of concern, these characteristics are somewhat vague and will require considerable specification before they can be precisely measured. In this book we've tried to identify specific competencies that characterize effective coaches, and we've expanded these into usable checklists to monitor coaching behaviors. We encourage you to use these checklists when selecting assistant coaches. Specifically, when selecting assistants, look for concrete evidence beyond the interview that the prospective assistants are able to do some or all of the following:

Avoid the pitfalls of effective behavioral coaching (Chapter 2)

Skillfully assess the fundamentals (Chapter 3)

Positively teach fundamental skills (Chapter 4)

Select appropriate individualized strategies for decreasing repetitive errors (Chapter 5)

Positively motivate practice and endurance training (Chapter 6)

Effectively involve the athletes in decreasing problem behaviors (Chapter 7)

Plan and implement effective conditioning programs (Chapter 8)

Help athletes use sports psyching to improve performance at competitions (Chapter 9)

Skillfully set pre-season goals and conduct post-season evaluations (Chapter 10)

Plan and manage practices effectively (Chapter 11)

Help the head coach in budgeting and management of equipment and facilities (Chapter 13)

Be well organized and manage time well (Chapter 14)

Help the coach in all other aspects of managing an athletic program (Chapter 16)

Maintain good relationships with athletes, game officials, colleagues, administrators, and parents (Chapter 16)

MANAGING ASSISTANT COACHES DURING THE SEASON

Let's assume that you have completed your pre-season preparation, met with the parents, registered the athletes, and you're already several practices and perhaps two or three games into the season. You are likely experiencing considerable pressure from a variety of sources concerning the way the season is progressing. The pressures that you are experiencing may influence you to focus your attention more and more on winning at all costs. It is important, however, to remember that you have considerable help and support from assistant coaches, a team captain, equipment managers, volunteer parents, and others in carrying out your responsibilities. To the extent that you have responsibility for managing your "helpers," your important functions parallel those of managers in any organization, and include planning, leading, delegating, organizing, controlling, and evaluating. In a film about management made by the American Management Association, Lawrence Appley said, "When you do things yourself you are a technician. When you get things done through others you are a manager." Using these definitions, an effective coach obviously must be both a good technician and a good manager.

Over the past decade and a half there has been a growing body of evidence to demonstrate that "organizational behavior management" is a practical and highly effective approach for managing people in organizational settings. Drawing on such sources as Albrecht (1978), Fournies (1978), Fredericksen (1982), the *Journal of Organizational Behavior Management,* and O'Brien et al. (1982), this section presents two checklists to help coaches effectively deal with assistant coaches during the season. The questions contained in the checklists could also be applied to the coaches' dealings with team captains and others for whom they have management responsibility.

Fig. 12-1 identifies a number of behaviors of the coach that are likely to guarantee that assistant coaches will be less than satisfactory and unlikely to change. If you do many of these things, you're headed for trouble. Accordingly, they are referred to as "danger signals." At regular intervals during the season (approximately every 1 or 2 months), we would encourage you to use this checklist to assess your management performance with your assistants. If you score a number of yes answers, then you should definitely heed the danger signals. How? We strongly recommend that you do whatever is necessary so that you can subsequently answer yes to most of the questions on the checklist in Fig. 12-2.

Loyalty, rapport, mutual respect, and cooperation are some of the terms that might be used to describe an ideal relationship between a head coach and the assistant coaches. Head coaches want their assistants to take pride in their work. However, it's one thing to acknowledge the value of such a relationship, and quite another for you as head coach to behave in ways that lead others to describe your relationship with your assistant coaches in glowing phrases. If you are sensitive to the danger signals, and if you continually try to practice the desirable management behaviors, then you will greatly increase the chances that others will refer to your relationship with your assistants as showing loyalty, mutual respect, cooperation, and rapport. More important, your athletes are likely to gain maximum benefit from you and your assistants.

C H E C K L I S T

Danger Signals for Managing Assistants _____

By *assistant coach* we mean a salaried individual with considerable training who has been hired as an assistant coach. not a parent volunteer who is "helping out." As a coach dealing with assistant coaches. do you:

1. Assign many small distinct jobs rather than complete "missions" or areas of responsibility (so that your assistant frequently asks. "What do I do next?")? Yes____ No____

2. Frequently talk *at* your assistants. rather than getting them involved? Seldom ask your assistants for their ideas and opinions? Always give commands and rarely ask questions? Yes____ No____

3. Frequently find fault. criticize. blame. or accuse your assistants whenever problems or unexpected difficulties arise? Yes____ No____

4. Frequently give feedback in terms of vague generalities. rather than being specific? Concentrate on general attitudes rather than on specific behaviors? Yes____ No____

5. Frequently prod assistants to do more. do it faster. and get better results. but rarely praise them for the good work they have already done? Yes____ No____

6. When there is a problem. rarely ask an assistant if he or she is aware of it? Rather. do you assume an assistant knows when a problem exists. what has to be done to solve it. and is capable of solving it? Yes____ No____

7. Assume assistants should solve problems because it is their job. and therefore not praise them when they do solve problems? Yes____ No____

8. Frequently use your authority to silence debate about a problem area? Yes____ No____

9. Frequently correct assistants in front of athletes? Yes____ No____

FIGURE 12-1

C H E C K L I S T

Desirable Behavior for Managing Assistants _____

By *assistant coach* we mean a salaried individual with considerable training who has been hired as an assistant coach. not a parent volunteer who is "helping out." As a coach dealing with assistant coaches. do you:

1. Frequently praise assistants for jobs well done?   Yes____   No____
2. Delegate whole projects. areas of responsibility.   Yes____   No____
   or complete problems to be solved?
3. Specifically identify high performance standards   Yes____   No____
   in the form of coach's checklists. and expect your
   assistants to self-monitor and live up to them?
4. Consult with your assistants beforehand on all   Yes____   No____
   matters concerning them and their areas of responsibility. and allow them to have input?
5. Use coaching clinics and meetings to cooperative-   Yes____   No____
   ly solve problems and plan for new developments?
6. Encourage your assistants to continuously ana-   Yes____   No____
   lyze their own areas of responsibility and to
   search for ways of performing more effectively?
7. Encourage your coaches to follow "a coaching   Yes____   No____
   creed" (page 380) and ethical guidelines for effective behavioral coaching?
8. When necessary. use your authority in a straight-   Yes____   No____
   forward. nonapologetic. nonmanipulative man-
   ner. but without embarrassing assistants in
   front of athletes?
9. Always provide rationale for changes in assis-   Yes____   No____
   tants' duties and areas of responsibility?
10. Positively acknowledge and discuss potential   Yes____   No____
    benefits of suggestions made by assistants (rath-
    er than immediately citing numerous reasons
    why the suggestion will not work)?

FIGURE 12-2

Reprinted with special permission of King Features Syndicate, Inc.

SELECTING AND MANAGING TEAM CAPTAINS AND
TEAM MANAGERS

Do you remember Jim Dawson, the coach of the Clifton Junior
High basketball team in Columbus, described in Chapters 1 and 7?
His basketball players could earn points and an "Eagle Effort" award
for performance on lay-up drills, jump shooting drills, free throw drills,
and encouragement of teammates at practices. The points were tabu-
lated and graphed by student managers. And then there was Coach
Keedwell from the Manitoba Marlins, described in Chapter 3. She and
the author enlisted the help of Clayton Cracklen and other psychology
students to record and graph the frequency of improper turns and
unscheduled stops of swimmers during sets. Do you remember
Michelle Hume, the professional figure skating instructor described in
Chapter 7? She trained university student volunteers to attend practices of the St. Anne's Figure Skating Club and to keep track of the
frequency of jumps and spins and the amount of time that skaters
spent off-task during practices. In almost every chapter, we have described actual, data-based projects to demonstrate the effectiveness of
behavioral coaching for improving the performance of athletes in a
wide variety of sports. In all such cases, the Number 1 characteristic of
effective behavioral coaching that was described in Chapter 2 pre-
vailed. That is, the coach emphasized specific, detailed, frequent measurement of athletic performance, and the use of those measures to
evaluate the effectiveness of specific coaching techniques. Some of the
necessary data can be obtained by you and your assistant coaches.
However, team managers, team captains, parent volunteers, and the
athletes themselves are integral components of effective behavioral
coaching.

Your first step in selecting team managers or parent volunteers is
to list in writing the things they will do and the amount of time in-

volved. What do you want them to do? What athletic behaviors will they be monitoring? What are the minimum number of practices per week that you would expect them to attend in order to accept their volunteer services? How much training time will be required for them to reliably use the data sheets? What type of interaction will they have with the athletes? How will you introduce them to the athletes? How will you judge their degree of interest and the probability of their reliable participation throughout the season? If you have more applicants for the student manager or parent volunteer positions than you need, what criteria will you use for selection purposes? If you and your assistants spend some time answering these questions before the season begins, you stand a good chance of obtaining valuable and necessary volunteer support for practicing effective behavioral coaching.

What about a team captain? From a player's point of view, a team captain should be willing to discuss with the coach issues of concern to the players, collect ideas from all of the team members to present to coaches, be positive and set a good example at practices to help make practices fun, organize team activities away from the athletic environment, and encourage other players in various ways, both on and off the field. From a coach's perspective, a team captain will show the behaviors characteristic of a "coachable" athlete, be a good student, hustle at practices, encourage other players, show sportsmanlike behavior, show leadership on and off the field, and be receptive to new ideas from the coaches. The new ideas would include getting the athletes involved in considerable self-monitoring of important practice and game behaviors. At a team meeting at the start of the season, the coach should outline the desirable behaviors of a team captain and discuss them with the players. Whether the captain is elected by the team or appointed by the coach, it is valuable for the team to understand the considerations that go into the selection of a captain.

SUMMARY

Most head coaches will tell you that assistant coaches are indispensable. If anything, the practice of effective behavioral coaching makes assistant coaches even more valuable. When selecting assistant coaches, several definite pitfalls are to be avoided. First, do not select an assistant coach who has a totally different coaching philosophy from yours. Second, do not evaluate an applicant primarily in terms of his or her athletic accomplishments. People who are outstanding athletes are not necessarily outstanding coaches. Third, do not select an assistant who is a carbon copy of yourself. An assistant with different, complementary strengths to yours will be most valuable. Fourth, do

Organizing and Administering Athletic Programs

not select an assistant primarily on the basis of performance in an interview. We strongly recommend that you adopt a competency-based approach for selecting and evaluating assistants. This means that you must identify coaching competencies that you believe to be critical for effective assistant coaches, and choose assistants who show those competencies. Competencies of potential applicants can be assessed by examining their performance in terms of the various coaching checklists at the end of the chapters in this book.

During the season, consult with your assistants before identifying specific areas of responsibilities for them. An effective management strategy consists of identifying minimum performance standards on the coachs' checklists, requesting your assistants to frequently self-monitor their performance using the checklists, and regularly evaluating their performance yourself and giving them feedback. Finally, using Figs. 12-1 and 12-2, we would encourage you to self-evaluate your own management performance on a monthly basis to maximize the chances that your relationship with your assistants includes loyalty, mutual respect, cooperation, and rapport.

Team captains and team managers are also important contributors to a successful season. The guidelines for selecting and managing assistants and the general organizational behavior management strategies outlined in this chapter can also be applied to the task of selecting and managing team captains and team managers.

Coach's Checklist

General guidelines for selecting and managing assistant coaches are summarized in the checklist in Fig. 12-3. We suggest that you use the checklist as a convenient reminder to ensure that you follow all of the recommended guidelines.

Review Questions

1. List four pitfalls to be avoided when selecting assistant coaches.
2. Briefly describe what is meant by the competency-based approach recommended by the authors when selecting assistant coaches.
3. List five functions of a manager in an organization.
4. According to Lawrence Appley, what is the difference between a technician and a manager? Is a coach a manager or a technician or both?
5. The number one characteristic of effective behavioral coaching is that it emphasizes specific, detailed, and frequent measurement of athletic performance and the use of those measures to evaluate the effectiveness of scientific coaching techniques. But taking all those

C O A C H ' S   C H E C K L I S T

Selecting and Managing Assistant Coaches _____

SCORING KEY: √ = *Satisfactory (performed by coach at appropriate times)*
X = *Less than satisfactory*

Date

Selecting Assistant Coaches

1. List specific pitfalls to be avoided when selecting assistant coaches
2. List specific competencies that you would want your assistant coaches to demonstrate
3. List specific character behaviors that you expect to be typical of your assistants
4. If possible. observe your assistants in action to correctly assess their competencies in applying effective behavioral coaching procedures
5. If you cannot directly observe assistants in action. use typical assessment devices (interviews. references) to attempt to judge presence of specific competencies and desirable character behaviors in candidates

Managing Assistant Coaches

1. Consult with your assistants to identify specific areas of responsibility for them
2. Identify minimum performance standards for your assistants on coach's checklists
3. Instruct your assistants to frequently self-monitor their performance, using checklists
4. Regularly (monthly) evaluate your assistants on coach's checklists and provide feedback
5. Monthly, self-evaluate your own management behaviors, using danger signal checklist for managing assistants
6. Monthly, self-evaluate your management performance, using desirable behavior checklist for managing assistants

FIGURE 12-3

observations is time consuming. Describe several strategies that a busy coach might consider to make it possible to collect important observations on the behavior of athletes.

6. What is a coach likely to look for when selecting a captain? What are athletes likely to look for in their captain?

Mini-Lab Exercises

1. The purpose of this exercise is to give you some experience using the danger signal checklist for managing assistants. If you currently coach and you have an assistant coach who is responsible to you, use the danger signal checklist to evaluate your own performance. Alternatively, approach a coach whom you know and ask for assistance in helping you to complete this assignment. Be sure to indicate that the results will be confidential. Ask that coach each of the questions on the danger signal checklist and record his or her answers. Now select two of the items to which the coach answered "yes" on the danger signal checklist. Describe, in a paragraph, specific behavior of the coach in specific instances that led to those "yes" answers.

2. The purpose of this exercise is to give you some experience using the desirable behavior checklist for managing assistants. If you currently coach and you have an assistant coach who is responsible to you, use the desirable behavior checklist to evaluate your own performance. Alternatively, approach a coach whom you know and ask for assistance in helping you to complete this assignment. Be sure to indicate that the results will be confidential. Ask that coach each of the questions on the desirable behavior checklist and record his or her answers. Now select two of the items to which the coach answered "no" on the desirable behavior checklist. Describe, in a paragraph, specific behavior of the coach in specific instances that led to those "no" answers.

References

Albrecht, K. (1978). *Successful management by objectives: An action manual.* Englewood Cliffs, N.J.: Prentice-Hall.

Fournies, F.F. (1978). *Coaching for improved work performance.* New York: Van Nostrand.

Frederiksen, L.W., ed. (1982). *Handbook of organizational behavior management.* New York: Wiley.

Journal of Organizational Behavior Management. New York: Haworth Press.

O'Brien, R.M., Dickenson, A.M., and Rosow, M.P., eds. (1962). *Industrial behavior modification: A management handbook,* New York: Pergamon Press.

Sabock, R.J. (1985). *The coach,* 3rd ed. Champaign, Ill.: Human Kinetics Publishers.

Selected Readings

Blanchard. K.. and Johnson. S. (1982). The one-minute manager. New York: William Morrow.

Blanchard. K.. and Lorber. R. (1984). Putting the one-minute manager to work. New York: William Morrow.

Blanchard. K.. Zigarmi. P.. and Zigarmi. D. (1985). Leadership and the one-minute manager. New York: William Morrow.

13

Budgets, Equipment, and Facilities

We suspect that, as a university student planning a career as a coach, you haven't given much thought to the role of budget preparation and financial management in coaching. You might even think, "That stuff's for accounting majors. What's it doing in a book on coaching?" You might be surprised to learn that experts argue that financial management should be the Number 1 topic in almost any organization, because financial support is essential to an organization's establishment and development (Vanderzwaag, 1984). Coaching is no exception. Wise use of money is no doubt one of the factors influencing administrators when they evaluate the performance of a coach. For some coaches, their job may depend as much on their money management skills as on their won/lost record. Moreover, many of the decisions that you will make as a coach will stem from a financial base. Thus, financial management is an important responsibility, and must be carried out with care and knowledge.

How much do you need to know about financial management? As you advance in your coaching career, you will undoubtedly acquire a detailed knowledge of this topic. At some point it may be necessary for you to learn in considerable detail about such approaches as line-item budgeting, PPBES (Planning, Programming, Budgeting, and Evaluation System), zero base budgeting, cost analysis budgeting, and highly technical aspects of computerized budgeting (e.g., *see* Jensen, 1983; Pestolesi and Sinclair, 1978; Vanderzwaag, 1984). We assume that you are not yet at that level. A beginning coach is often provided with a set practice schedule, a set game schedule, and a set budget within which to work. However, you should have at least passing acquaintance with some of the above topics. In this chapter we review some of the basic considerations of budget preparation, outline some strategies for administering a budget, review guidelines for purchasing and caring for equipment, discuss possible areas of responsibility for caring for your playing facility, and review some pitfalls to be avoided in money management. As in other chapters, we provide checklists to remind you of the things that need to be done before and during the season.

BUDGET PREPARATION

A budget is basically a written statement of anticipated revenues and probable expenditures over a given period of time. As indicated in the introduction, as a beginning coach you will likely be expected to operate within a budget prepared by someone else. Sooner or later, however, you will likely become involved in the preparation of a budget. It is important, therefore, that you have some knowledge of typical approaches to budget preparation.

What do you do when you are asked to submit a budget proposal for your sport for the coming year? If you have never prepared a budget before, a reasonable first step is to obtain copies of budgets from previous years. An examination of income and expenditures over several preceding years will give you a reasonable expectation of probable trends. It will also alert you to purchase dates of equipment that may have to be replaced. These will be listed as anticipated expenditures in your proposed budget. If you have been hired for a new program in a new school, and there are no previous budgets for you to review, then you might enquire about examining the budgets for your sport at schools of similar size in your district.

Careful study of previous budgets can teach you a lot about the intricacies of preparation of budget proposals. It will also raise lots of questions. Your next step is to talk to a number of individuals who can help you obtain answers to these questions. Important people to talk to early in the process are the comptroller or accountant and the athletic director for your school or organization. In addition to being able to answer lots of questions that will be raised from your scrutiny of previous budgets, these people can also inform you of various forms to be completed, number of copies to be made, channels through which your budget proposal will pass, and the backgrounds of the persons who will likely be present when you're expected to present and defend your proposal.

An early step in any budget preparation process must include the taking of an inventory of supplies and equipment on hand, and assessment of their state of repair. This will help you determine what will be needed during the coming season. If you coach at a large school, chances are that computer printouts are available to help you take inventory of current equipment and supplies. An important person to talk to about inventory is the equipment manager. The equipment manager can alert you to equipment that must be replaced during the coming year, and can be a valuable resource to help you peruse catalogues and identify probable costs of new items.

The next step is to consider your goals and priorities for the coming season. What do you hope to accomplish with individual athletes and with the team? Are there particular innovations that you wish to add to your practices that will have cost implications? Are there particular opponents that were underrated last year? Perhaps you may want to have them scouted this year. Review the priorities identified from completing the various forms in Chapter 10 (pre-season planning) and Chapter 14 (time management) to help you identify additional items that you will want to add to the budget.

Another category of expenditures are those related to home games and away games. Some teams have trip managers that help coordinate and organize costs associated with competitions. With the help of such a person, we suggest that you fill out an expenditure sheet such as the one shown in Fig. 13-1 for each home game and each away game for the coming season.

After you have collected the necessary information, you will be expected to transfer the information to a standard budget summary form used by your organization. Although each organization has its own version of budget forms, most contain similar categories. A sample of a budget proposal form is shown in Fig. 13-2.

One question that inevitably arises is whether to submit your best and honest guess of your actual expenses or to "pad" your budget. Some people pad their budget on the assumption that funds will be cut and it's best to have a little bit of padding to give away. We recommend, however, that you include only those items that can be realistically and easily defended. There are two problems with padding the budget. First, credibility is easily lost but not easily regained. Because "you can't fool all of the people all of the time," padding might gain something for you in the short run, but will likely cost you in the long run.

Expenditure Sheet for Home Games _____

Visiting team _____   Date _____

Items	Projected Costs for 19___	Actual Costs
Advertising		
Ambulance (stand-by)		
Announcer		
Custodians		
Facility clean-up (in addition to custodians)		
Facility rental		
Guarantees for visiting team		
Officials		
Pregame meal		
Printing of programs		
Scorers		
Security officers		
Ticket crew		
Timers		
Ushers		
Videotaping or game films		
TOTAL		

FIGURE 13-1

Summary of Budget Proposal for 19_____

Item	Last Year's Costs	Projected Costs for Current Year	Proposed Costs for 19__
Administrative salaries			
Advertising			
Assistant coach's salary			
Auxiliary security officers (for home games)			
Awards			
Books			
Cleaning uniforms			
Coaches' clinics			
Equipment			
Films			
Guarantees for visiting teams			
Home game costs (ticket sellers, ticket takers, custodians)			
Insurance (health, medical, liability)			
Laundry			
Officials			
Payroll taxes			
Physical examinations			
Printing (programs)			
Recruiting (off campus)			
Repairs and maintenance			
Scouting			
Student assistant salaries			
Supplies and postage			
Telephone			
Travel (meals, transportation, overnight lodging)			
Uniforms			
Videotaping or game films			
TOTAL			

FIGURE 13-2

Second, once administrators consider you to be a coach who typically pads the budget, they are likely to cut funds from your budget in subsequent years without actually determining whether there is a definite need for those funds.

Thus far we have talked about determining proposed expenditures. What about income? In most cases, submission of budget proposals means submission of proposed expenditures. Although you will no doubt have some general idea of the approximate income that might be available for you, this is usually controlled by senior administrators. In some schools, sports receive their funds from budget appropriation. In other cases, athletic gate receipts provide a source of revenue. Additional sources of income for athletics include special student fees, uniform or facility use fees, fund raising by booster clubs, donations from various foundations or companies or individuals, concessions from program or food and beverage sales at athletic contests, and special fund raising events such as walk-a-thons. It is important for you to have some general idea of both the sources and amount of funds that might be available. But it is the adequacy of the justification of expenditures on which your budget proposal will stand or fall. Two of the more common budget preparation procedures for arriving at expenditures are line-item budgeting and PPBES.

Line-Item Budget

If you follow the guidelines outlined, and submit a budget summary similar to that summarized in Fig. 13-2, you will have completed what is referred to as a conventional, or line-item, budget. Quite simply, this type of budget has a specific line for each item (e.g., awards) and function (e.g., scouting). Each line typically includes a request for the amount of funds for that item or function for the coming year, and the amount that was spent on that item or function during the current or preceding year. A weakness of this approach is that items tend to be included in budgets because they were there in previous budgets rather than on the basis of analysis of the potential value of that item for next year's program. If accountability mechanisms are weak or nonexistent, it is possible that some items may be retained in a budget as long as 3 or 4 years after they should have been eliminated or drastically reduced.

Planning, Programming, Budgeting, and Evaluation System

An approach that is becoming increasingly popular in public schools is the PPBES (originally PPBS). If followed appropriately, this approach requires a coach to be much more accountable than does the conventional line-item budgeting approach.

The *planning* component of PPBES requires a coach to identify specific goals or objectives for athletics in terms of measurable accomplishments. Effective behavioral coaching as described in this book is very compatible with PPBES. For example, a coach who has completed the pre-season goal-setting sheets for physical, technical, tactical, and psychological preparation of athletes (*see* Chapter 10), could easily summarize those goals for budget preparation purposes. The *programming* phase of PPBES identifies specific strategies and activities that the coach will follow during the coming season to accomplish the goals. As with the planning phase, effective behavioral coaching strategies can also help the coach complete this aspect of the PPBES approach. The strategies for motivating athletes, decreasing problem behaviors, sport psyching, and the many other strategies outlined in this book could be followed by a coach in accomplishing goals for the season. The *budgeting* component of PPBES requires that the coach outline the components of the budget that will make it possible to implement the program outlined in the programming phase. Often this requires little more than taking the line-item budget (Fig. 13-2) and submitting it as is, along with some indication as to how each item relates to the program strategies. The *evaluation* aspect has two main components. First, the person to whom the coach submits the budget is expected to analyze whether the proposed program will likely lead toward the proposed goals, and whether the proposed budget is adequate for the proposed program. The second aspect of evaluation will occur at the end of the season. Both the coach and the person to whom the budget was submitted (and probably others) are expected to evaluate whether the accomplishments were worth the costs. Here again, the effective behavioral approach to coaching can be extremely valuable. The many data sheets proposed in this book that are recommended for use by the coach during the season will provide ample data on the accomplishments of the athletes.

Often, budget requests exceed the funds available for the coach to carry out everything that was proposed for the coming season. In such cases the administrator is likely to return the budget to the coach with a request for funding prioritization. The PPBES approach can be valuable when priorities must be established within a particular budget. The coach will be able to reexamine the planning component of PPBES and prioritize the goals set for the season. This then makes it possible to identify priority expenditures during the third phase of PPBES to ensure that available funds will go toward the programs that the coach will follow during the coming season to accomplish the high priority goals.

BUDGET ADMINISTRATION

An important part of administering your budget involves acquiring good bookkeeping habits. Good bookkeeping includes neatness, accuracy, and keeping records up to date. An important rule of thumb is, when you spend it, record it. If you coach a sport that involves a relatively small budget and is not much more than a one-person operation, you might be able to get by with a ledger (Quint, 1981). A ledger is a lined card or sheet of paper with several columns. On each line, spaces are provided to record the date, a brief description of the expenditure, the amount of each entry in dollars and cents, and a column to indicate the remaining balance in your budget. Increasingly, organizations are using microcomputers to store such records. Although microcomputers make for easy information storage and retrieval, they nevertheless serve the basic function of the old-style ledger kept by accountants in a loose-leaf notebook.

As your budget and operation increase in size and number of persons involved, we recommend that you develop control cards for administering the budget in several major areas of expenditure. At a minimum, you might consider developing separate control cards for the subcategories of petty cash, supplies, equipment, home games, and away games. For example, Fig. 13-1 could easily be modified to serve as a useful control card for monitoring expenses of home games. Additional hints for administering your budget are provided in the following sections.

PURCHASING AND CARING FOR EQUIPMENT

Whether you were given a set budget at the start of the year, or were intimately involved in the details of budget preparation, you will likely have responsibility for the equipment used in your sport. Knowledgeable purchasing and responsible caring for equipment and supplies can enhance your credibility with those who control the finances in the organization. There are likely some approved procedures that you must follow in purchasing equipment. It is also likely that there is some room for creative planning on your part. We suggest that you ensure that you can adequately answer the following questions:

1. How do you get and pay for equipment?
   a. Do you have to deal through a central purchasing department at your school or agency?
   b. Do you use a standard purchase requisition form?
   c. Do you pay directly and then submit your receipts to get your money back?
   d. Do you have to send out information to several dealers to obtain competitive bids?

   e. Can you shop around and purchase from dealers directly?
   f. Do you work with equipment technicians or equipment attendants?
   g. Does your school have an equipment advisory committee that you must check with?
   h. Should you give preference to local dealers?
   i. Is there a minimum lead time required in order to ensure delivery when you need it?
   j. Can you capitalize on short-term sales?
2. How do you decide what equipment to buy?
   a. Have you asked various dealers to put you on their mailing list or to send their representatives to talk to you on a regular basis?
   b. Have you checked equipment displays at various sport conferences?
   c. Have you considered setting up an annual show in which you would invite dealers to present their equipment lines, and invite coaches to view the displays?
   d. Have you asked your athletes for their preferences?
   e. Have you asked the trainer to check items for durability and safety?
   f. Have you asked the equipment attendant to check items for ease of care and maintenance?
3. How do you care for equipment?
   a. Has all the equipment been appropriately marked and tagged? Do you have an accurate record of all equipment, including size, general condition, and date placed in service?
   b. Do you have an adequate monitoring system for athletes to sign out and return equipment?
   c. Have you prepared a list of do's and don'ts to review with the athletes concerning proper care and use of equipment?
   d. Have you reviewed manufacturers' recommendations for cleaning equipment after use?
   e. Have you reviewed manufacturers' recommendations for drying and storing uniforms after practices and games?
   f. Have you reviewed manufacturers' recommendations for cleaning and storing equipment during the off-season?
   g. Have you enquired about typical storage problems (e.g., rust, mildew), and strategies for minimizing them?
   h. Have you encouraged your equipment attendants to develop efficient and time-saving methods of equipment room operation?

DEVELOPING AND CARING FOR YOUR HOME FACILITY

The extent to which coaches are involved in developing and caring for the home facility varies tremendously from one school to the next. At one extreme, the coach may have little more to do with the facility than sticking a few stakes in the ground to adjust a cross-country running course in a local park that is totally cared for by a local service organization. At the other extreme, a coach might have considerable input into the planning, construction, and maintenance of a sports facility. If you should find yourself in the latter position, we would encourage you to carefully examine such sources as Flynn (1980), Glading (1980), Grant (1980), Jensen (1983), Pestolesi and Sinclair (1978), and Resick et al. (1979). Also, each year the January issue of *Scholastic Coach* emphasizes athletics and physical education facilities. Another useful source is a planning checklist available from *Planning Facilities.**

We will assume you will be hired to coach a sport for a school or club that already has an approved facility. Your responsibilities concerning the facility for your sport can vary widely. We recommend that you obtain a clear understanding of your responsibilities in terms of the following.

1. Safety standards. Does your facility meet at least the minimum expected safety standards for athletes, spectators, and officials? What are your responsibilities in ensuring a safe facility? This is discussed in more detail in Chapter 16.

2. Scheduling. Do you share the facility with other teams? Coaches? Physical education classes? The general public? If so, carefully examine your goals with respect to practices, and concerning possible unscheduled exhibition contests, to ensure that all relevant persons have been notified of the upcoming schedule and of your needs.

3. Accommodations for home and visiting teams. Conduct a thorough review of the dressing rooms, equipment rooms, training room, and other aspects of the facility reserved for use by the home and visiting teams. Do they meet your minimum expectations? Can improvements be made within your existing resources? Sometimes facilities that are less than optimal can be improved considerably by projects involving the team or various segments of the community. What

---

*American Alliance for Health, Physical Education, Recreation and Dance, 1900 Association Dr., Reston, VA 22091.

can you do to make your facility one that your athletes will be truly proud of? If they have a stake in some minor remodeling or decorating, they are much more likely to be especially cooperative in upkeep.

4. Cleaning, upkeep, and repair. Who is responsible for janitorial services? Get to know those individuals personally. A positive relationship with janitorial staff can contribute considerably to the service provided? How about upkeep and repair? You may be blessed with a school or club that has a lot of money and a top-notch facility. On the other hand, you may be coaching in an area with a tight budget and a home facility that is somewhat run down. Once again, projects involving the team or the community and a little paint, spit, and polish, could make a big difference.

5. Security and local regulations. Are there full-time security staff to look after the facility? What are your responsibilities with respect to such tasks as locking up after practices, double checking to ensure the facility has been vacated, checking windows and doors? Are there local ordinances or regulations regarding the facility that you should know about? All of these areas should be checked out ahead of time.

6. Spectator services. Spectator services at a facility can include parking, seating, washrooms, concessions, and crowd control. In each of these areas, clearly determine your areas of responsibility. If you are coaching in a local community where you have considerable influence and responsibility in any or all of these areas, you might brainstorm with community representatives over various strategies for improving spectator services. These can vary from minimal adaptations, such as signs and ropes to improve movement, to considerable improvement in comfort and shelter for spectators.

PITFALLS TO BE AVOIDED

In Chapter 12 we presented a danger signal checklist for managing assistants, that is a number of behaviors of the coach that are likely to guarantee that an assistant coach will be less than satisfactory and unlikely to change. In this chapter we present a danger signal checklist for behaviors of the coach that are likely to guarantee that money management will be less than satisfactory and unlikely to be approved by administrators. At regular intervals during the season (approximately every 2 months), we encourage you to use the checklist in Fig. 13-3 to monitor your money management. If you score a number of "yes" answers, you're heading for danger. In such cases, reexamine the guidelines in this chapter and take the necessary steps so that you can answer "no" to the questions on the danger signal checklist.

CHECKLIST

Danger Signals for Managing Money _____

As a coach preparing and administering a budget, do you:

1. Present "padded" or grossly inadequate budgets   Yes_____   No_____
   that may cause you to lose your credibility?
2. Fail to meet your deadline with your budget pro-   Yes_____   No_____
   posal because of lack of communication and plan-
   ning?
3. Leave records of financial agreements and trans-   Yes_____   No_____
   actions in your pockets, at the gym, on the front
   seat of your car, and numerous places?
4. Decide that it is not necessary to record expenses   Yes_____   No_____
   during out-of-town trips on your control cards?
5. Update financial information every month or two,   Yes_____   No_____
   or when you get around to it?
6. Allow unauthorized flow of petty cash?   Yes_____   No_____
7. Leave petty cash in obvious places and unse-   Yes_____   No_____
   cured?
8. Allow unauthorized persons to collect money?   Yes_____   No_____
9. Accept gifts and favors from salespersons that   Yes_____   No_____
   could obligate you to buy from them?
10. Allow high-pressure salespersons to interrupt   Yes_____   No_____
    your "quiet" time?
11. Choose equipment that does not meet allowable   Yes_____   No_____
    standards but that you can get for a "good price"?
12. Leave the computerized purchasing system to as-   Yes_____   No_____
    sistant coaches to understand rather than mas-
    tering it yourself?
13. Decide it is not necessary for you to be familiar   Yes_____   No_____
    with the financial procedures followed by your
    school for purchasing equipment and supplies?
14. Decide it is not necessary for your athletes to sign   Yes_____   No_____
    out equipment (after all, they're all honest)?

FIGURE 13-3

SUMMARY

Budget preparation and management is an important area of a coach's responsibilities. Two of the common budget preparation procedures are those of line item budgeting and PPBES budgeting. A line item budget includes a specific line (with a dollar value) for each object and function during the coming season. PPBES budgeting requires a coach to *plan* for specific goals during the coming season, *program* strategies to accomplish those goals, *budget* funds necessary to accomplish the program, and *evaluate* the adequacy of the budget to achieve the goals prior to the season, as well as the extent to which the goals were met following the season. An important aspect of administering a budget is the purchase and care of equipment. Another important aspect is the cost of out-of-town trips. Coaches should prepare separate control cards for sub-categories of petty cash, supplies, equipment, home-games, and away-games. An important rule of thumb for administering the budget is, "when you spend, record it." Often, coaches also have a responsibility of managing their home facilities. In such cases, coaches must clearly determine their duties in the sub-categories of safety, scheduling, security and regulations, facilities for home and visiting teams, cleaning and repairs, and spectator services. The chapter concluded with a danger signal checklist to remind the coach of money management practices to be avoided.

Coach's Checklist

The checklist in Fig. 13-4 outlines the recommendations in this chapter. We suggest that you use the checklist as a convenient reminder to ensure that you follow all of the recommended guidelines.

Review Questions

1. List seven steps that you might follow in preparing a budget.
2. Describe the essential characteristics of line-item budgeting.
3. Describe how effective behavioral coaching can be compatible with each of the four steps of the PPBES budgeting system.
4. What is a control card? In what five categories should control cards be used in administering a budget?
5. Briefly list four rules of good bookkeeping.
6. What are the disadvantages of padding a budget?
7. List five people that you should talk to before buying equipment.
8. List five subareas in which you as coach should clearly determine your responsibilities concerning care of your facility.

COACH'S CHECKLIST

Managing Money

	Date of Assessment					
Budget Preparation						
1. Review budgets from previous years.						
2. Seek input from comptroller and athletic director.						
3. Take inventory of supplies and equipment and assess needs for coming season.						
4. Seek input from equipment manager.						
5. Make list of budget needs in relation to your proposed goals and priorities.						
6. Seek input from trip managers.						
7. Transfer budget to standard budget summary forms.						
Administering the Budget						
1. Prepare separate control cards for subcategories of petty cash, supplies, equipment, home games, and away games.						
2. Establish clear rules for management of petty cash.						
3. When you spend it, record it.						
4. Review Danger Signal Checklist (p. 306) every couple of months.						
Managing the Facility						
1. Clearly determine your responsibilities in subcategories of safety, scheduling, security and regulations, facilities for home and visiting teams, cleaning and repair, and spectator services.						

FIGURE 13-4

Mini-Lab Exercises

1. Choose a piece of equipment for a sport that you played or hope to coach. Prepare what you consider to be a reasonable list of do's and don'ts to review with athletes concerning proper care and use of that equipment.
2. Choose a sport that you played or hope to coach. Approach a coach that you know who coaches that particular sport. Volunteer your services to help the coach take an inventory of supplies and equipment. Based on your inventory, assess the supplies and equipment needs for that coach for the upcoming season, and submit them to him or her for feedback.

References

Flynn. R. (1980). Timely topics in facility planning. Journal of Physical Education and Research **51**:19.

Glading. J. (1980). The "Big Apple" beats the athletic facility's crunch. Journal of Physical Education and Research **51**:28.

Grant. N. (1980). A facility goes underground. Journal of Physical Education and Research **51**:30.

Jensen. C.R. (1983). Administrative management of physical education and athletic programs. Philadelphia: Lea & Febiger.

Pestolesi, R.A., and Sinclair, W.A. (1978). Creative administration in physical education and athletics. Englewood Cliffs, N.J.: Prentice-Hall.

Quint, B.G. (1981). Clear and simple guide to bookkeeping. New York: Monarch Press.

Resick, M.C., Siedel, B.L., and Mason, J.G. (1979). Modern administrative practices in physical education and athletics. Reading, Mass.: Addison-Wesley.

Vanderzwaag, H.J. (1984). Sport management in schools and colleges. New York: Wiley.

Selected Readings

Hobson. A. (1983). The pulse of the market changes. Coaching Review **6**:29-31.

Hogan. P. (1982). The nuts and bolts of playground construction. vol 3. Champaign. Ill.: Leisure Press. Human Kinetics Publishers.

Mackenzie. V. (1983). Stopwatches on the market. Coaching Review **6**:21-24.

Mountjoy. T. (1982). Finding dollars in depressed times. Coaching Review **5**:17-19.

14

Time Management Techniques for Coaches

Studies of successful individuals in different walks of life who are considered to be effective time managers have revealed numerous commonalities (Douglass and Douglass, 1980; Hanel et al., 1983; Mackenzie, 1975; Reynolds and Tramel, 1979). They plan and schedule important activities on a daily basis, knowing that an hour of effective planning and scheduling can save 2 hours in execution. They have well-organized office or work settings, with some consideration given to economy of movement to get, use, replace, file, and store things. They schedule time to relax, both mentally and physically, rather than running around like a chicken with its head cut off. They've learned how to minimize the amount of time wasted in ineffective meetings, inefficient delegation, and the seemingly uncontrollable interruptions that plague many of us in our work. Finally, they've learned how to minimize personal time wasters and maximize personal time savers. All of these practices can also be very beneficial for coaches. In this chapter we describe strategies to help you juggle your time and energy between coaching responsibilities, a full-time job, and your personal life—strategies to help you make the most of available time.

TIME SAVERS AND TIME WASTERS

A time saver is anything that decreases a time waster. But what is a time waster? There are three broad classes of personal time wasters. First, many people would agree that behaviors that are more or less synonomous with "doing nothing" are a form of time wasters. Examples include daydreaming, doodling while sitting in your office, sitting in the cafeteria drinking coffee and socializing for an hour at a time. A second class of personal time wasters includes those that are more or less synonomous with inefficiency. It's possible to appear to be constantly busy (and not wasting time according to the first class of time wasters), yet waste a lot of time. Examples of such time wasters in an office include having a disorganized desk or work area so that you spend much time searching for things, or switching often from one task to the next so that time is wasted familiarizing yourself with the previously unfinished tasks (when once would have been sufficient), or having a single file folder in which all of your correspondence is inserted chronologically so that time is wasted searching for information on a particular item that was inserted 2 or 3 weeks before.

The third class of time wasters is rarely recognized, yet it is probably the most important potential class of time wasters when considered over a lifetime. The third way to waste time is to continually work on low-priority activities and postpone high-priority activities. Obviously, some activities have a much higher payoff for you than others. Also, many high payoffs are long delayed in that they occur only after a great deal of activity on your part. For example, a high salary, good job, prestige, and other things that go along with an important promotion are obtained only after much hard work. The thrill and ecstasy of winning an Olympic gold medal occurs only after many years of intensive training. If you decide that a goal with long-term payoffs is really a high priority, then you should try to spend some time each day working toward that goal. If, instead, you spend all of your time working on lower priority activities with lesser but more immediate payoffs, that constitutes a form of time wasting. For example, suppose that you coach at a high school. Suppose further that you decide that getting a master's degree in physical eduction is something that you really want to do. To be accepted into the school that you want to attend, you must score well on the Graduate Record Exam. The date for the exam is four months away. You're now sitting at your desk wondering how you should spend the next couple of hours. You could go to the bank and get some money for the weekend and drop some clothes off at the laundry; you could prepare the practice plan for tomorrow's practice;

you could grade yesterday's exam papers; or you could spend some time studying for your Graduate Record Exam. If you have really decided that getting into graduate school is your highest priority, then performing any of the other three activities before first doing some studying is wasting time. Of course, the other three activities are not time wasters like those in the first two broad classes above. The lower priority activities do have payoffs that are fairly immediate, and sooner or later those activities must be done. However, the payoffs for those activities are much lower. From this point of view, time management skills, in part, increase the chances that you will perform activities leading to delayed but highly valued consequences while decreasing the chances that you will perform only lower priority activities that have more immediate but lower value consequences.

TIME MANAGEMENT STRATEGIES
Step 1: Evaluate Current Time Management Skills

The checklist in Fig. 14-1 is designed to help you determine what kind of a time manager you are by assessing the extent to which you engage in good time management behavior. We don't want to show you up as a poor time manager, and we don't want to scare you away from the rest of this chapter. Rather, the questionnaire is a quick, convenient way of prompting you to think of potential time wasters and time savers. More important, it will provide you with a yardstick to use later to measure your progress in acquiring time management skills, and a source of reward for improving.

After completing the checklist, total your points (subtracting the total minus score from the total plus score). If your total score is 25 or better, you are already a good time manager. Any score less than 25 means there is room for improvement.

Step 2: Identify Priority Activities and Goals

List specific activities to be time-lined. Many of your duties and responsibilities must be met during certain times of the year. We've provided a partial list of these activities in Fig. 14-2. No doubt you will be able to add to that list. Your task at this time is to go through the list, roughly estimate the amount of time required to perform the activities, and write in the deadlines by which you would like the activities to be completed during the next season. For now, don't try to prioritize them.

Identify personal goals for the coming year. In addition to necessary activities, you no doubt have some personal goals that you would like to accomplish during the coming year. A problem that many

Text continued on p. 319.

Time Waster/Time Saver Factors

Read each time waster/time saver pair of items. For each pair, circle the number on the rating scale that is most typical of you.

SCORING KEY: −2 = *Almost always*
                  −1 = *Often*
                    0 = *Sometimes*
               +1 = *Often*
               +2 = *Almost always*

Time Wasters	−2 −1 0 +1 +2	Time Savers
Paperwork I keep paperwork such as junk mail, memos, etc., in a single pile so that I repeatedly handle the same paper while searching for individual items.	−2 −1 0 +1 +2	I minimize paper handling. The first time I look at my paperwork I categorize it and place it in one of four piles: top priority, medium priority, low priority, waste basket
Paper work Copies of my letters, schedules, medical waiver forms, etc., are scattered all over my office or back of my car	−2 −1 0 +1 +2	Copies of my letters, schedules, medical waiver forms, etc., are placed in folders and inserted alphabetically in a well-organized filing cabinet.
Organization of books and coaching manuals Players and coaches borrow my books and coaching manuals, and I'm never sure where they are when I need them.	−2 −1 0 +1 +2	I use a formal sign-out system for keeping track of items that I lend to others.
Office distractions Noises, sights and sounds from the window and open door of my office distract me.	−2 −1 0 +1 +2	I keep my office area organized to decrease daydreaming, looking out the window, and such.
Office distractions I keep materials for more than one project on my desk.	−2 −1 0 +1 +2	My desk top contains only the project on which I'm currently working.

FIGURE 14-1

Time Wasters	-2	-1	0	+1	+2	Time Savers
Telephone calls I accept calls as they come in, and make calls to others as they occur to me.	-2	-1	0	+1	+2	I group my telephone calls whenever possible so that I make them and accept them all at one time, to reduce disruptions.
Drop-in visitors I talk to visitors when they come to my office at any time.	-2	-1	0	+1	+2	I post the times when I am available for drop-in visitors.
Long-term planning I work on tasks as I think of them.	-2	-1	0	+1	+2	I keep a detailed written list of long-term goals and duties and review them approximately once a month.
Deadlines I do things as I think of them or as they are brought to my attention.	-2	-1	0	+1	+2	I set reasonable deadlines for important activities and schedule the related work in my planning calendar.
Prioritizing I do things during the day as they occur to me or are brought to my attention.	-2	-1	0	+1	+2	Each morning I write out my priority activities for the day.
Daily scheduling I do things during the day as they occur to me or as they are brought to my attention.	-2	-1	0	+1	+2	I schedule my time each morning for the rest of the day so that I can be sure to accomplish my top-priority activities.
Scheduling personal work time I do things as I think of them or as they are brought to my attention.	-2	-1	0	+1	+2	Each work day I try to schedule a specific "quiet time" during my "prime time" to do top-priority paperwork and planning without interruptions.

Continued.

Time Waster/Time Saver Factors—cont'd _____

Time Wasters	−2 −1 0 +1 +2	Time Savers
Planning calendar I do things and go places without taking my planning calendar.	−2 −1 0 +1 +2	I take my planning calendar with me when I do things or go places.
Planning for practices and meetings I go to practices and meetings (for which I am responsible) without a written plan.	−2 −1 0 +1 +2	I prepare a written plan or agenda for practices and meetings for which I am responsible.
Personal organization at practices At practices, I don't have the schedules, forms, and materials that I need.	−2 −1 0 +1 +2	At practices, I keep a well-organized coaching manual with me that contains the practice routine, game schedule, goals for the season, and other relevant information that athletes and assistants frequently ask for.
Communicating with staff I review my priorities with my staff whenever they ask me about them.	−2 −1 0 +1 +2	I schedule a time to review my objectives and priorities with my key staff on a daily or weekly basis.
Assignments for staff I tell my staff things as I think of them.	−2 −1 0 +1 +2	I set specific deadlines for assignments to staff, and immediately follow up on projects that staff have submitted to me by those deadlines.
Serving on committees I serve on committees whenever asked.	−2 −1 0 +1 +2	I ask for an estimate of the time commitment, check my schedule and my priorities before agreeing to serve on committees.

FIGURE 14-1, cont'd

Coaching Activities To Be Time-Lined _____

Activities To Be Time-Lined	Deadlines	Priorities	Estimated Time to Complete
1. Budget submission			
2. Budget allocation			
3. Equipment ordering			
4. Equipment storing			
5. Facilities evaluation and improvement			
6. Selecting coaches			
7. Inservice for coaches			
8. Nutrition plan			
9. Conditioning plan			
10. Charts for attendance. team and individual feedback, public posting, etc.			
11. Meetings of league officials and coaches of other teams			
12. Team playbook or manual			
13. Medical and waiver forms			
14. Practice schedule			
15. Assessment forms for basic skills			
16. Game schedule			
17. Road trips			
18. Officials. time keepers, and score keepers			
19. Safety rules for facilities and equipment			

FIGURE 14-2   *Continued.*

Coaching Activities To Be Time-Lined—cont'd ___

Activities To Be Time-Lined	Deadlines	Priorities	Estimated Time to Complete
20. First-aid and medical coverage for games and practices			
21. Sample practices			
22. Try-outs			
23. Equipment dispersal			
24. Assessing basic skills			
25. Season goal setting with team			
26. Season goal setting with individuals			
27. Other			

FIGURE 14-2, cont'd

coaches face is that personal goals tend to get shoved aside until the necessary daily activities are completed. That often leaves little or no time for personal goals. At this point, consider several questions. What potential accomplishments during the next year would give you the most satisfaction? The most recognition from your fellow coaches? The most appreciation from the athletes that you coach? The best chance of promotion? The biggest pay raise? The highest evaluation from your boss? What do you really want out of your job? Every workday, you should spend at least some time working toward your top-priority goals, those goals with the greatest potential payoff for yourself. Therefore, a critical step in effective time management is to identify priority personal goals and activities leading to them. Writing out priority goals and the steps that lead to them constitutes the first step in accomplishing those goals, and in minimizing time spent on the less important activities that seem to occupy many of us through much of a typical working day. The form provided in Fig. 14-3 will help you complete this task.

Try to list the goals so that they read specifically and identify quantitative results. Avoid general qualitative statements. For example, rather than "Develop a personal exercise plan to get in shape," it would be better to write "Develop a personal exercise plan to keep my weight at 160 pounds and to earn 30 aerobic points per week." Wherever possible, identify goals in terms of specific time commitments. For example, rather than "Help children with homework each week," it would be better to write "Schedule a minimum of 2 hours per child per week to help with homework."

Identify long-term career goals. The final step in planning for the coming year is to consider your own long-term career goals. Have you seriously thought about what you would like to be doing 5 years from now? Ten years from now? For the rest of your life? As with other goals, thinking about and actually writing out long-term goals is an important step in time management. The guide for identifying long-term career and personal goals shown in Fig. 14-4 will help you to complete this step.

Step 3: Prioritize Goals

Alex McKenzie has said, "Eighty percent of our payoffs come from 20% of our activities." There is absolutely no doubt that some of our activities have a much higher payoff than others. If you feel that you tend to spend considerable time performing a wide variety of activities that have little or no payoff, then there is probably room for improvement in your time management skills.

Text continued on p. 326.

Personal and Career Goals for Current Year _____

Goals	Priorities	Deadlines	Estimated Time to Complete
Work-related goals (teaching or other work goals for the year; special projects; other)			
Family/friendship goals (spouse or roommate; children; vacation; other relatives; house or apartment projects; other)			

FIGURE 14-3

Goals	Priorities	Deadlines	Estimated Time to Complete
Educational goals (university courses; inservice courses; coaching or other conferences; other)			
Personal health, exercise, recreational goals (exercise/dieting program; sports you yourself play; other)			

Guide for Identifying Long-Term Career and Personal Goals

The following categories will prompt you to think of long-term career and personal goals. If you are serious about long-term personal planning. then "brainstorm" your goals.

	Goals for Next 5 Years	Priorities	Lifetime Goals	Priorities
Education				
Extra courses				
Extra degrees				
Career				
Target job or position				
Geographic location				
Target salary				

FIGURE 14-4

	Goals for Next 5 Years	Priorities	Lifetime Goals	Priorities
Target retirement date				
Special projects				
Health				
Exercise program				
Dieting goals				
Family				
Spouse activities				

Continued.

Guide for Identifying Long-Term Career and Personal Goals—cont'd

	Goals for Next 5 Years	Priorities	Lifetime Goals	Priorities
Family—cont'd Child/parent activities				
Home style and location				
Vacations				
Financial planning				
Special projects				

FIGURE 14-4, cont'd

	Goals for Next 5 Years	Priorities	Lifetime Goals	Priorities
Social Relationships				
Friendships				
Personal improvement goals				
Other				

The next important step in our program is that of prioritizing goals and activities for the coming year. In Figs. 14-2, 14-3, and 14-4 you have completed three forms, listing activities to be performed at certain times of the year, your personal goals for the coming season, and some of your long-term career and personal goals. If we were bookies, we would give you odds on two things: First, you will not accomplish all of the goals and activities listed on those three forms. Second, failure to prioritize and deliberately schedule time for top-priority activities will ensure that many of your important personal, top-priority goals will get shoved aside.

The time has come to prioritize. Review the activities and goals listed on the three forms and put an A beside all of those that are absolutely top priority. Review the remaining categories and put a B beside all of those that you would really like to do if you can find the time. Put a C beside all of the remaining items. (This ABC prioritizing strategy was first described by Lakein in 1973.) Then go back over the A items and number them in order of priority. This gives you a list of your top-priority activities and goals for the coming year.

Step 4: Set Deadlines

Review all of the A items and estimate as closely as possible the total amount of time needed to complete each item. Where appropriate, identify specific deadlines by which they must occur. Next, prepare a monthly or yearly overview. For example, you might make 12 photocopies of the Monthly Planning Page (Fig. 14-5), or prepare a large (approximately 3 feet by 3 feet) yearly calendar. Now enter the deadines and required work time for all of the top-priority A items on your monthly or yearly planning calendar. Consider the amount of time that you normally have available to work on these items. Also consider your commitments in all of the categories listed above. It's important not to plan coaching activities in total isolation from other commitments. This is a critical step because it will give you some idea of how far in advance you will have to start working toward various goals in order to use the time that you have available for those goals and complete them by the prescribed deadlines.

Step 5: Adopt Time Management Calendar

Adopt an effective daily, weekly, and monthly planning system. One possibility is to prepare your own calendar system using 12 copies of the monthly calendar shown in Fig. 14-5, and copies of the Weekly Planner shown in Fig. 14-6.

The calendar system will greatly assist in managing your time most effectively. It requires that you take about half an hour at the start of each week to plan the week. In addition to weekly planning, take approximately 10 minutes each morning to plan the day. Finally, the monthly overview page will help you keep track of important meetings or deadlines scheduled more than a month in advance. Guidelines for using this system follow.

1. Plan at the start of each week (Fig. 14-6)
   a. In appropriate time slots, mark off all of the commitments related to work that cannot be changed. These include meetings, time to be spent on projects, staff attendance sheets that must be completed, and so on. Schedule only those activities that must be completed. Be sure to check your monthly overview page for any deadlines or meetings previously recorded for that week.
   b. If possible, reschedule meetings (and schedule new meetings) near the end of the day. People tend to shoot the breeze less in meetings scheduled near quitting time. Meetings where you must be especially alert are exceptions.
   c. Review each scheduled meeting to see if it can be more effi-

Text continued on p. 332.

Monthly Planning Page

Month					19	
Sunday	Monday	Tuesday	Wednesday	Thursday	Friday	Saturday
AM						
Noon						
PM						
Evening						
AM						
Noon						
PM						
Evening						
AM						
Noon						
PM						
Evening						

FIGURE 14-5

Sunday	Monday	Tuesday	Wednesday	Thursday	Friday	Saturday
AM						
Noon						
PM						
Evening						
AM						
Noon						
PM						
Evening						

Weekly Planner

Month _____. 19_____

Date _____ Monday Activities	Estimated Time	Delegate to	P.	Date _____ Tuesday Activities	Estimated Time	Delegate to	P.	Date _____ Wednesday Activities	Estimated Time	Delegate to	P.

8:00			
8:30			
9:00			
9:30			
10:00			
10:30			
11:00			
11:30			
12:00			
12:30			
1:00			
1:30			
2:00			
2:30			
3:00			
3:30			
4:00			
4:30			
5:00			
Evening			

FIGURE 14-6

Time	Date _____ Thursday Activities	Estimated Time	Delegate to	P.	Date _____ Friday Activities	Estimated Time	Delegate to	P.	Date _____ Saturday Activities	Estimated Time	Delegate to	P.
									8:00			
									9:00			
									10:00			
									11:00			
									12:00			
									1:00			
									2:00			
									3:00			
									4:00			
8:00									5:00			
8:30									6:00			
9:00									7:00			
9:30									8:00			
10:00									9:00			
10:30									10:00			
11:00									Date _____ Sunday Activities			
11:30												
12:00												
12:30									8:00			
1:00									9:00			
1:30									10:00			
2:00									11:00			
2:30									12:00			
3:00									1:00			
3:30									2:00			
4:00									3:00			
4:30									4:00			
5:00									5:00			
Evening									6:00			
									7:00			
									8:00			
									9:00			
									10:00			

ciently handled by telephone. If so, schedule a telephone call and cancel the meeting.

d. If you have a secretary who can screen telephone calls, schedule a time near the end of the morning or afternoon to return all calls. Otherwise, keep a list of calls to be made, and make them all at one time. This decreases interruptions at other times of the day.

e. Review your high-priority goals, and write in those steps that are most important for you to work on during the coming week.

f. If possible, block in a "quiet hour" (preferably during the morning) each day for you to work on your high-priority activities.

g. If you have a secretary, review your calendar so that he or she will know what you have scheduled.

2. Plan at the start of each day (Fig. 14-6)

a. Review the scheduled activities for the day. Add any additional activities that you can think of, including those that didn't get completed the previous day. This might also include personal items (e.g., going to the bank to get money for the weekend).

b. Prioritize those activities that have not yet been scheduled. Identify the most important activity and put a 1 beside it in the column labeled P. Using consecutive numbers, continue to prioritize the other activities.

c. For each of the prioritized activities, write in the "Delegate to" column those that can be effectively delegated to one of your staff.

d. For each of the remaining prioritized activities, estimate the time to complete them, and enter it under "estimated time."

e. Schedule the prioritized activities in the available time slots. When you run out of time slots, forget about the remaining activities. If you have followed our system effectively, you are already taking care of your high-priority activities; the others can be postponed.

f. For most people, it is wise to underschedule. Many people require at least an hour of unscheduled time during the day to take care of the daily "crises" that are impossible to postpone or avoid.

g. As you complete each activity during the day, check it off your list. This provides visual feedback on the proportion of scheduled activities that you are accomplishing.

3. Schedule activities for the subsequent month (Fig. 14-5)
   a. If any activity or deadline is identified for a subsequent month, be sure to record it *only* on the appropriate one-page monthly planner, so that you have a monthly overview at the start of each month.

Step 6: Manage Meetings Effectively

A survey of managers from 14 countries, by time management consultant Alex Mackenzie (1975), revealed that meetings were the third most frequently listed time waster. Regular use of the checklist in Fig. 14-7 will greatly reduce your time wasted in meetings.

Step 7: Delegate Effectively

An important strategy for improving time use efficiency is effective delegation. However, inappropriate delegation of authority and responsibility can lead to frequent interruptions, conflicting expectations, and much time wasted on both sides. When delegating to your assistant coaches and other staff, clearly identify the results, performance standards, and deadlines that you expect to be met. Also, review and identify resources and any additional training that may be needed in order for your assistants to carry out the responsibilities that you delegate to them. Then follow up, by the deadlines agreed on, projects that staff have submitted to you. And finally, praise your staff for appropriately handling delegated responsibilities.

Step 8: Evaluate Time Savers and Time Wasters Regularly

If you have followed all of the preceding steps, you are well on your way to effective time management. To ensure that your time management skills are maintained, we recommend that you self-evaluate time savers and time wasters weekly, using the checklist in Fig. 14-8.

SOME MISCONCEPTIONS ABOUT TIME MANAGEMENT

Before concluding this chapter, let's discuss some common misconceptions about time management. First, effective time management does not necessarily mean becoming a compulsive clock watcher or frequently being upset about being late or wasting a minute (and in turn influencing others to become upset). Effective time management means working smarter, not harder. Second, although you may feel that you can find more time, you can't; you already have all there is—24 hours each day. Time is the one commodity in the world that's equally distributed among everyone, at least within our lifetimes. Third, time management is not something that you learn once and

Text continued on p. 338

C H E C K L I S T

Evaluating Effectiveness of Meetings _____

Select a recent meeting that you attended or, if possible, chaired. Put a check in the appropriate column opposite each statement, to reflect your observations about the particular meeting. If a particular item does not apply, check "Not applicable."

SCORING KEY: 1 = *Yes*
                   2 = *Generally yes*
                   3 = *Generally no*
                   4 = *No*
                   5 = *Not applicable*

____ I chaired the meeting.
____ I did not chair the meeting.

Date of meeting _____

	Day	Month	Year	1	2	3	4	5

Preliminary Organization

1. Notice of meeting was given at least 2 days in advance.
2. Agenda was distributed prior to meeting or was agreed on as first order of business.
3. Agenda items were specific and detailed enough to provide adequate prompts for preparing meeting.
4. Meeting started at prearranged time.
5. Minutes of previous meeting were read and approved.
6. Those in attendance gave thought to their contributions beforehand and had written notes concerning their participation.
7. Someone was assigned to take notes to prepare minutes.
8. Duration of meeting was determined in advance or at start of meeting.
9. Meeting room was prearranged, and meeting was free of outside distractions.

NOTE: The more "yes" answers the better; the more "no" answers the more time is being wasted.

FIGURE 14-7

	1	2	3	4	5
Participation by Those in Attendance					
1. Every individual attending needed to be there throughout meeting.					
2. Decision was made for at least one item of business.					
3. If action was required, tasks were assigned to specific individuals.					
4. Deadlines for reporting results of action were agreed on.					
5. Discussion was restricted to items on agenda.					
Management by Chairperson					
1. Participants were kept to one topic at a time.					
2. Participants were prompted when they discussed irrelevant issues.					
3. Chairperson summarized main parts of discussion prior to voting.					
4. Meeting followed appropriate parliamentary procedure.					
5. Chairperson terminated meeting on time.					

C H E C K L I S T

Evaluating Time Savers/Time Wasters Regularly

Use this checklist to evaluate your time management behaviors during the past week. If you score some of the items in "Generally no" or "No" column, you have room for improvement.

SCORING KEY: 1 = *Yes, all opportunities*
                2 = *Generally yes, more than half of opportunities*
                3 = *Generally no, less than half of opportunities*
                4 = *No, not at all*
                5 = *Not applicable*

	1	2	3	4	5
Personal Time Savers					
1. Prepared written weekly plan at beginning of work week.					
2. Prioritized and scheduled daily activities each workday morning.					
3. Scheduled "quiet hours" during "prime time" for each workday.					
4. Worked on most important tasks first each day.					
5. Used "prime time" to work on high-priority tasks.					
6. Set reasonable deadlines for all important activities.					
7. Meet majority of deadlines each day.					
8. "Grouped" phone calls each day.					
9. Posted times I was available for drop-in visitors.					
10. Dealt with routine paperwork once each day.					
Time Savers Involving Myself and Others					
1. Kept non-work-related conversation to reasonable amount during phone calls and when talking to drop-in visitors.					
2. When situations such as short-term "crises" or drop-in visitors pressured me to rearrange priorities, I was politely assertive about sticking to schedule.					

FIGURE 14-8

	1	2	3	4	5
3. Reviewed daily objectives each morning with key staff, and informed all staff immediately about job-related changes, objectives, and priorities.					
4. When I delegated responsibilities, indicated both results desired and deadlines.					
5. Used written communications with staff to delegate effectively.					
6. Took time to express appreciation to staff when they completed work effectively and efficiently.					
7. Refused to let staff shift work to me that should be done by them.					
8. Used Meetings Checklist to evaluate all meetings.					

My worst time waster this past week was _____

_____

_____

_____

_____

_____

To minimize this time waster next week, I will _____

_____

_____

_____

_____

_____

_____

that stays with you for the rest of your life. Unfortunately, you can't spray yourself with "time management deodorant" in the morning and "be good for the whole day." Rather, like dieting or exercising, good time management practices become habit only after regular practice and frequent attention . As shown in Fig. 14-9, disorganization breeds disorganization; organization breeds organization.

SUMMARY

Effective time management means learning to make the most of available time. It means learning to work smarter, not harder. Time management skills increase the chances that you will perform activities leading to delayed but highly valued consequences, while decreasing the chances that you will perform only lower priority activities that have more immediate although lower valued consequences. Effective time management requires that you identify both short-term and long term personal and professional goals that have the highest payoffs. It requires that you prioritize those goals, task analyze them into activities that can be accomplished on a daily or weekly basis, set deadlines for their accomplishment, and time-line them. Effective time managers use a planning calendar to prompt them to take steps to accomplish their goals in order to maximize their payoffs. Finally, time management techniques help you to minimize time wasters and maximize time savers so that important priority goals are more likely to be accomplished.

Coach's Checklist

The checklist in Fig. 14-10 outlines the steps to be taken for effective time management. We suggest that you use the checklist as a convenient reminder to ensure that you follow all of the recommended steps.

Review Questions

1. Briefly describe the three different types of time wasters.
2. For each of the three different types of time wasters, describe an example that applies to you.
3. Briefly outline the characteristics of Lakein's ABC prioritizing strategy.
4. When you identify a deadline to be met or a meeting to be attended in any month, why is it advantageous to record it only on an appropriate one-page monthly planner (as opposed to also recording it on your daily and weekly planners)?
5. List at least three reasons why meetings are often a waste of time.

From Turla, P.A., and Hawkins, K.L.

FIGURE 14-9
Personal organization is important part of effective time management. **A,** *Time waster: Distractions.* **B,** *Disorganization breeds disorganization.* *Continued.*

FIGURE 14-9 cont'd

C, Time saver: Only project being worked on is on desk. D, Organization breeds organization.

COACH'S CHECKLIST

Effective Time Management _____

	Date Completed					
1. Evaluate your current time management skills by completing Time Waster/Time Saver Checklist (Fig. 14-1).						
2. Prepare list of all your work activities and responsibilities to be time-lined (Fig. 14-2).						
3. Identify personal and career goals for current year (Fig. 14-3).						
4. Identify long-term career and personal goals (Fig. 14-4).						
5. Use ABC prioritizing system for preparing list of top-priority goals and activities (From Figs. 14-2, 14-3, 14-4).						
6. Add deadlines for completion of all top-priority activities identified in step 5.						
7. Photocopy 12 copies of Monthly Planner (Fig. 14-5) and insert dates for coming season.						
8. Transfer all deadlines for your top-priority activities and goals to appropriate month on Monthly Planner.						
9. Photocopy sufficient number of copies of Weekly Planner (Fig. 14-6) for use during coming season.						
10. Organize daily-weekly-monthly planning calendar system in three-ring binder.						
11. Use checklist (Fig. 14-7) to evaluate effectiveness of at least one meeting per month.						
12. Use written communications with staff to improve delegation.						
13. Use checklist (Fig. 14-8) to evaluate time savers/time wasters at least once per week.						

FIGURE 14-10

6. Briefly describe three common misconceptions about time management.
7. In four or five sentences, describe what effective time management is all about.

Mini-Lab Exercises

1. Identify your personal and career goals for the coming year by completing Fig. 14-3.
2. Identify your long-term career and personal goals by completing Fig. 14-4.
3. Use the checklist in Fig. 14-7 to evaluate formally the next meeting that you attend.

References

Douglass. M.E.. and Douglass. D.N. (1980). Manage your time. manage your work. manage yourself. New York: AMACOM. A Division of the American Management Associations.

Hanel. F.. Martin. G.. and Koop. S. (1983). Fieldtesting of a self-instructional time management manual with managerial staff in an institutional setting. Journal of Organizational Behavior Management 4:81-96.

Lakein. A. (1973). How to get control of your time and your life. New York: New American Library.

Mackenzie. R.A. (1975). New time management methods for you and your staff. Chicago: Dartnell Corporation.

Reynolds. H.. and Tramel. M.E. (1979). Executive time management: Getting twelve hours of work out of an eight hour day. Englewood Cliffs. N.J.: Prentice-Hall.

Selected Readings

Ferner. J.D. (1980). Successful time management: A self-testing guide. New York: Wiley.

Kozoll. C.E. (1984). No time for wasting time. Coaching Review 7:30-32.

Kozoll. C.E. (1985). Coaches' guide to time management. Champaign. Ill.: Human Kinetics Publishers.

Turla. P.. and Hawkins. K.L. (1983). Time management made easy. New York: E.P. Dutton.

15

Sociological, Philosophical, and Ethical Aspects of Coaching

To a large extent, this book has dealt with specifics—the how-to-do-it aspects of effective behavioral coaching. Among other things, we describe how to identify desirable athletic behaviors in observable terms, frequently monitor and chart athletic behaviors, and adopt a consistent positive approach to changing behaviors of athletes. We include lots of checklists to help you deal with the details of effective behavioral coaching. However, although a coach deals in specifics on a day-to-day basis, a coach must also consider the broader framework. One discipline dealing with broader issues in sports is sports sociology. Another such discipline is the philosophy of sport. A subtopic of the philosophy of sport is ethics. In this chapter we examine some of the sociological, philosophical, and ethical aspects of coaching. Specifically, we discuss some aspects of aggression and violence in sport, and review implications for coaching youth. We then discuss ethics of coaching under the subtopics of winning, losing, coach-athlete relationships, sportsmanship, confidentiality, and protecting the rights of athletes.

The issues that we address and the suggestions that we make in this chapter are directed at coaches of young athletes (ages 8 to 18 years) in grade school, junior high, or high school sports and in agency-sponsored youth programs. Although many of these issues are pertinent to college, international, and professional athletics as well, some of the recommendations in this chapter may not be appropriate for these groups.

SOCIOLOGICAL ASPECTS OF SPORT

Sociology has been defined as "the scientific study of social structures and social processes" (Leonard, 1980). Social structures of interest to sports sociologists cover a wide range, including coach-athlete dyad, team, league, professional athlete union, and the crowd or audience in a packed stadium. Social processes of interest to sports sociologists also cover a wide range, and include racial discrimination, aggression and violence by athletes, fan violence, gender role socialization, and sexism, to mention a few. It is beyond the scope of this text to discuss all of these issues and to review the considerable data and research. One topic that we will discuss, however, concerns aggression and violence by athletes.

AGGRESSION AND VIOLENCE IN SPORT

"Hit him hard and hit him low, and if he gets up, hit him again."
"If you can't beat them in the alley, you can't beat them on the ice."
"The fans wanted violence, and we gave it to them."
These quotes are from coaches of football, ice hockey, and lacrosse. Although the coaches involved coached adults in professional sports, we suspect that some coaches of young people in those same sports have made similar comments at one time or another. As expressed by Bredemeier and Shields (1985), "to be good in sports you have to be bad." "You have to play aggressively to win" is a comment that one is likely to hear from coaches of most sports. Obviously, the degree and type of aggression varies from sport to sport. Boxing and American football involve direct aggression against an opponent. In sports that supposedly have little body contact, such as basketball and soccer, flying elbows and pushing and shoving are common. In sports such as racquetball or tennis, the aggression is more indirect, and in sports such as golf, aggression is directed against objects.

Some Causes of Aggression in Sport

What contributes to the development of aggressive behavior in athletes? In the long run, we assume that aggressive behavior, like other behavior, is controlled primarily by its consequences. If an athlete is excessively aggressive, it may mean scoring more goals or points, winning, receiving money or scholarships, immediate crowd support, immediate peer support, positive coach feedback, and overcoming a more skilled opponent. It may also involve the removal or termination of the prospect of losing, a form of escape conditioning. What events trigger an episode of aggression? They can include observation of someone else being aggressive and getting away with it (modeling), instructions from the coach either directly or indirectly, self-instructions (e.g., "This guy is too good, but if I take him out of the game we can still win."), and reflex reaction to threat. Moreover, some athletes may have been taught that the referees are there to enforce certain rules, but within those they can do whatever the referee will let them get away with. They may have learned to give up the kinds of self-control that they show outside the athletic environment and to put their behavior in the hands of the officials (the enforcers of the rules) and their coaches (whom many athletes have learned to see as responsible for all decisions). It may be this factor that has led many athletes to show a type of Jekyl and Hyde behavior. Some football players, for example, are soft spoken, considerate, and friendly off the field, but extremely mean, nasty, and rotten on the field. As expressed by Bredemeier and Shields (1985), the morals that control their normal everyday behavior simply don't apply in the athletic environment.

ASSERTION VERSUS AGGRESSION

To put aggression in sports in the proper context, it helps to distinguish between aggression and assertion. Aggression has been defined as "any form of behavior directed toward the goal of harming or injuring another living being who is motivated to avoid such treatment" (Baron, 1977). Quite simply, it means acts that are intended to inflict pain or injury. In terms of this definition, a coach should never encourage an athlete to be aggressive (boxing is a possible exception, although some might debate whether boxing is a sport). Within the context of sport, assertion has been defined as "robust, physically forceful play not meant to harm another player" (Bredemeier and Shields, 1985).

COACHING STRATEGIES TO DEVELOP ASSERTION AND CONTROL AGGRESSION

In terms of the above definitions, coaches should encourage athletes to be proudly assertive in their play, to hustle, to try to score points, and to try to win. Coaches should not teach athletes to harm or injure another athlete in the course of practice or competition.

1. **Teach "play by the rules."** In terms of their behavior toward officials and others, and in terms of instructions to athletes, coaches should teach athletes to play within the rules. They should specifically encourage athletes in contact sports that taking cheap shots or deliberate late hits is simply not acceptable.

2. **Teach sportsmanship.** Coaches are extremely important as models for athletes, especially young athletes. Shaking hands with the opposing coach and acknowledging that the opposing team played well (win or lose) helps to set a good example for the players. In terms of athletic behavior, for example, if a lineman makes a quarterback sack, standing over the fallen quarterback and glaring at him is poor sportsmanship. Offering a hand to help him up or patting him on the back is good sportsmanship.

3. **Teach respect for opponents as people.** A coach should not talk about the other team as "animals" or "jerks." They're people who have feelings, desires, and hopes, like anybody else. Modeling respect for the opponents as people sets a good example for athletes.

4. **Teach emotional control.** Coaches who rant and rave, have prolonged arm-waving arguments with officials over decisions, or who threaten and holler at opponents provide poor role models for their athletes. On the other hand, coaches that show consistent emotional control, such as Bud Grant of the Minnesota Vikings or Tom Landry of the Dallas Cowboys, provide a much better model for young athletes.

By permission of Johnny Hart and News America Syndicate.

5. **Teach assertion in response to cheap shots by opponents.** What happens if an opponent gives a cheap shot—a late hit in football, a cross-check in hockey, or an elbow in basketball? How should athletes on the receiving end be taught to handle that type of situation? In our view, young athletes should be told something like "Whenever one of their team gives you a shot, let them know in every way possible that it's only going to make you play harder. The way you jump up quickly,

the way you get right back into the play, the body language you show, the encouragement you give your teammates are all ways to let them know that that kind of stuff only makes you a better athlete. If you do that consistently, you'll be the winner, and they'll be the loser. That way, you don't have to resort to their tactics."

6. **Watch your language.** Consistently use technically correct words and avoid jargon that implies aggression and violence. For example, talk about making a tackle instead of making a hit. Say "Use your body to make a good body check" rather than "Knock him on his can." Statements such as "Hit him hard," "Take him out," "We should be wiping the floor with these guys" imply violent aggression. They are unnecessary and should not be used by a coach. Every sport has acceptable language for describing aspects of the sport, for example, tackling, body checking, maintaining your position, running interference.

By permission of Johnny Hart and News America Syndicate.

7. **Teach "coping self-statements" for athletes to deal with situations that might trigger aggression.** To maintain self-control when playing against a frustrating or irritating opponent in a contact sport, an athlete might be taught to think things like "I'm not gonna let him get to me. I'm not going to take any dumb penalties"; "Every time she does that, I'm gonna play harder and harder"; "He is deliberately trying to throw me off my game to intimidate me. All they're doing is giving me more and more incentive." Other examples of coping self-statements are described in Chapter 10.

PHILOSOPHICAL AND ETHICAL ASPECTS OF COACHING

When you interview for a coaching job, it is likely that someone will ask, "What is your coaching philosophy?" You might even be asked, "Do you follow a specific code of ethics?" How will you answer such questions? One meaning of philosophy is "a system of principles for guidance in practical affairs" (American College Dictionary, 1969). Thus, when we speak of a philosophy of coaching, we're talking about a set of attitudes or basic principles that guide a coach's behavior in practical situations. One meaning of ethics is "the rules of conduct recognized in respect to a particular class of human actions" (American College Dictionary, 1969). In that sense, a code of ethics is also a set of rules or principles that help to guide practical behavior in everyday situations. You can see that philosophical and ethical aspects of coaching are interrelated.They refer to the system of personal values, attitudes, beliefs, and principles that guide your behavior as a coach. Although ethics is generally considered a subtopic of philosophy, we use the terms interchangeably.

Several approaches to ethics are available to coaches and physical educators. Ziegler (1980) outlined five major philosophical approaches to ethical decisions, and recommended that a scientific-ethics approach would be best for the present and the future. Fraleigh (1984) recommended an approach that submits each guideline in an ethical code to a philosophical analysis of its moral foundation. From a behavioral perspective, ethics refer to certain standards of behavior that are developed by a culture or subculture and that promote the survival of that culture or subculture (Skinner, 1953, 1971). For example, one of the standards that we recommend is that coaches use more positive reinforcement than negative reinforcement when dealing with young athletes. This standard of behavior should promote the long-term survival of sports in our culture by increasing the number of people in society who participate and enjoy participation in sports (Dickinson, 1977). It is beyond the scope of this book to compare and contrast the different approaches to ethics; interested readers are referred to the selected readings listed at the end of this chapter.

A coaches ethical behavior will include both the understanding of the rules of a particular game and an attitude toward following those rules according to the true spirit of the game. Ethics involves a whole lot more, however, than simple adherence to the written and unwritten rules of the sport. In addition to attitudes and behaviors toward aggression versus assertion, discussed in the previous section, subtopics requiring ethical behavior for a coach include winning, losing, dealing with athletes, sportsmanship within the rules, confidentiality, and protecting the rights of athletes.

Winning

No matter what some coaches say about winning, their behavior implies a "win at all costs" philosophy. In the heat of battle, such coaches are likely to use only the best players, despite prior statements that everyone will get a chance to play; scream at officials and referees, despite prior suggestions that such behavior is unsportsmanlike; or schedule an injured "star" player in the championship game, even though aggravating the injury may have severe long-term consequences for the athlete. With such coaches, you might find youngsters in tears, being screamed at by the coach, or youngsters whose self-image is destroyed because they were cut from the team at the ripe old age of 10 years, or never got to play in the "big" game.

Some parents also place far too much emphasis on winning. Some parents force their children to live, sleep, eat, and drink a particular sport, even though the child would rather do other things. Some parents have been known to force a son to repeat one of the early grades so that he'll be bigger and stronger for high school football, presumably with images of an illustrious college career and a lucrative professional contract somewhere in the future. At competitions involving their kids, parents of opposing teams have been known to scream obscenities at each other across the playing field or rink, or heap abuse on and sometimes punch out referees because a call went against their child.

Most people would agree that such examples represent the worst in youth sports in America. Such instances are potentially harmful to the athletes involved and to the long-term survival of desirable sports ideals. It's the win at all costs philosophy of some coaches and parents that provides ammunition for critics who argue that competitive sports programs for youth should be eliminated entirely. In our view, however, eliminating competitive youth athletes is neither necessary nor likely. What is needed is a change from a win at all costs philosophy to one that focuses on individual and team development and improvement, independent of the outcome of a contest. As expressed in Chapter 2, this can be accomplished in part by encouraging young athletes to set performance goals. The more they reach those goals, the more they have won, regardless of the score at the end of the game. Winning in the sense of beating another person or team has its own rewards. The coach doesn't need to emphasize those. What a coach does have to do is to encourage athletes to look and feel and act like winners if they achieve realistic individual and team goals, regardless of the outcome of a particular contest. Moreover, this definition of winning should be encouraged through emphasis on the positive approach and with full consideration for social validation from the athlete's point of view.

Losing

For years, many Americans have held the view that athletic participation helps an individual to develop strong character, leadership, responsibility, honesty, and a sense of fair play. Others have challenged this claim, arguing that sports builds characters rather than character (Tutko and Bruns, 1976), causes spectator and player mis-behavior, rowdyism, and violence (Yeager, 1977), and that athletics have been prostituted by materialistic values (Miller, 1980). Events such as the 1985 trial in a Pittsburgh federal court (Lacayo, 1985) concerning use of drugs by professional baseball players have led to criticism of values that can be developed through sports competition. The truth is that contingencies surrounding participation in athletics have the potential to be highly beneficial to the development of an individual, or to teach that individual to be dishonest and unethical. One of the important determinants of which will occur is the attitude of a coach toward losing. After a loss, some coaches holler and scream at their athletes, put down certain athletes in front of the team, public-ly name individuals responsible for the loss when talking to the media, blame officials, and indirectly put the blame on the athletes by saying such things as "They made too many mental errors" or "They just didn't execute properly." Between games, some coaches also make speeches to their athletes that imply that they're a bunch of losers.

In our view, such an approach can only do harm. An athlete who loses already feels bad. Nothing can be gained from additional humilia-tion and fear engendered by a raving coach. Some coaches seem to think that the team will play better next time if he reads the riot act after a loss. However there's absolutely no evidence to support that view. In addition, some players in some contests will play up to their full potential and still lose. They already feel bad about losing; one of the coach's tasks is to help them feel a sense of pride for playing up to their full potential.

It's also important for a coach to help athletes put a sports contest in perspective in the events of the world, especially when coaching children and adolescents in school- and agency-sponsored sports pro-grams. If a team wins the big game, everybody should feel happy for a few hours, maybe even for a couple of days. If a team loses the big game, it's okay to feel unhappy for an hour or two. But either way, there are still thousands of starving children in Africa. There's still a danger of nuclear war between the superpowers. For the athletes them-selves, there are still the immediate problems of doing well in school, getting along with girlfriends and boyfriends, choosing a career, and going on to make a living and raise a family. Does one sporting event at the grade school, junior high, or high school level really make that much difference? Hardly. We don't mean to imply that *trying* to win is unimportant. The long hours of planning, the thoughts and dreams and discussions of winning the championship, the weeks and months of hard work and skill acquisition, and the experience of the competition itself—all can contribute tremendously to the development of an individual athlete. But when the big game is finally over, lets keep it in perspective and get on with life. Tomorrow's another day.

Coach-Athlete Relationship

Cooperation and respect are two of the things that you would like from your athletes. Patience, tolerance, and a sense of humor on your part will encourage your athletes to like you, and liking you will encourage cooperation. Respect, however, is based on your display of knowledge of the game, your efficiency in organizing and running practices and competitions, and coaching techniques that produce change in a positive direction. Young athletes don't want much. They simply expect you to be an excellent teacher and a super person. They want you to be serious but have a sense of humor. They want you to be firm but not strict. They want you to be an authority figure but kind and understanding. They want you to be parent and a friend. Most of all, they want to believe that you're an adult they can trust. See? They don't expect much. But then, if you couldn't be all that they expect, you wouldn't be a coach. Right? So how do you go about providing the right atmosphere for good relationships with your athletes?

The first step is to control the chaos. Young people are spontaneous, combustible, and filled with undirected energy. And nothing sets them off faster than a confused, disorganized, hesitant coach who's supposed to be in charge. Conversely, nothing can capture their attention and calm their restless spirits faster than a quietly confident coach who has plans. The keys are organization and confidence. Never gather a group of young athletes at practice or competition without knowing what you want to say, having decided on a way to say it, and having a plan or schedule of activities to follow over the next few hours.

Athletes respond best to a coach who exudes easy confidence (not conceit, bluster, or bravado). Confidence. A quiet but easily heard voice, a relaxed body, and an easy smile that says quite clearly, "I like young people." If you don't like young people, don't even *think* about trying to coach them. If noise, corny jokes, or sheer exuberance are distasteful to you, you're in the wrong profession. And no one will know that faster or better than the athletes. Your first step, then, in good coach-athlete relations is to be the person who directs their movements in an organized way, and the adult who is confident enough to provide that direction without being "bossy."

The second step is to be honest. Two areas of honesty are particularly important. The first is the willingness to say, "I don't know." The second is the willingness to say "I'm sorry." Too often, coaches attempt to convey to athletes the impression that they have all the answers. A good teacher and a good coach has a strong enough ego to be able to admit it when he or she doesn't have all the answers or makes a mistake, and the courage to say, "I'm sorry."

The third step is to be objective. It is inevitable that, as a human being, you may prefer some athletes over others. But if you want to succeed as a coach, no one should ever be able to tell which athletes are your favorites. As a coach, you must treat your athletes equally; correct their mistakes as you see them, help all of them change inappropriate behaviors, and try to teach all of them healthy values.

Although it's important to treat your athletes equally in the sense of not giving your favorites preferential treatment, it's also important to recognize that each athlete is an individual. Some may be stubborn, some may be withdrawn, some may be outgoing. And because of such characteristics, you may help your athletes develop to their fullest potential by using different approaches with different athletes. Thus, although they must be treated equally in terms of attention, adherence to team rules, and dealing with violations of team rules and regulations, they must also be treated as individuals in terms of one-on-one personal interactions.

Sportsmanship Within Rules

Coach A and Coach B both know the rules of basketball, backward and forward. Coach A teaches her players defensive strategies to be followed after the opposing team has a foul shot. Coach B teaches her players to move slightly just before the person shoots, to let out a heavy sigh, to cough, and in other ways "rattle" an opponent preparing to shoot a foul shot. Coaches X and Y both know the rules concerning attendance requirements and geographic locations for the inner-city high schools. Coach X holds open baseball tryouts for students eligible to attend his high school. Coach Y recruits three players from "just over the line" and convinces them to use the address of a "cousin" so that they can try out for his baseball team.

These kinds of examples are never-ending. Most coaches know the rules. Some teach their athletes to play the game according to the rules and, in both verbal behavior and actions, consistently play within the spirit of the game. Other coaches see the rules as a challenge. They consistently violate the spirit of the rule, the written rule itself, or both. Such coaches are teaching values to their athletes that, in the long run, are detrimental. These are the coaches that critics of athletics point to when they argue that sport does not build character. If coaches show the worst in their behavior, then critics can argue that sport brings out the worst in people in general. Coaches who show that type of behavior threaten the long-term survival of athletics.

Confidentiality

Of all the ethical values a good coach acquires, respect for other people's right to privacy is high on the list. A coach is in a position of responsibility and authority. A coach is often perceived as mature, responsible, knowledgeable, and someone a person can trust. This is especially true of the man or woman who is considered a "good coach." This person will often be placed in the role of counselor and advisor. He or she will be the recipient of some very personal confidences. Those confidences must always be respected for what they are: personal, private, and not for repetition outside the one-to-one relationship between parent/coach or athlete/coach.

Perceived as an adult who has influence over their child, parents will seek out the coach to confide their children's hopes, dreams, and fears about the athletic skills. The mother of a shy son who desperately wants to play third base may confide that wish to the coach because she knows the youngster would never dare to do so on his own. The father of the young woman with a slight heart murmur will confide his fears that his daughter may push herself too hard in order to prove she's as strong as any other athlete. Whatever the confidence, it's told to the coach on the assumption that the information will remain confidential. It's given in trust, and this trust must be protected. Whether the confidential information relates to the athlete directly or indirectly (such as the confession of a marriage breakdown that may affect the young athlete's attitudes or motivation), any discussion with a parent must be held in confidence.

The trickiest confidences of all may come from the young athlete. If you are a good coach, you will be respected and trusted. For a lot of young athletes, particularly those in the adolescent age group, the coach may be the only adult the young person can talk to. And not all of the discussions will be related to sports. After all, if you're wise enough to know how to achieve a perfect tennis serve, maybe you also know how to explain the confusion of adolescent sexuality. In some cases, you will be able to offer advice. Of course, no one expects you to have all the answers. When you don't, just say so. Regardless of whether you can solve the problems the athletes bring to you, remember that each athlete expects you to keep confidences to yourself. The one thing you cannot promise, however, is that you will withhold all information from a minor's parents. If you do that, you may find yourself in a position whereby you've promised not to tell the athlete's parents that he or she has a drug problem, is contemplating suicide, or is thinking of running away from home to join a religious cult. The final responsibility, both legally and morally, for a minor's welfare belongs to the parent or legal guardian. Beyond that, however, whatever an athlete confides to you in private conversation must remain inviolate.

Finally, confidentiality must be respected with regard to those issues, discussions, or situations that arise between you and your assistant coaches, the principal of your school, or the organizers who oversee the sports programs. What happens between you and other administrators is not for publication for athletes or parents. (Your relationship with significant others is discussed in Chapter 16.)

Protecting Rights of Athletes

The athlete who participates in an amateur sports program must be protected regarding is or her rights as a human being. Coaches, assistant coaches, volunteers, and parents must all be aware of those rights and be willing to ensure that each athlete is treated fairly. The greatest responsibility for protecting an athlete's rights, however, rests squarely on the shoulders of the coach. These rights have been encoded in a Bill of Rights for Young Athletes (Thomas, 1977).

1. *Right to participate regardless of ability.* In politics it's known as equal time. In amateur sports, it means that each person is allowed an equal opportunity to practice and to play. It also means that each person on the team, regardless of height, weight, sex, race, religion, or present state of clumsiness, is considered part of the team. If you play only the most graceful, strongest, or most talented young athletes, you are in a sense degrading your own skill as a coach—that wonderful talent a good coach has to make a silk purse out of a sow's ear, so to speak.

2. *Right to participate on level commensurate with developmental level.* In general, young athletes must be allowed to play according to their abilities and age level. They should not be asked to play like adults. It also means that coaches must realize there is, to some degree, no such thing as a typical 10-year-old, 12-year-old, or 14-year-old. Young people will have growth spurts at different ages. To expect any athlete to perform beyond his or her current developmental level is to expect too much. That's why a good behavioral coach carefully assesses

and records present skill levels and begins to teach each person, not at the level where he or she "should" be, but at the level where they are. Additional discussion of the importance for coaches to consider the developmental level of athletes is provided in Chapter 6.

3. *Right to qualified leadership.* The young athlete is entitled to a coach who is qualified, who knows the game, is familiar with good coaching techniques, and who operates from an ethical approach to amateur sports. This also means that all members of the coaching staff should be willing and able to attend coaching courses, seminars, or workshops designed to continuously improve and update their skills. In addition, each member of the coaching staff should be willing to monitor (or have monitored) his or her coaching skills on a regular basis. And each person should be flexible enough to change those skills that need improvement.

4. *Right to participate in a safe and healthy environment.* All equipment used in practice or competitive play must be safety approved. Before and at regular intervals throughout the season, coaches should make safety inspections of athletic equipment (e.g., helmets, face guards, rackets, skates) to ensure that no one is using substandard equipment. (Safety standards are discussed further in Chapter 16.) In addition to the physical environment, a healthy environment includes the mental or emotional environment to which an athlete is exposed. This is where a coach's personal and professional behaviors with respect to ethics can enhance or harm the young athlete in his or her care.

5. *Right to share in decision making.* Built into the behavioral coaching approach are techniques for ensuring that young athletes participate in the decision-making process with regard to their sport (*see* Chapter 2).

Reprinted with special permission of King Features Syndicate, Inc.

Organizing and Administering Athletic Programs

6. *Right to have fun.* Sports participation for youth should be enjoyable. No one's life or mental health should depend on the outcome of a game. Remember always that, to a young athlete, a part of the joy of sports rests in the effort, the trying, the sheer expenditure of physical energy, and the striving to win (as opposed to winning). One thing that really matters to young people is to have fun, to enjoy sports participation. Make sure that the athletes you coach end up feeling that way about their sport. Remember, when the umpire starts the game he shouts, "Play ball!" He doesn't yell, "Work!" Young people don't work tennis, work hockey, or work squash. The catchword is play. Let them play!

7. *Right to be treated with dignity.* Young athletes do have opinions. Respect them. Also, never forget that you are working with people—people with feelings and sensitivities about fitting in and being one of the gang. All athletes that you coach, regardless of size, shape, sex, race, or religion, must be treated with courtesy, respect, and dignity.

SUMMARY

One of the issues examined by sports sociologists is the problem of excessive aggression and violence in sport. After reviewing some of the causes of aggression, we suggested that a distinction should be made between aggression and assertion. An aggressive act is one intended to inflict pain or injury. Assertion, on the other hand, is robust, physically forceful play within the context of a sport that is not meant to harm another player. To encourage assertion and control aggression, coaches should (1) teach athletes to play by the rules; (2) teach sportsmanship; (3) teach respect for opponents as people; (4) teach athletes to show emotional control; (5) teach athletes to behave assertively against cheap shots from opponents; (6) model appropriate sports language and avoid using words that imply violence and aggression; and (7) teach coping self-statements for athletes to use to deal with situations that could trigger aggression.

Important philosophical and ethical aspects of coaching include the identification of attitudes, rules, and principles to guide a coach's behavior in practical situations. Desirable principles discussed include (1) defining "winning" in terms of individual and team development that is independant of the outcome of a contest; (2) keeping losing in a proper perspective and encouraging athletes to feel a sense of pride for playing up to their full potential, irrespective of the score at the end of the game; (3) showing cooperation, respect, honesty, organization, and knowledge of the game, to develop desirable coach-athlete relationships; (4) showing sportsmanship by playing within the spirit of the rules and within the letter of the rules; (5) maintaining confidentiality of personal information from others that was given in confidence; and (6) protecting the rights of athletes. The Bill of Rights for Young Athletes includes the right to participate regardless of ability; the right to participate on a level comensurate with the athlete's developmental level; the right to qualified leadership; the right to participate in a safe and healthy environment; the right to share in decision making; the right to have fun; and the right to be treated with dignity.

Coach's Checklist

Guidelines for ethical behavior with athletes are summarized in the form of a checklist in Fig. 15-1. We suggest that you use the checklist to self-evaluate and maintain your personal ethics at the highest level.

Review Questions

1. List several topics that have been studied by sports sociologists.
2. In general, what are some causes of aggression in sports?
3. What specific events might trigger an episode of aggression by an athlete?
4. Differentiate assertion and aggression.
5. Briefly list seven steps that coaches can take to encourage assertion and control aggression in their athletes.
6. In a sentence, what do we mean by philosophical and ethical aspects of coaching?
7. What position do the authors take on winning? Do you agree or disagree with their position? Defend your answer.
8. According to the authors, how should coaches interact with athletes after a loss? Do you agree or disagree? Defend your answer.
9. What are some of the things that will earn for a coach respect from her or his athletes?
10. Briefly list three steps that coaches should take to foster good coach-athlete relationships.
11. Should a coach of young athletes maintain complete confidentiality regarding confidence shared by those athletes? Why?
12. Briefly list the specific rights contained in the Bill of Rights for Young Athletes.

COACH'S CHECKLIST

Ethical Behavior with Athletes —————————

SCORING KEY: 1 = *Almost never*
3 = *Sometimes*
5 = *Almost always*

	1	2	3	4	5

1. To develop assertion and control aggression, do you, by word and deed:
   a. Model "playing within rules" to your athletes?
   b. Model good sportsmanship toward opponents and officials?
   c. Model respect for opponents as people (and refrain from referring to them in derogatory terms)?
   d. Model emotional control to decisions made by officials?
   e. Encourage athletes to behave assertively in face of "cheap shots" from opponents?
   f. Use acceptable sports jargon and avoid words implying aggression and violence?
   g. Teach "coping self-statements" to athletes to deal with situations that might trigger aggression?
2. At competitions, do you focus more attention on individual and team development and improvement rather than "win at all costs" philosophy?
3. When contests are lost, do you help athletes experience a sense of pride for playing up to their potential and for making improvements, rather than blaming athletes or referring to them as losers?
4. When contests are lost, do you put loss in proper perspective?
5. Do you show honesty with athletes by saying "I don't know" and "I'm sorry" if and when appropriate?

FIGURE 15-1

	1	2	3	4	5
6. Do you treat athletes equally in terms of attention and adherence to team rules and dealing with violations of team rules?					
7. Do you treat athletes individually and respect their differences in one-on-one personal interactions with them?					
8. Do you teach your athletes to play game according to both written rules and spirit of game?					
9. Do you maintain confidentiality with all those who share confidences with you?					
10. Do you respect "Bill of Rights for Young Athletes." including:					
a. Right to participate regardless of ability					
b. Right to participate on level comensurate with athlete's developmental level					
c. Right to qualified leadership					
d. Right to participate in safe and healthy environment					
e. Right to share in decision making					
f. Right to play as child and to have fun					
g. Right to be treated with dignity?					

Mini-Lab Exercises

1. Assume that you are a coach and that you are doing your best to follow the ethical guidelines described in this chapter. However, you become aware that the coach of an opposing team is behaving unethically in several ways. Moreover, his unethical behavior appears to be giving his team the advantage, to the point where you might lose an important contest against that team. Should you:
   a. Behave unethically yourself in order to even your team's chances?
   b. Approach the coach directly and express your concerns to try to convince him to behave in an ethical fashion?
   c. Take your concerns to the league officials in the hope that they will deal with the situation in a prompt and fair manner?
   d. Adopt several of the above strategies?
   e. Adopt some alternative strategies?

   Describe the course of action that you think you should follow, and explain why you think it would be the best approach to take.
2. In this chapter we have outlined a number of guidelines for coaches to follow to practice acceptable ethical behavior. Outline at least 10 additional steps that might be taken by educators, school administrators, fans, and athletes to increase the probability of coaches practicing acceptable ethical behavior. Feel free to brainstorm in any direction. Your answer could include additions to university curricula in coach preparation programs, posting of locker room slogans (e.g., "Honor your opponent"), encouragement of fans at a football game to cheer one good play by the opposition in each quarter, and so on.

References

American College Dictionary (1969). New York: Random House.

Baron, R.A. (1977). Human agression. New York: Plenum.

Bredemeir, B.J., and Shields, D.L. (1985). Values and violence in sports today. *Psychology Today* 19(10):22-32.

Dickinson, J. (1977). A behavioral analysis of coaching. Princeton, N.J.: Princeton Book Co.

Fraleigh, W.P., (1984). Right actions in sport: Ethics for contestants. Champaign, Ill.: Human Kinetics Publishers.

Lacayo, R. (1985). The cocaine agonies continue. Time September 23:74

Leonard, W.M. II. (1980). A sociological perspective of sport. Minneapolis: Burgess Publishing.

Miller, D.M. (1980). Ethics in sport: Paradoxes, perplexities, and a proposal. Quest **32**:3-7.

Skinner, B.F. (1953). Science and human behavior. New York: Macmillan.

Skinner, B.F. (1971). Beyond freedom and dignity. New York: Alfred Knopf.

Thomas, J.R., ed. (1977). Youth sports guide for coaches and parents. Washington, D.C.: AAHPER Publications.

Tutko, P., and Bruns, W. (1976). Winning is everything, and other American myths. New York: Macmillan.

Yeager, R.C. (1977). Savagery on the playing field. Readers Digest July:21-23.

Zeigler, E.F. (1980). Application of a scientific ethics approach to sport decisions. Quest 32:8-21.

Selected Readings

Boutilier, M.A., and Sangovanni, L. (1983) The sporting woman. Champaign, Ill.: Human Kinetics Publishers.

Dyer, K.F. (1982). Challenging the men: Women in sport. St. Lucia: University of Queensland Press.

Loy, J.W. Jr., Kenyon, G.S., and McPherson, B.D. (1981). Sport, culture and society: A reader on the sociology of sport, 2nd ed. Philadelphia: Lea & Febiger.

Magill, R.A., Ash, M.J., and Smoll, F.L., eds. (1982). Children in sport. Champaign, Ill.: Human Kinetics Publishers.

McKay, J., and Pearson, K. (1984). Objectives, strategies, and ethics in teaching introductory courses in sociology of sport. Quest 36:134-146.

Snyder, E.E., and Spreitzer, E.A. (1983). Social aspects of sport, 2nd ed. Englewood Cliffs, N.J.: Prentice-Hall.

Terry, P.C., and Jackson, J.J. (1985). The determinants and control of violence in sport. Quest 37:27-37.

Managing an Athletic Program: Additional Considerations

If coaches put into practice the guidelines offered in previous chapters, they will be well on their way to successful management of their athletic programs. Specifically, they will have:

Worked out assessment systems for evaluating the fundamentals (Chapter 3)

Familiarized themselves with the checklists for teaching new skills, decreasing errors, motivating athletes, and decreasing problem behaviors (Chapters 4, 5, 6, and 7)

Developed conditioning and nutrition programs for their athletes (Chapter 8)

Prepared a sports psyching program to help their athletes maximize performance in competition (Chapter 9)

Identified some subgoals for skill development, physical conditioning, psychological preparation, tactical strategies, and style of play to accomplish a variety of end results (Chapter 10)

Prepared some sample practice plans (Chapter 11)

Hired assistant coaches (Chapter 12)

Prepared budgets, ordered and stored equipment, and put practice
and play facilities in shape (Chapter 13)

Identified and prioritized some goals for the season (Chapters 10
and 14)

So what's left? To paraphrase a popular song, When you've done
your very best, all there is, is all the rest! In one sense, a coach's work is
never done, and we're certainly not going to pretend that "all the rest"
is described in this chapter. However, there are a few critical areas of
successful coaching that haven't been covered in previous chapters,
including public relations; injuries, liabilities, and insurance; and a
strategy for managing the many checklists contained in earlier chapters. Because these areas are important to your success in managing
an athletic program, they should be given thoughtful consideration.

PUBLIC RELATIONS
Dealing with Athletes

In Chapter 15 we discussed several steps that you might take to
develop positive relationships with your athletes. We don't want to
repeat those suggestions here, but we do want to emphasize the importance of your relationship with your athletes for public relations in
general. Your athletes can be your most effective ambassadors.

As a coach, your behavior is under constant scrutiny. Your knowledge, or lack of it, at practice, your praising or reprimanding of certain
players, fairness or favoritism that you show your athletes, your sin-
cerity or glibness when discussing personal problems with athletes,
your patience or intolerance—these and any other of your qualities will
be frequent topics of conversation in the community. Between athlete
and family at the dinner table, between athletes and friends at the
drive-in restaurant or other hangout, at local businesses where your
athletes have part-time jobs, wherever your athletes happen to be in
the community—your actions and activities will be discussed. If
they're discussed positively, your position and sport in particular,
and the athletic program in general, will benefit. If words like patience,
tolerance, knowledgeable, honest, fair, firm, trustworthy, and organized are commonly used, you can have no better public relations.
Never forget, however, that those words depend on the behaviors that
you show in your dealings with athletes and others.

Dealing with Colleagues and Teachers

In one sense, your first responsibility as a coach is to yourself and
your profession. Coaching, regardless of where you coach, is a job that
requires professional behavior. Coaching is a job that carries with it

considerable responsibility, and each man or woman who chooses to accept a position as a coach must also be willing to accept the challenge of living up to that responsibility. Part of that task involves ethical behavior with respect to fellow coaches, assistants, and volunteers who help you carry out your coaching responsibilities. In behavioral coaching, the best safeguard against messing up is to clearly identify those behaviors that you think are important, and to find a means to keep track of or measure whether you are, in fact, performing them. That's why we've provided checklists at the end of each chapter.

Whether you coach the sport at a school with the biggest budget or the smallest budget, whether it involves the most athletes or the fewest athletes, whether it's the focus of frequent media attention or mentioned briefly once a year, it's important for you to respect your colleagues and the sports that they coach. The students will benefit most from an athletic program that offers quality instruction and opportunities to participate in a wide variety of sports and at a wide variety of levels. Moreover, during the past two decades intramural sports have received increased attention, sometimes at the expense of interschool competitions. Support for your particular sport will be determined by funding, facilities, general community support for sports in general, recent successes or failures of your particular sport and other sports, and a host of other factors. In the long run, however, your sport can't help but benefit from a strong overall athletic program and a positive, supportive atmosphere between you and your fellow coaches.

Cooperative interaction with teachers begins with communication. At the start of a season, provide teachers with a practice and game schedule, including departure times for out of town trips (if they are during school hours). Offer apologies in the event that classes will be missed by athletes participating in your sport. Invite teachers to come to the athletic events to observe their student athletes. In addition, dealing with teachers requires that you remember one important thing: As much as you love football, or tennis, or any sport, there's another world out there. It includes mathematics, history, carpentry, art, music, and literature among other things. Your subject, sports, is no more and no less important than these. You may, however, find that your coaching job is considered the most "glamorous" of the teaching positions at a given school. That could lead to resentment on the part of some teachers. You can diffuse that resentment by demonstrating your respect for other teachers' chosen subjects. And you can help others to understand your subject by sharing your teaching methods, your problems, and your enthusiasm. You can also share your needs. For example, you've got an important high school game coming up in 2 weeks. You want to have a good turnout of the student body to cheer your team on. You tell your problems to Matty West, the art teacher. She says, "You think you've got problems! I need a commercial art project for my senior class, and I can't think of one that will have real meaning for my students." Now there's your chance, coach. How about combining forces with the art department? The art students could design and paint posters to advertise and attract the student body to your game! In one fell swoop, you've created good public relations. The art teacher will be pleased at your confidence in her students. And you'll get some free advertising for your game. It's all a matter of respect. Respect for those other worlds outside of sports that can be combined with yours to demonstrate a cooperative school spirit.

Dealing with Game Officials

There are two things to remember when dealing with game officials. Be polite. Be unemotional. Under the rules of most amateur sports, the coach is entitled to question a call, or to request clarification of an official's decision. That's where polite comes in. If you stand there like Lucy, screaming, "Blockhead!," you will not only make a fool of yourself, you will likely anger the official, who may then decide not to cooperate. Most of all, you will state quite clearly by your behavior that sportsmanship is a lost art. Remember both athletes and fans are watching you. If you're rude to the officials, your athletes or the fans may decide to imitate your behavior. Request clarification when necessary, but accept the call as final. If at some time you are convinced that an error was made, register a calm, formal protest.

If you treat the officials with respect, they will return the favor. Remember, they too are professionals, trained to do their job. Most of them do it right.

Dealing with Parents

Beyond your responsibilities to yourself, your profession, and your athletes, one of your main responsibilities is to the athletes' parents. In several chapters we have discussed protection of the rights of the athlete. Now let's talk about Mom and Dad! If you are working with and teaching young people, you are, in a sense, taking over the parents' responsibilities regarding their child. Although it may seem that a few parents don't care, most parents are very interested in their child's progress and development. As a coach, therefore, you can save yourself some problems by respecting the fact that Mom and Dad have a right to know. Moreover, if parents clearly understand the objectives of your coaching program, understand your expectations for their involve-

Sample Agenda for Parents' Clinic _____

1. Introduce coaches and other team officials who may be present.
2. Ask players and parents to introduce themselves.
3. Introduce administrators or others who may be present.
4. Briefly review the coaching philosophy.
5. Describe some specifics of the competitions or game schedule (number, duration, frequency) and distribute the schedule for the season.
6. Briefly review some specifics of practices (number, duration, frequency).
7. Briefly review some rules and regulations that everyone should know about (e.g., attendance requirements at practices).
8. Briefly review expenditures (e.g., equipment purchases) for which the players (and the parents) are responsible.
9. Discuss possible parental involvement and ask for volunteers (e.g., car pooling to games, timing or officiating at competitions, keeping team or league statistics, organizing a booster club, banquet, or social events).
10. Have a question and answer session (Be prepared to talk about such things as risk of injury, guidelines for playing time for specific individuals in contests, experience and background of coaches).
11. Distribute and describe the various medical, registration, and waiver forms.
12. Indicate the deadline for returning the forms and registration materials (allow at least 3 to 4 days).

FIGURE 16-1

ment, have clear lines of communication with you, and receive positive feedback for all of the various ways that parents can be helpful in conducting a season's activities, then their relationship with you and their support of their sons and daughters in the athletic program are likely to be positive and helpful. We therefore recommend that you hold a parent clinic or orientation program to coincide with athletic registration. Send out formal notices to parents of athletes whom you know will be involved, advertise in local newspapers in order to reach parents of newcomers, choose a time and location for the clinic that is likely to be most convenient for working parents, and prepare an agenda (Fig. 16-1).

An alternative to a parent clinic or orientation program is a letter to the parents of your athletes. This letter could summarize most of the things that you would have presented at the clinic. Mid-season and post-season newsletters on the team's progress are also advisable. Some coaches also arrange separate parent seating sections at home games in order to foster good relationships and overall support for the team.

Dealing with Administrators, Principals, and Presidents

You are responsible to the person or group who functions in an administrative capacity with respect to your athletic program. This can include the dean of the physical education department, committees, boards and board members, school principals, or community club presidents. Two important questions are: Who are these people? and What do you owe them? You could be dealing with some of the greatest people you could hope to meet, or some of the biggest pains in the kneecap you've ever met! Your position is particularly tricky if you are literally employed by these people, because you will inevitably crash headlong into the golden rule: He who controls the gold makes the rules. It is not a point to be taken lightly. It is also not something that should jeopardize your ethics. Every coach knows that sooner or later he or she will run across a board member who thinks team performance would drastically improve if the uniforms were pink and purple instead of black and white. Or perhaps you've met the dean, the principal, or the booster club president who has somehow managed to get his or her self-image tangled up with whether the team is winning, and is screaming for a trophy that he or she thinks will enhance personal prestige. As a coach, you must learn to live with such individuals. They go with the territory. But what, exactly, do you "owe" them in return for the salary they pay or the privilege of being their coach? We suggest that you owe the following:

- A clear, easy-to-understand description of your approach to coaching (to be given before you are hired)
- An organized coaching approach (such as effective behavioral coaching) that will turn out properly trained athletes and steady progress for each athlete
- A clear definition in behavioral terms of your personal ethics with respect to honesty, fair play, athletes' rights and sportsmanship
- An understanding of their focus on the budgetary aspect of the athletic program, and a concentrated effort to stay within that portion of the budget that is allotted to you
- Honesty about unsafe playing equipment or playing facilities that require over-budget assistance to correct

- Loyalty with respect to any and all public comments that reflect on their efficiency, personality, and attitudes. You don't have to lie or praise what you don't agree with. You simply deal with the problem directly. If you disagree with the administrators, tell them—not the local press or an angry parent.

The very nature of the behavioral approach, with its targeted goal systems, its systematic step-by-step procedures for achieving those goals, techniques such as reinforcement that are designed to improve chances of success, and the habit of recording data, is such that a behavioral coach is automatically accountable for his or her coaching approach. The data sheets, checklists, and procedures that are used in the behavioral approach to coaching provide solid evidence that the approach is working, that the players are getting good training, that the coach is living up to her or his own responsibilities to the players and the parents and to the organization or administration that hired the coach in the first place. In addition, the system is flexible and creative. Where the data indicates that an approach or procedure is not working, behavioral coaching provides for alternative methods and individual program planning that make exchanging the ineffective procedure easy and comfortable for all concerned. And always there is data to support maintaining the status quo or adapting a procedure that might produce better results. The benefits of being accountable with proof provided by recorded data are endless. It is an interesting fact that in our society few people can actually prove that they are doing the job they were hired to do. An effective behavioral coach can.

Dealing with Support Organizations

Successful public relations for a coach in many schools requires that you deal effectively with one or more organizations. Two such organizations that we would like to comment on are the booster club and the Parent-Teachers Association (PTA). A booster club or group is essentially a group formed for the purpose of supporting a particular sport or team. The support typically includes both money to pay for the high costs of an athletic team and strategies to increase fan support to fill the stands at competitions. When you accept a coaching position, you should find out whether a booster group existed for the previous coach and team. If not, you may consider starting one. Booster club members typically include local businessmen with both an interest in the sport and a desire to gain some advertising or community service outlet and former athletes in the community. The time that you might spend with a booster club at weekly luncheons or monthly meetings or postgame conferences can contribute a great deal to overall public relations for your program.

The second association that you might consider contacting is the PTA at your school. Parents and teachers lobbying through the local PTA can exert considerable influence on a sports program at a school. Also, it's quite possible that the majority of PTA members are either not interested in or know little about your particular sport. A presentation at a PTA meeting in which you describe your philosophy of coaching, your objectives for the season, and the benefits the student athletes might derive from participating in your sport could do wonders to develop overall public support for your program.

Dealing with News Media

The late Paul "Bear" Bryant, coach of the University of Alabama football team and one of the most famous and successful college coaches of all time, once said, "There's just three things I ever say. If anything goes bad, then I did it. If anything goes semi-good, then we did it. If anything goes real good, then you did it. That's all it takes to get people to win football games for you" (Lyons, 1981). If you consistently follow that philosophy, you are well on your way to having the media cover your sport in a way that will enhance your program. The emphasis on "we" rather than "I" is important when talking to any group about the performance of athletes. Whether it's to the PTA, the booster club, a parent group, the student body, fellow teachers, or the media, coaches can facilitate support for their team and their coaching by spreading the credit for successful performances.

In addition to the philosophy expressed by Coach Bryant for communicating to the media, it's also helpful to go out of your way to make specific statistical information available. Things such as an up-to-date team roster, information on the physical and game stats of specific players, and similar information about the opposition can be especially helpful to media people covering a contest. You might also remember that dealing with the media is like any other kind of situation: the more prepared you are, the better you will fare. Think of alternative outcomes for contests and how to talk about each. During the postgame press conference, what questions are likely to come up, and what you can answer? You might even think about how to invoke a little humor. For example, after a loss by the Houston Oilers, John Breen, former general manager said, "We were tipping off our play. Whenever we broke from the huddle, three backs were laughing and one was pale as a ghost."

INJURIES, LIABILITIES, AND INSURANCE

Do you remember our discussion of Coach Dick Mitchell in Chapter 1? He was the disorganized coach of the baseball team who showed up late for the first practice, had trouble finding the baseball equipment under the debris and empty food cartons in the back of his station wagon, forgot to bring his briefcase that he thought contained the schedules, and then had to leave when his wife reminded him of another appointment. The preceding chapters have identified a number of important preparatory activities to ensure that you don't wind up like Coach Mitchell. But there are several important items still to be discussed: safety precautions, injury prevention and treatment, legal liability, and medical insurance.

Reprinted with special permission of King Features Syndicate, Inc.

Safety Precautions, Injury Prevention, and Injury Treatment

Wheeling around the goal, I saw Archie get control of the puck. A quick glance up ice showed an opening down the left side. Tired after the long practice, dripping with sweat, I dug in for one more burst. With legs hurting, heart pounding, and breath coming in short gasps, I hit the red line in full stride. Archie laid up a perfect pass, right on the end of my stick. Glimpsing Duke's yellow sweater, I head-feinted to the left and pulled the puck over to the right. It should have been an easy shot on goal. But at the last moment, Duke's leg came out. An instant later, I was lying on the ice with the most excruciating pain in my right knee that I had ever known.

A segment from Paul Newman's movie "Slapshot"? No. It's a description of a check that prematurely ended the first author's senior year as a promising center with the Varsity hockey team at Colorado College. Normally, he would have easily avoided the outstretched knee of the defenseman. That day, because he was playing with considerable fatigue at the end of a long practice, he wound up with badly torn ligaments and a full-leg cast for 6 weeks. Are you aware that several million athletic injuries occur yearly in the United States? Perhaps more important, are you aware that the great majority of these injuries are initially seen and treated by the coach? And that a significant number of them can be prevented? In the Selected Readings are listed several books that provide detailed discussion of various topics in sports medicine. There is no doubt that topics of safety precautions and injury treatment must be addressed before the beginning of the season. We have attempted to simplify these topics by preparing a checklist in the form of a questionnaire (Fig. 16-2). We strongly encourage you to ensure that you can confidently answer or deal with the issues raised by the questions.

Legal Liability and Medical Insurance

We hope your coaching experience will be an outstanding success. We hope the individuals that you coach will thoroughly enjoy themselves, acquire some new skills, and want to pursue physical fitness as a lifelong goal. However, the unexpected can happen. In recent years there has been a dramatic increase in the number of lawsuits in sports. In these times, a coach simply cannot ignore the possibility of a suit. Accordingly, a portion of a coach's pre-season preparation must be directed at this possibility. An excellent source is the book *Coach's Guide to Sport Law* (Nygaard and Boone, 1985). Nygaard's research has indicated that when coaches are sued, the action usually stems from negligence. While we will not provide a detailed discussion of various legal considerations, we do strongly encourage all coaches to take three steps by way of pre-season preparation:

1. Familiarize yourself with some of the legal issues discussed by Nygaard and others.
2. Carefully ensure that the above questions concerning safety precautions and injury treatment are adequately attended to

Text continued on p. 376.

C H E C K L I S T

Safety Precautions, Injury Prevention, and Injury Treatment

Proper Equipment

1. What safety standards are available for your sports equipment?
2. Does your equipment meet or surpass available safety standards?
3. Do you have adequate numbers of equipment items for each athlete?
4. Does equipment properly fit each athlete?
5. Have you arranged to make periodic checks during season to ensure that equipment remains in good repair?

Safe Facilities

6. Are fields or courts level and free of holes? Are fields or courts appropriately soft (e.g., is part of football field like concrete or covered with gravel)?
7. Are fields or courts free of moveable items (e.g., sprinkler heads, track hurdles piled in end zone)?
8. Is there appropriate protective netting or padding (e.g., just behind baskets for basketball, or underneath chinning bars)?
9. Have locker room facilities for home and visiting clubs been adequately checked (e.g., so that lockers will not fall over, benches fall apart)?

Acceptable Weather

10. If your sport is played outdoors, have you identified climatic conditions under which you definitely will not allow your athletes to participate? (Although this is normally an official's decision for competitions, a coach should have his or her own independent standards for safety of athletes for competitions and practices.)
11. If your sport is played outdoors and in a climatic or geographic area where heat illness (heat stroke, exhaustion, fatigue) is a potentially serious problem, have you made arrangements to:
    a. Schedule practices during cooler parts of day?
    b. Schedule water breaks at regular intervals?
    c. Practice without heavy equipment or sweatsuits?
    d. Ensure that athletes are not taking salt tablets?
12. Have you taken steps to avoid dangers from extreme weather (frostbite, windburn, sunburn)?

FIGURE 16-2   *Continued.*

C H E C K L I S T

Safety Precautions, Injury Prevention, and Injury Treatment—cont'd

Concerning Athletes

13. Have you made arrangements to ensure that athletes complete appropriate informational, medical, and waiver forms including:
    a. Pre-season medical examination form (preferably from family physician who knows the individual)?
    b. Parental permission form for participation?
    c. Accident form listing family physician, home telephone number, and phone number of someone to call in case parents are not at home?
    d. Emergency medical treatment form on which parents give permission for emergency medical treatment of child if they cannot be first contacted?
14. Have you ensured or assessed whether your athletes are appropriately conditioned for demands of their sport?
15. Have you taken steps to ensure that your athletes will use equipment properly?
16. Have you prepared a set of rules to discuss with athletes to prevent potentially dangerous behaviors, such as horseplay with equipment?
17. Have you confronted athletes with possible debilitating outcomes of unethical plays (e.g., face-masking in football, undercutting in basketball)?
18. Because young teenagers of the same age can be considerably different in size and physical maturation, have you arranged for athletes to be grouped according to size and physical maturation in addition to age?
19. Have you arranged for adequate number of appropriately trained supervisors or spotters for all practices, games, and trips?
20. Because major injuries are more likely to occur when athletes become tired, have you identified ways to monitor fatigue of your athletes during practices and games?

FIGURE 16-2, cont'd

Treating Injury

21. Is first-aid kit available at all practices and games?
22. Do you have telephone numbers of local emergency services at all practices and games?
23. Where league rules require it, or when you consider it necessary, have you made arrangements for a physician or emergency vehicle to be in attendance at all contact-sport games?
24. Have you and your assistant coaches read and discussed procedures for:
    a. Transporting injured athlete?
    b. Cuts, scrapes, bruises, bloody nose?
    c. Cardiopulmonary resuscitation?
    d. Strains and sprains?
    e. Heat injury?
    f. Standard student accident report forms (available in virtually all public schools)?
    g. Proper period of rest and exercise before allowing injured athlete to reenter practice or competition?

before and during the season. If you deal with all of those questions and follow the ethical guidelines we have described, you will, in our opinion, have met all of your legal and ethical responsibilities as a coach.

3. Because the unexpected can happen, we strongly recommend that you consider registering with a liability insurance protection plan.

YOU AND ALL THOSE CHECKLISTS: A MANAGEMENT STRATEGY

Throughout this book, we have emphasized the importance of frequent monitoring of performance of athletes and coaches alike during practices and games. We have emphasized that behavioral coaching requires a lot of time and effort. One of the things that helps to make effective behavioral coaching possible (and effective) is the involvement of assistant coaches, team managers, and volunteers to help with monitoring. Another important ingredient is self-monitoring by the athletes. To effectively use all of the checklists, however, it is necessary for a coach to have an overall plan. Specifically, we will describe a strategy that will make it possible for you to use most or all of the checklists presented. An important aspect of the strategy is to spread your use of the checklists over a full year. There are some for use during the off-season, some for during the pre-season, some for during the season; and there are post-season evaluations. Obviously, the duration of the season and the off-season varies considerably from sport to sport. The swimming season, for example lasts a full 11 months for top-level performers. For other sports, the season is much shorter. To illustrate the strategy, we have divided the year into 1 month preseason, 5 months in-season, 5 months off-season, and 1 month postseason. With this in mind, we recommend the strategy outlined in Fig. 16-3. This strategy recommends that particular checklists be used during particular times of year. It immediately becomes obvious from examining Fig. 16-3 that much of the work of coaching in many sports is done during the off-season and the pre-season. If you follow this strategy, you will find yourself using (or reviewing) one or two checklists each week. We believe this strategy helps to make effective behavioral coaching a viable approach for most coaches in most situations.

A COACHING CREED

Why do you want to coach? Are you sure you're cut out for it? Are the rewards that you will encounter likely to be sufficient to keep your interest and involvement at the level necessary to be successful? Throughout this book, we have emphasized practical, useful guidelines for coaching to get better results and make the sport enjoyable for athletes and coaches. In this last section, we would like to reemphasize a point made in Chapter 1. Coaching is work, and being good at it sometimes requires hard work. Sabock (1985) suggested that a coach, at one time or another, will be expected to fulfill the roles of teacher, disciplinarian, salesman, public relations person, guidance counselor, diplomat, organizer, detective, psychologist, judge and jury, leader, father or mother figure, dictator, politician, actor, director, field general, citizen of the community, and citizen of the school. Also, with increasing research in sports psychology, physiology, medicine, sociology, and sports equipment, there is a tremendous body of literature for coaches to attempt to master. So why do you want to coach? You may have fantasies of wealth, glamor, and fame; but you must realistically remember that these come to relatively few coaches and are typically short-lived. Moreover, fans and administrators can be very fickle. Thus, in the final analysis, the most important rewards are the natural pleasurable consequences of the day-to-day activities involved in working with athletes. We believe that the guidelines of effective behavioral coaching outlined in this book will help you become the kind of coach who can wholeheartedly ascribe to the Coaching Creed (Fig. 16-4).

SUMMARY

This chapter discusses several critical areas of successful coaching not covered in previous chapters. One such area is professional, athletic, and parental relationships. Professional relationships include those with teachers and fellow coaches, game officials, and administrators. A part of the challenge of successful coaching is to deal ethically and responsibly with teachers and fellow coaches. Game officials are fellow professionals, and must be treated with respect and dignity. Positive relationships with administrators are built on effective communication, a clear understanding and agreement on each others' positions on critical issues, a clear understanding of areas of responsibility, and acceptance of strategies for accountability. To develop and maintain positive relationships with athletes, you must show patience, tolerance, a sense of humor, honesty, objectivity, and a level of competence and knowledge of the game that will earn their respect. Finally, you have responsibilities to the athletes' parents. If parents clearly understand your expectations and the objectives of your program, have clear lines of communication with you, and receive positive feedback for their involvement in the season's activities, then their relationship with you and their support of the athletic program are likely to be positive and helpful.

Organizing and Administering Athletic Programs

Yearly Plan for Using Checklists for Effective Behavioral Coaching

	Off-Season					Pre-Season	In Season Early	Mid	End	Post-Season		
Month:	1	2	3	4	5	6	7	8	9	10	11	12
Time management: Review personal and career goals and time-saver checklist (Chapter 14).	X			X			X			X		
Time management: Prioritize and time-line (Chapter 14)	X			X			X			X		
Budget preparation and management (Chapter 13)		X			X			X			X	
Selection of assistant coaches (Chapter 12)		X										
Management of assistant coaches (Chapter 12)							X		X		X	
Pre-season planning (Chapter 10)			X									
Purchase equipment (Chapter 13)				X								
Care for home facility (Chapter 13)				X								
Select conditioning activities that match energy requirements of game (Chapter 8)					X							
Develop assessment systems for evaluating fundamentals (Chapter 3)					X							
Prepare nutrition program for athletes (Chapter 8)					X							
Prepare practice plans (Chapter 11)					X							
Review checklist of Safety Precautions and Injury Treatment (Chapter 16)					X							

FIGURE 16-3

						Pre-Season	In Season			Post-Season
		Off-Season					Early	Mid	End	
Month:	1	2	3	4	5	6	7	8	9	10	11	12
Prepare list of "good news" and "bad news" behaviors for athletes (Chapter 7)					X							
Announce and prepare for parent meeting (Chapter 16)					X							
Use conditioning checklist (Chapter 8)						X	X	X	X	X		
Use skill development checklist (Chapter 4)						X	X	X	X	X		
Use error reduction checklist (Chapter 5)						X	X	X	X	X		
Use checklist for motivating practice and endurance training (Chapter 6)						X	X	X	X	X		
Use checklist for decreasing problem behaviors (Chapter 7)						As needed						
Use sports psyching checklist (Chapter 9)						X	X	X	X	X	X	
Do post-season evaluation (Chapter 10)												X

A Coaching Creed

Be a resource person able to assist the athlete to develop his or her athletic potential and self-dependency.

Recognize individual differences in athletes and always think of the athlete's long-term best interests.

Aim for excellence based on realistic goals and the athlete's growth and development.

Lead by example. Teach and practice cooperation. self-discipline. respect for officials and opponents and proper attitudes in language. dress. and deportment.

Make sport challenging and fun. Skills and techniques need not be learned painfully.

Be honest and consistent with athletes. They appreciate knowing where they stand.

Be prepared to interact with the media. league officials. and parents. They too have important roles to play in sport.

Coaching involves training by responsible people who are flexible and willing to continually learn and develop.

Physical fitness should be a lifelong goal for everyone. Encourage athletes to be fit all year. every year. and not just for the season.

Reprinted with permission from Coaching Association of Canada.

FIGURE 16-4

Another important area discussed is injuries. liabilities. and insurance. Specific steps are outlined that should be taken concerning safety precautions. injury prevention. and injury treatment. We also recommend that you consider registering with a liability insurance protection plan.

This chapter also describes a management strategy to help you effectively use the various checklists throughout this book. A yearly plan is presented, with recommendations for using some checklists during the off-season. some during the pre-season. some during the in-season. and some during the post-season. The chapter concludes with The Coaching Creed.

Coach's Checklist

This last checklist (Fig. 16-5) summarizes the steps to take to ensure that you meet necessary additional considerations for managing

Additional Considerations for Managing Athletic Program

SCORING KEY: ✔ = *Satisfactory (performed by coach at appropriate times)*
X = *Less than satisfactory*

Date

To Whom Are You Responsible?

1. Communicate with teachers at start of season and provide them with practice and game schedules.

2. Prepare list of specific ethical behaviors that guide your interactions with athletes and game officials.

3. Prepare agenda for parents' clinic to be conducted at start of season.

4. Prepare written list of your responsibilities to administrators who hired you and discuss with them.

Injuries, Liabilities, and Insurance

1. Complete Checklist of Safety Precautions, Injury Prevention, and Injury Treatment so that you can answer "yes" to all 24 questions and their subquestions.

2. Familiarize yourself with legal issues in coaching (Nygaard and Boone, 1985).

3. Subscribe to liability insurance protection plan for coaches.

You and All Those Checklists: A Management Strategy

1. Make photocopies of all of the Coach's Checklists in this book. Obtain a yearly planning calendar that you can post on the wall in your office, and pencil in the specific dates when you plan to use the checklists as recommended in Fig. 16-2. As you use the checklists during the year, mark them off on the calendar.

"A Coaching Creed"

1. Photocopy "A Coaching Creed" (p. 380) and post it in a conspicuous place in your office.

FIGURE 16-5

an athletic program beyond those described in previous chapters. As with all of the preceding checklists, we encourage you to self-monitor your performance regularly, and to have an assistant coach periodically provide feedback to ensure that you practice effective behavioral coaching to the fullest extent possible.

Good luck! And happy coaching!

Review Questions

1. In what sense can your athletes be your most effective ambassadors?
2. Describe three steps that you can take to improve your relationships with teachers of the athletes that you coach or hope to coach.
3. List two categories of behavior that should be applied to a coach's interaction with game officials.
4. Describe an important prerequisite to starting the season on a positive note with parents of athletes.
5. When you are hired as a coach, what do the authors suggest that you owe those who hired you? Do you agree or disagree? Defend your answer.
6. Describe Bear Bryant's philosophy for dealing with athletes. Why is it also a good philosophy for dealing with the media?
7. What three steps do the authors recommend that you take concerning preseason preparation and legal liability? Do you agree or disagree? Defend your answer.

Mini-Lab Exercise

1. Identify a sport that you have played or hope to coach. Describe how you might try to respond to or deal with each of the 23 items concerning safety precautions, injury prevention, and injury treatment. Limit your answers to three or four sentences per item.

References

Lyons, W. (1981). Bryant aims at mark he doesn't care about. The Charlotte Observer, Nov. 13:C-15.

Nygaard, G., and Boone, T.H. (1985). Coach's guide to sport law. Champaign, Ill.: Human Kinetics Publishers.

Sabock, R. (1985). The Coach, 3rd ed. Champaign, Ill.: Human Kinetics Publishers.

Selected Readings

Arnheim, D. (1985). Modern principles of athletic training: The science of sports injury prevention and management, 5th ed. St. Louis: Times Mirror/Mosby College Publishing.

Fraleigh, W. (1984). Right actions in sport: Ethics for contestants. Champaign, Ill.: Human Kinetics Publishers.

Haycock, C.E., ed. (1980). Sports medicine for the athletic female. New York: Putnam.

Mirkin, G., and Hoffman, D. (1978). The sportsmedicine book. Boston: Little, Brown.

Newman, S. (1983). Dealing with pain. Coaching Review 6:25-31.

Puhl, J.L., and Brown, L.H. (1985). The menstrual cycle and physical activity. Champaign, Ill.: Human Kinetics Publishers.

Credits

Chapter 2

Pp. 16-17, from Martin, G., and Hrycaiko, D. (1983). Effective behavioral coaching: What's it all about? Journal of Sport Psychology **5**:8-20. Champaign, Ill.: Human Kinetics Publishers.

Chapter 3

P. 40, from Martin, G., and Hrycaiko, D. (1983). Effective behavioral coaching: What's it all about? Journal of Sport Psychology **5**:8-20. Champaign, Ill.: Human Kinetics Publishers.

Pp. 42, 43, from Komaki, J., and Barnett, F. (1977). A behavioral approach to coaching football: Play execution of the offensive backfield on a youth football team. Journal of Applied Behavior Analysis **10**:657-664. Copyright (1977) by the Society for the Experimental Analysis of Behavior, Inc. Reprinted with permission of the publisher and authors.

Chapter 4

P. 60, from Hoehn, R.G. (1984). Coaching Review **7**:40-42. Reprinted with permission from Coaching Association of Canada.

P. 62, from Simek, T.C., and O'Brien, R.M. (1981). Huntington, N.Y.: B-Mod Associates. Reprinted with permission.

Chapter 5

P. 83, from Buzas, H.P., and Ayllon, T. (1981). Behavior Modification **5**:372-385. Copyright © 1981. Reprinted by permission of Sage Publications, Inc.

P. 85, prepared by Scott Martin, point guard for Men's Basketball Team, University of Manitoba, 1984-1986.

P. 90, from Koop, S., and Martin, G.L. (1983). Journal of Applied Behavior Analysis **16**:447-460. Copyright (1983) by the Society for the Experimental Analysis of Behavior, Inc. Reprinted with permission of the publishers and authors.

Chapter 6

Pp. 110-112, from the National Coaching Certification Manual, Coaching Theory, Level 2, Ottawa, Ontario, 1981, pp. 5-21. Reprinted with permission from the Coaching Association of Canada.

P. 116, from Martin, G.L., LePage, R., and Koop, S. (1983). Applications of behavior modification for coaching age-group competitive swimmers. In Martin, G.L., and Hrycaiko, eds., Behavior modification and coaching: principles, procedures and research. Springfield, Ill.: Charles C Thomas, Publisher.

P. 120, prepared by Paul Milton, former Assistant Coach, Bishop University Ice Hockey Team.

P. 122, from Rushall, B.S. (1975). Swimming Technique 11:103-106. Reprinted with permission.

P. 127, from Daniels, D.B. (1983). Coaching Review 6:16-17. Reprinted with permission from the Coaching Association of Canada.

Chapter 7

P. 139, from Martin, G.L., LePage, R., and Koop, S. (1983). Applications of behavior modification for coaching age-group competitive swimmers. In Martin, G.L., and Hrycaiko, eds., Behavior modification and coaching: principles, procedures and research. Springfield, Ill.: Charles C Thomas, Publisher.

Pp. 144-145, 146, 148, from Hume, K.M., Martin, G.L., Gonzalez, P., et al. (1985). A self-monitoring feedback package for improving freestyle figure skating practice. Journal of Sport Psychology 7:333-345. Champaign, Ill.: Human Kinetics Publishers.

Chapter 8

P. 171, from the National Coaching Certification Manual, Coaching Theory, Level 1, Ottawa, Ontario, 1979. Reprinted with permission from the Coaching Association of Canada.

P. 189, from Nutrition for the Athlete (1971). Reprinted by permission of the American Alliance for Health, Physical Education, Recreation and Dance, 1900 Association Drive, Reston, Va. 22091.

Chapter 9

Pp. 216-217, paraphrased from Martin, G.L., and Pear, J.J. (1983). Behavior modification: What it is and how to do it, 2nd ed. Englewood Cliffs, N.J.: Prentice Hall.

P. 226, prepared by Paul Milton, former Assistant Coach, Bishop University Ice Hockey Team.

Chapter 10

Pp. 246-247, 248-249, from Basketball Development Model (1983). The document in its entirety available from Basketball Canada, 333 River Road, Vanier, Ontario K1L 8H9. Reprinted with permission from Basketball Canada.

P. 255, from Rushall, B.S., and Wiznuk, K. (1985). Athlete's assessment of the coach: The Coach Evaluation Questionnaire. Canadian Journal of Applied Sport Sciences 10:157-161. Reprinted with permission. Single copies of the Coach Evaluation Questionnaire, standardized scoring instructions, scoring procedures, and answer sheets may be obtained from Dr. B. Rushall, San Diego State University, Department of Physical Education, San Diego, CA 92182.

P. 256, from the National Coaching Certification Manual, Coaching theory, Level 2, Ottawa, Ontario, 1979, pp. 5-21. Reprinted with permission from the Coaching Association of Canada.

Chapter 11

Pp. 270-271, from Locke, E.A., and Latham, G.P. (1985). The application of goal setting to sports. Journal of Sport Psychology 7:205-222. Champaign, Ill.: Human Kinetics Publishers.

Chapter 14

Pp. 339-340, from Time Management Made Easy by Peter A. Turla and Kathleen L. Hawkins. Copyright © 1984 by Peter A. Turla and Kathleen L. Hawkins. Reproduced by permission of the publisher, E.P. Dutton, a division of New American Library.

Chapter 16

P. 380, reprinted with permission from the Coaching Association of Canada.

Author Index

Subject Index

A

Adenosine triphosphate, 166, 182
Aerobic, 166-171
Aggression in sports, 344-347
Amino acids, 183
Anaerobic alactic, 166, 171-174
Anaerobic lactic, 166, 171-174
Anxiety, assessment of, 212-213
Applied behavior analysis, 11
Applied sports psychology
  characteristics of, 200-203
  definition of, 200
  some myths about, 205-207
Assessment
  accuracy of, 43-45
  of anxiety, 212-213
  of assistant coaches, 282-284
  behavior and, 15-18, 31-32
  benefits of, 45-47
  and ethical considerations, 47-48
  figure skating, 142-145
  football, 37-42, 123-125

Assessment—cont'd
  form versus results, 15
  foul-shooting in basketball, 85
  of game performance in basketball, 250-251
  general areas with beginners, 14
  hockey, 36-39, 120
  of important practice behaviors, 272-273
  of personal goals, 319-325
  of physical factors for high school basketball, 243-244
  of pitching in softball, 60
  of problem thoughts before competition, 208
  of psychological preparation for basketball, 245-251
  of sports psyching techniques attempted, 234-235
  of tactical skills in basketball, 245-249
  of team performance during competition, 229-231
  of technical skills in basketball, 243-247

Assessment—cont'd
  positive reinforcement, 66-70
  swimming, 16-17, 34-36, 138-139
  of time management skills, 313-316
Assistant coaches
  managing, 284-288
  selecting, 282-284
Athletes
  developmental level and performance, 109-114
  rights of, 354-356
Attitude, 3, 140-141

B

Ballet, 92
Baseball, 47, 59-60, 121, 270
Basketball
  assessment of game performance, 250-251
  foul-shooting, 85
  goals for practice, 270
  motivation at practice, 3-4, 117-119
  physical preparation for, 243-244
  practice drill, 73-74
  psychological preparation for, 249-251